Girls, Boys and Junior Sexualities

Girls, Boys and Junior Sexualities takes an insightful and in-depth look at the hidden worlds of young children's sexualities. Based upon extensive group interviews and observation, the author illustrates how sexuality is embedded in children's school-based cultures and gender identities. From examining children's own views and experiences, the book explores a range of topical and sensitive issues, including how:

- the primary school is a key social arena for 'doing' sexuality;
- sexuality shapes children's friendships and peer relations;
- being a 'proper' girl or boy involves investing in a heterosexual identity;
- children use gendered or sexual insults to maintain gender and sexual norms.

Grounded in children's real-life experiences, this book traces their struggles, anxieties, desires and pleasures as they make sense of their emerging sexualities. It also includes frank and open discussions of the pressures of compulsory heterosexuality, the boyfriend/girlfriend culture, misogyny and sexual harassment.

Girls, Boys and Junior Sexualities is a timely and powerful resource for researchers, educationalists and students in childhood studies, sociology and psychology and will be of great interest to professionals and policy makers working with young children.

Emma Renold is lecturer in Childhood Studies at the Cardiff School of Social Sciences, Cardiff University.

Girls, Boys and Junior Sexualities

Exploring children's gender and sexual relations in the primary school

Emma Renold

RoutledgeFalmer
Taylor & Francis Group

LONDON AND NEW YORK

First published 2005 by RoutledgeFalmer
2 Park Square, Milton Park, Abingdon, Oxon OX14 4RN

Simultaneously published in the USA and Canada
by RoutledgeFalmer
270 Madison Ave, New York, NY 10016

RoutledgeFalmer is an imprint of the Taylor & Francis Group

© 2005 Emma Renold

Typeset in Bembo by GreenGate Publishing Services, Tonbridge, Kent
Printed and bound in Great Britain by TJ International, Padstow, Cornwall

British Library Cataloguing in Publication Data
A catalogue record for this book is available from the British Library

Library of Congress Cataloging in Publication Data
A catalog record for this book has been requested

ISBN 0-415-31496-8 (hbk)
ISBN 0-415-31497-6 (pbk)

To Rohen and Dean, with love

Contents

Foreword

I am very honoured to have been asked by Emma to write the foreword to her book. People sometimes ask you (it's a good interview question) to name a book by someone else that you wish you'd written yourself. Emma's book is firmly on my list of these books.

Girls, Boys and Junior Sexualities is a major contribution to the growing field of literature about children's sexualities. But it is more than that. Based on rigorously collected and analysed empirical, ethnographic data, the book helps us to think about childhood, about sexualities and about schools as sites of cultural negotiation and struggle in new and interesting ways. Using detailed, nuanced and multi-layered descriptions of the contexts of schooling and the children's own cultural worlds as revealed by participant observation and interview, a picture is drawn of two schools in a semi-rural setting in the east of England. The descriptions given are evocative and rich – what Clifford Geertz would have called 'thick' – in the best tradition of ethnographic work. By the end of the book, one feels one knows, personally, Alison and Sophie, Tom and Pete, and the other children in this account. These schools, Tipton and Hirstwood, are not only instantly familiar – the subject of numerous other descriptions of primary schools from the UK, Australia and the US, but also peculiarly individual. The book doesn't stop at description, however, but draws us into a highly nuanced theoretical account of children's school-based sexualities.

One of the successes of the book is that it does all this whilst remaining eminently readable – I found myself describing it to a friend as 'gripping' when I was in the middle of it. It introduces and explains difficult and abstruse theories of sexuality (for example those of Judith Butler) in ways that render them clear, understandable and relevant for practitioners working with children (whether as teachers, social workers, carers, etc.) and policy makers. At the same time, the dialogue with such theorists challenges and refines their ideas through engagement with empirical data in ways that will be important for academics concerned with childhood and/or sexuality studies.

Emma, herself, has outlined the main 'findings' (her quote marks) of the book in her final chapter. In this foreword, I don't wish to repeat what she has said there, but would like to draw attention to some of the most striking aspects of the book. It is tempting, when writing about children's masculinities and femininities, to over-emphasise the ways in which they invest themselves in dominant versions of gender at the expense of recognising the many, often subtle, ways in which the same children may resist them. Even those of us who are anxious to avoid essentialising masculinity and femininity can end up doing so, simply through this tendency to stress the hegemonic. This is something that Emma manages to avoid. She shows us clearly how children move between discourses and subject positions, how they both inhabit and resist dominant forms and how their resistance often ends up reinforcing the very features of the dominant forms that they wish to resist and even destabilise. In this way, she gives substance to Foucault's claims that where there is power there is also resistance and that counter-discourses can end up buttressing dominant ones in the discursive field. Or to draw on Raymond Williams' formulation, the emergent can very easily be recuperated by/into the dominant form (Williams 1977). Of course, others have said this or something similar, but I have rarely seen it so well demonstrated as in *Girls, Boys and Junior Sexualities*.

In the final chapter, Emma considers how her work might be used to construct sex and relationships education in such a way that it might provide children with 'really useful knowledge' (Johnson 1979), not in the utilitarian sense in which this phrase is so often used by educational managers these days, but in the much more important sense of knowledge which is critical and progressive, empowering for those (originally working-class people) who are able to develop it, learning not only from teachers (or even organic intellectuals) but from each other. What neither the radical educators of the nineteenth century, nor Richard Johnson in his influential essay about them, considered was the capacity for children to be makers and sharers of such really useful knowledge in their own rights. It is this capacity that Emma demonstrates so well throughout the book and argues for in her final chapter.

In this way, Emma has provided us with pointers to thinking sexuality education (or sex and relationships education) 'Otherwise' in practice and in policy. What she does not discuss overtly in the same way are the fruitful avenues for future research that her work opens up. I would like to make a few suggestions here.

First, there is her careful refinement of the concept of Otherness. Her account of how girls and boys can 'Other' others, 'be' Other and 'do' Other is a really rich seam that needs exploration in all kinds of contexts and in relation to all kinds of differences that make a difference. Emma has discussed gender, sexuality and class in her book but, because of the demographics of her school populations, has not taken on questions of race/ethnicity, nation and migration (including asylum), dis/ability and age. These are all intersecting areas and differences that could yield significant insights in further detailed and rigorous ethnographic work.

Second, as Emma herself points out, there is almost no work published that investigates issues of gender and sexuality (and the way they intersect other differences) outside schools. The tantalising insights that Emma offers from comments made to her by children indicate that things might seem much less fixed and more fluid were we able to investigate children's relationship cultures beyond the school walls. This is an area ripe for investigation and one which I hope that people involved in childhood studies will take on board in the near future. The difficulties of access are, of course, enormous – but we now know that children-as-pupils are not exactly the same as children-as-playmates/friends out of school, children-as-family members or children-as-neighbours (to name but a few other discursive positions they might occupy). Furthermore, work in all areas of childhood studies indicates the importance of generational relations in children's lived experiences. Thinking of ways to overcome the difficulties of access outside school may therefore be the next important development in this field of study.

Third, there is the question of what comes before and what follows the junior sexualities of girls and boys in the later years of primary schooling. There is very little work on children younger than ten or eleven (with the notable exceptions of Bhana 2002; Connolly 1995, 1998, 2004; Epstein 1995a, 1995b; Walkerdine 1981) and almost none of what research there is deals with children under the age of compulsory schooling. Yet we know that gendered identities are usually well established by the age of two or three, that parents, carers and workers in day care and nurseries constantly support and reinforce (hetero)gender and that very young children are active meaning makers in many areas of their lives and clearly this includes gender and sexuality. So I would like to see studies as good as this one of nurseries and day care facilities which take children from babyhood onwards and which trace, in nuanced detail, the ways in which even babies and toddlers are inscribed in (hetero)gender and (hetero)sexuality. At the same time, the studies of primary schools and the studies of secondary schools have rarely been accompanied by studies that take us across the divide between the two phases of schooling. Rosalyn George begins to do this in her study of girls' friendships (George 2004), in which she traces the development and progress of her research participants as they move from primary to secondary school, but much remains to be done about the impact on constructions of gender and sexuality of this key transition in children's lives.

Readers of this foreword will, by now, have worked out that I think they should read *Girls, Boys and Junior Sexualities* without further delay. I am confident that it will prove to be a key text in the several fields to which it contributes: gender and sexuality studies; childhood studies; the sociology and cultural study of education.

Professor Debbie Epstein
Cardiff University
July 2004

Acknowledgements

There are many people I would like to thank and who have each, in their different ways, contributed towards this book.

First, my thoughts and special thanks must go to the children who participated in the research. Without their articulate, illuminative comments, this project would not have been possible. I hope I have 'done justice' to the time they invested in the research and the wide range of experiences they chose to share with me. Thanks of course to the two schools and the two class teachers who made their participation possible.

This book is based upon my PhD research. I thus want to acknowledge and thank the (then) department of education at Cardiff University for their financial support of a studentship. Thank you to John Fitz, my doctoral supervisor and to Sara Delamont who took the time and effort to read the original thesis and whose comments and positivity gave me a much needed boost of confidence. Thanks to RoutledgeFalmer and the editors Alison Foyle and Priyanka Pathak who have fully supported this project and for granting me numerous extensions.

A special thank you also to Alison Parken for offering and then making the time to proof read the book. Her catalogue of comments and questions in the margins made the final editing more bearable.

A big THANK YOU goes to Debbie Epstein who first encouraged me to turn the thesis into a book back in 1999. Since coming to the School of Social Sciences at Cardiff University in 2003, Debbie has been an inspiration and the source of much support.

Some of my early ideas and some of the data have been presented in various forms in journal articles and at a number of conferences. This book builds upon this work and the comments and questions that they generated. Acknowledgement goes to Taylor & Francis and the journals *Gender and Education, Educational Review, British Journal of Education Research* and *British Journal of Sociology of Education*.

Special thanks and love to all my family, especially my mum, Jan, whose long term interest and enthusiasm has been a constant source of strength. Apologies to all my friends, especially Mandy, Jayne and Dale, for turning down dinners and parties to get the book finished!

There are many colleagues and friends who have shaped the ways I think about children, childhood, gender and sexuality. Many are in the School of Social Sciences' 'Sexualities and Gender' and 'Childhood' Research Groups: Sandy Allan, Amanda Coffey, Debbie Epstein, Sally Holland, Gabrielle Ivinson, David Mellor, Maire Messenger-Davies, Jonathon Scourfield, Merryn Smith, Terry Rees and Valerie Walkerdine. Thanks also to: Paul Connolly, Becky Francis, Mary Kehily, Mairtin Mac an Ghaill, Rob Pattman and Chris Skelton.

This book is dedicated to Dean Stroud and our daughter, Rohen (age 3). Over the past three years Rohen has opened my eyes to the heteronormativity of daycare centres and has spurred me on to complete this project.

My final thanks go to Dean for all his love and endless support. For always being there, encouraging me and keeping me going.

Chapter 1

Sexualising gender, gendering sexuality

Some introductions

They (the boys) won't let us play … unless you're going out with one of them

(Hayley, aged 10)

I haven't got a girlfriend […] I'm more into football

(Timothy, aged 10)

You need some boys to talk to sometimes, not just all girls, all the time. But you don't want to get in a … like a relationship with them … BUT YOU STILL DO!

(Harriet, aged 10)

They say I'm gay … they say I'm like a girl

(Damien, aged 10).

This book explores the salience of sexuality in children's accounts of being and becoming 'girls' and 'boys' during their final year of primary school.[1] As the children's quotes above illustrate, it traces how gender and sexuality suffuse and shape the informal world of children's peer group cultures and social relations in diverse and powerful ways. Exploding the myth of the primary school as a cultural greenhouse for the nurturing and protection of children's (sexual) innocence, it vividly illustrates how children locate their local primary school as a key social and cultural arena for doing 'sexuality'.[2] In the chapters that follow I explore girls' and boys' struggles, anxieties, powers and pleasures as they individually and collectively make sense of their gender and sexual identities within a local and global culture that expects nothing less than a 'compulsory heterosexuality' (Rich 1983; Jackson and Scott 2004).

The ethnographic research upon which this book is based (see Renold 1999) was conducted and written against a media and policy backdrop of competing representations of contemporary children in late capitalist societies as knowing and doing 'too much too soon', yet 'not quite ready' for sexual knowledge or activity (see Epstein and Johnson 1998). The year of the millennium witnessed a string of UK media moral panics in which childhood was being represented as a time of presumed innocence and under attack. The *Guardian* (UK broadsheet newspaper), for example, ran stories with headlines such as, 'Innocence on the line' (Gerard 1999), 'The end of innocence' (Birkett 2000) and 'Too much too young' (Ellen 2000). Meanwhile, the Department of Education and Employment (DfEE 2000) issued new Sex and Relationship Education guidance encouraging schools to develop policies and programmes that are 'responsive to children's needs', providing they are 'age-appropriate' and don't encourage 'any early sexual experimentation'. The impetus and rationale to write a book on junior sexualities was fuelled by the dearth of published research on children's day-to-day sexual cultures and identity-work beyond representations of dangerous sexualities (e.g. sexual abuse) or outside of a 'sex education' framework. As Sue Scott, in her plenary to the 2004 British Sociological Association Conference, stated: 'there is a tendency to bracket off sex and sexuality as a special area of human life at the very edges of the social and cultural' and ignore both 'sexuality as everyday practice' and 'the institution of heterosexuality'. This is especially the case when it comes to children and childhood (see Jackson and Scott 2004).

Children's presumed innocence, sexuality as everyday social practice and institutionalised heterosexuality are key themes that punctuate children's own gendered narratives of being a 'girl' and 'boy'. They are also themes that permeate the following chapters that make up this book. One of the book's central aims is to situate sexuality firmly at the centre of how we conceptualise and theorise children's gendered childhoods. In particular, the book invites us (adults) to think differently about the place and performance of gender and sexuality in children's childhoods from the standpoint and experience of children themselves.

The purpose of this first chapter is to outline and offer a number of introductions. First, I introduce and critically explore a number of key theoretical concepts and perspectives (from feminist to queer theories) that collectively offer a theoretical framework sensitive to the complexities of children's gendered, generational and sexual social worlds. Next, I reflect upon how I came to research children's informal and often private school-based gender/sexual cultures. Finally, I explore what it means to undertake research that privileges the subjective experiences of children themselves and how this approach and my theoretical framework both inform and ultimately shape the structure of the following chapters.

Using theory to think Otherwise: feminist, poststructuralist and queer theories

The impact of social constructionst perspectives over the past 30 years or so has contributed significantly to our understanding of how sexuality and gender are shaped and reshaped by the societies and cultures within which we live. Feminist accounts have troubled the relationship between (biological) sex and (social) gender by arguing how the category 'sex' (e.g. male/female) is the product of 'gender' (rather then the other way around) thus laying the blame for gender inequalities at the door of society rather than biology. Contemporary socio-historical accounts that literally trace the *making* of sex (Lacquer 1990) and (hetero/homo)sexuality (Foucault 1978; Weeks 1981, 1986; Katz 1996) have been pivotal in disrupting essentialist truths and dualisms about the 'nature' of sex, gender and sexuality as something fixed, natural, stable and coherent. It is not the purpose of this section to offer a full excavation of this literature on gender and sexuality theory in Western culture, primarily because comprehensive reviews already exist (see Weeks 1985, 1986; Hawkes 1996; Richardson 1996). Rather, I critically explore how my engagement with feminist poststructural, socio-cultural and queer perspectives (particularly the work of Bronwyn Davies, Valerie Walkerdine and Judith Butler) each provide ways of troubling and simultaneously making sense of the kinds of gendered and sexual identities and relations of primary school girls and boys. In brief, feminist poststructuralist and socio-cultural perspectives enable a thinking Otherwise about the contradictory and multiple ways in which children experience and negotiate the gendered category 'girl' and 'boy' (and the power of gender norms). Queer theory enables a thinking Otherwise about the heteronormativity of these gender identities and the sexualisation of gender and the gendering of sexualisation in children's identities more widely.

Touched by feminist poststructuralism

I have found feminist appropriations of poststructuralist perspectives (see Weedon 1987) especially useful in challenging old and opening up new and exciting ways of conceptualising and deconstructing the social processes through which we become gendered. Particularly powerful has been the deployment of the term 'discourse' (as socially organised frameworks of knowledge and meaning) in exposing how certain regulatory 'truths' about gender (e.g. 'boys are boisterous', 'girls are weak') come about and create and control particular ways of thinking, feeling and acting as 'normal' and 'natural'. Bronwyn Davies' research in Australian primary schools was one of the first to deconstruct how young children's gender identities are constituted through discourse and discursive practices. This approach enabled her to fracture the simplistic (yet all powerful) sex/gender binary of 'male/masculinity' and 'female/femininity' and illustrate how children engage with a range of multiple masculinities and femininities, while simultaneously exploring how the rigid male/female dualism is produced and reproduced. There is now a growing body of empirical research within the field of gender and education that explores *gender* as *multiple and relational* (see Francis and Skelton 2001a). Many gender theorists now recognise the plurality and diversity of masculinities and femininities *and* the pushes and pulls of the gender dualism which binds together sex/gender categories (e.g. masculinity with male, femininity with female) – thus how masculinity and femininity are co-constructed in opposition to each other (e.g. male is not to be female and vice versa, see Davies 1989b, 1993a).

A further significant shift over the last two decades, particularly in the work of Bronwyn Davies and Valerie Walkerdine, has been locating children not as passive recipients imprinted upon or 'socialised' by 'society', but making room for the *child as active agent* in the gendering process and fully implicated in the construction and maintenance of their social and cultural worlds (Davies 1989a). Attributing greater agency and self-knowledge to children's 'doing' of gender is particularly important given the historical denial of children as active constructors and mediators of their identities and social worlds more widely (James and Prout 1998).[3] Feminist research into young children's gender identities and relations has always been concerned with integrating and exploring the relationship between the 'being' (via child-centred methodologies) 'becoming' (self in process) and 'doing' (child as active and agentic) of gender (see Davies 1989a, 1993a; 1993b; Walkerdine 1989a, 1990; Jones 1993; Rhedding Jones 1994, 1996; Francis 1997). In particular, I have found the concepts of 'performativity' (Butler 1990) and 'positioning' (Davies and Harre 1991) especially productive in thinking through children's ongoing struggles in being, doing and becoming gender/ed and the costs and consequences of projecting or transgressing normative gender identities.

Performative genders and positioning: challenges and possibilities

The idea that 'gender' is not something that you 'have' but something that you 'do' and continually 'do' ('re-do') through everyday social and cultural practices has been developed by Judith Butler (see Harrison and Hood-Williams 2002) through the concept of 'performativity'. In her book, *Gender Trouble* (1990), Butler emphasises the citational nature of identity where gender is actualised through a series of repetitive performances that constitute the illusion of a 'proper', 'natural' or 'fixed' gender. Identity is thus understood to be the effect of these on-going performances. Butler explains:

> The effect of gender is produced through the stylization of the body and, hence, must be understood as the mundane way in which bodily gestures, movements, and styles of various kinds constitute the illusion of an abiding gendered self ... significantly if gender is instituted through acts ... then the *appearance of substance* is precisely that, a constructed identity, a performative accomplishment which the mundane social audience, including the actors themselves, come to believe and perform in the mode of belief.
>
> (Butler 1990: 140–1)

For Butler, then, 'gender' does not pre-exist behind the 'performances' of gender. Rather, gender comes into being through performance (see Bell 1999). And it is these gendered expressions ('stylized acts') continually produced and reproduced that constitute the fiction of a coherent stable identity and give the illusion of a fixed set of gender norms. It is this performative metaphor and the notion of gender as 'illusory' that I have found an invaluable theoretical resource. This is not just because I had come across a concept that fully reflected my everyday observations of children's reiterative performances as they attempted to project an 'abiding gendered self', but in making sense of children's despair at the impossibility of this task. It also assisted me in mapping how gender norms through constant citation come into being and are held in place and how gender norms are undermined and can be destabilised in the course of these reiterations. This last point, however, is more problematic and warrants a little more explanation.

Butler draws attention to the subversive potential of performative genders in two related ways. First, through a wilful transgression and violation of gender norms that expose other gender performances and thus 'gender' as less than real. And second, how gaps and cracks in performances open up discursive spaces and create possibilities for alternative gendered performances. Both accounts, however, are problematic. As the following chapters illustrate, children (as each others' harshest critics) were more than ready to expose the gaps, cracks and transgressions of other children who constantly struggled to pull off convincing gender performances (i.e. those girls and boys who actively engaged and challenged existing gender norms, see Chapter 7). But they did so often in ways that consolidated and reinforced rather than undermined or thwarted gender norms.

The concept of performativity has been instrumental in recognising the 'doing' and 'living' of gender as much more contradictory than other studies on children's gender relations would have us believe. However, as Butler herself questioned in 'Bodies that Matter' (Butler 1993; see also Jackson 1996; Lloyd 1999; Richardson 2000), transgressive acts do not necessarily result in the subversion of gender norms, but can serve to reinforce them, depending upon social context and audience. Paying attention to the constraints as well as the possibilities of enacting non-normatitve gender/sexual performances, as I do throughout this book, thus involves attending to the social space and social relations within which gender performances occur. As Moya Lloyd explains below:

> It is easy to over-emphasize the discontinuities in gender performance; to present them as indicative of disruptive behaviour. What is occluded, as a consequence, is the space within which performance occurs, the others involved in or implicated by the production, and how they receive and interpret what they see.
>
> (Lloyd 1999: 210)

To explore the ways in which gender performances are enacted and interpreted by children through everyday social relations, Davies and Harre's (1991) notion of 'interactive' and 'reflexive' positioning has been particularly useful to differentiate between and explore the intentional and unintentional ways in which children position/are positioned by others ('interactive') and how they position themselves ('reflexive'). Chapter 7 is dedicated to mapping the costs and consequences of those girls and boys who dare to deviate from and resist gender normative performances and the significance of space and audience in creating the possibilities for their individual and collective transgressive acts. However, as Davies (1989b: 235) illustrates in her discussion of agency, power and the rigidity of the male/female binary, 'doing gender' (and 'sexuality') in non-normative ways is not simply a matter of choice, 'but involves grappling with both subjective constraints and the constraints of accepted discursive practices'. Paying attention to the ways in which identities are constructed (through social interaction) within a nexus of power relations, which involves conceiving of power (and thus discourse) as both a repressive and productive force (Foucault 1977), is an all important step in making sense of the ways in which 'doing boy' and 'doing girl' can be both constraining and empowering in different contexts.[4] Thus while I recognise and explore the fluidity and shifting nature of gendered power relations, I also recognise the ways in which power (via discursive formations) can operate in regulatory and constraining ways, what Foucault referred to as 'major dominations' (see Ramazanoglu 1993: 240). Thus, I will be referring to hegemonic and dominant discourses, identities and postitionings, but also attending to emergent/transformative discourses and thus those who are marginalised within dominant discourses (Cain 1993). And one of the most marginalised discourses, or configuration of discourses, when it comes to children's gendered childhoods, is that of sexuality.

Queering gender and compulsory heterosexuality: outing the ordinary

The socially constructed, multiple and 'performative' nature of gender has been widely recognised, but much less so can be said of sexuality and specifically heterosexuality. When sexuality has been the focus of social analysis and theorising, this work has tended to focus upon sexual minorities (i.e. the sexual Other). Heterosexuality has, until relatively recently, remained an invisible, unexamined and taken-for-granted norm (see Richardson 2000). Early feminists and proponents of queer theory, however, have radically interrogated, problematised and thus rendered visible the ways in which heterosexuality is not only socially constructed but fundamental to the social, cultural and material conditions that shape and regulate our everyday lives. Adrienne Rich's (1983: 21) powerful conceptualisation of heterosexuality as 'compulsory' was one of the first to draw attention to the institutionalisation of heterosexuality as something that is 'imposed, managed, organised, propagandised and maintained by force'. Since then there has been an expanding literature specifically examining the interaction and intersection of heterosexuality and gender, particularly (although by no means exclusively) by those theorists associated with what has come to be known as 'queer theory' (e.g. Butler 1990, 1993; Sedgwick 1990, 1997; Dollimore 1991; Warner 1993; Sinfield 1994).

Described as the 'grandchild of academic feminism and gay liberationist theory' (Hostetler and Herdt 1998: 2), queer theory builds on and employs general poststructuralist perspectives and confronts the binary focus of sexual and gender categories:

> Queer theory is linked to forms of politics which deliberately seek to break down the fixed boundaries between the hetero/homo, gender and other binaries to multiply sexual categories and ultimately dissolve them, insisting that 'queer' itself is not some bounded community, or not only so, but is everywhere.
>
> (Johnson 1997: 9)

While there is much debate over what constitutes 'queer theory' (see Hostetler and Herdt 1998), the radical shake-up of the relationship and inter-dependency of gender and sexuality has provided some complex (and challenging) theoretical accounts of the gendering of sexuality and the sexualisation of gender (see Butler 1990, 1993; Sedgwick 1990; Wilton 1996, 2004). For many, proponents of queer theory have provided the conceptual space from which to expose and contest the hegemony of heterosexuality and the politics and practice of heteronormative and heterosexist social worlds.

In my own research, Judith Butler's conceptualisation of how gender is routinely spoken through a 'heterosexual matrix' has been pivotal in thinking through the ways in which children's normative gender identities as 'girls' and 'boys' are inextricably tied to dominant notions of heterosexuality, as Butler sets out below:

> I use the term *heterosexual matrix* ... to designate that grid of cultural intelligibility through which bodies, genders, and desires are naturalized ... a hegemonic discursive/epistemological model of gender intelligibility that assumes that for bodies to cohere and make sense there must be a stable sex expressed through a stable gender (masculine expresses male, feminine expresses female) that is oppositionally and hierarchically defined through the compulsory practice of heterosexuality.
>
> (Butler 1990: 151)

Here, Butler is arguing that the 'real' expressions of masculinity and femininity (what she defines as 'intelligible genders') are embedded and hierarchically structured within a presupposed heterosexuality. In other words, to be a 'real' boy or girl would involve desiring or growing up to desire the opposite sex, such is the power of the 'heterosexual imaginary' (see Ingraham 1996). Alternatively, to deviate from normative 'masculinities' and 'femininities' (or 'unintelligible genders') can throw heterosexuality into doubt (e.g. consider the 'homosexualisation' of boys who step outside normative gender boundaries). Disrupting the linear story that there is first a sexed subject which expresses itself through gender and then through sexuality, Butler exposes the developmental path of sex, gender and desire to be wholly illusory and further illustrates, along with other identity theorists (Hall and du Gay 1996), how this 'illusion' (i.e. the 'hegemony' and ubiquity of the heterosexual matrix) is maintained through the policing and shaming of 'abnormal' or Other sexual/gendered identities (Butler 1993). Constituting both heterosexuality and gender as inherently unstable by showing how each depends upon the contrasting presence of an Other for their reference point (as 'normal' and 'natural') exposes their compulsory *and* fragile nature. Indeed, the power *and* fragility of normative gender/sexual identities and the costs and consequences of transgressing gender/sexual boundaries are central themes in children's own accounts, where 'doing gender' is simultaneously 'doing sexuality'.

To foreground the heterosexualisation of gender and to confront the naturalisation of heterosexuality in the chapters that follow, I will be drawing upon Chrys Ingraham's term, 'heterogender' (and sometimes heterofemininity and heteromasculinity). I will also be deploying Butler's notion of 'heterosexual hegemony' (Butler 1993) which I feel is a significant and necessary theoretical development from the more universal 'heterosexual matrix' because it can not only account for shifting, multiple and hierarchical heterosexualities but also recognise the possibility that 'this is a matrix which is open to rearticulation [and] which has a kind of malleability' (Butler 1993). Exploring the multiplicity of heterosexualities and the regulative power of hegemonic heterosexuality is particularly important in this study, where I was unable to record any fixed or singular notion of heterosexuality. Rather, girls and boys were performing and 'practising heterosexuality' (Epstein 1993b) in multiple and diverse ways that could at different moments and in different contexts subvert and maintain hierarchical normative gender/sexual power relations (for further discussion on the theorisation of heterosexualities see Jackson 1996 and Richardson 1996, 2000).

Queering childhood, schooling sexualities

A number of researchers who have been exploring the school as a specific social and cultural arena for the production and reproduction of gender and sexual identities have been inspired by some of the theoretical developments within queer theory (see Haywood and Mac an Ghaill 1995, 1996; Laskey and Beavis 1996; Kehily 2002; Epstein *et al.* 2003) . Much of this research, however, has centred on the domain of the secondary school and thus the sexual cultures and relations of young women and men (particularly men). There is, nevertheless, a small but expanding body of research queering childhood sexualities and interrogating the gendering of sexuality and the sexualisation of gender with children in their pre-school (Boldt 2002; Robinson 2002), elementary (Boldt 1996; Letts and Sears 1999) and junior years (Epstein *et al.* 2001a, 2003). Indeed, one of the broader projects of queer theory, that of 'queering' existing theory (Sedgwick 1990; Warner 1993) and in doing so rendering visible those sites and spaces not usually associated with sexuality, is certainly something that these latter studies have accomplished. Also, each, in their different ways, has confronted and disrupted not just the binaries of sexuality, gender and ethnicity, but the sedimented generational binary of child/adult (see Chapter 2).

One of the projects of this book is to encourage what could be described as a 'queering' of childhood. That is, paying attention to the multiple and contradictory ways in which sexuality is constitutive of both the subject 'child' and the social and cultural institution of 'childhood'. 'Queering childhood' involves not just the queering of sex/gender and sexual binary oppositions such as male (masculinity)/female (femininity) and heterosexual/homosexual, but also the generational binaries adult/child and sexual/asexual. More specifically then, queering childhood pushes us to identify and think Otherwise about (and thus trouble) the (hetero)gendered and (hetero)sexualised nature of identity categories such as 'girl', 'boy' and 'child' and foregrounds the heteronormativity of children's childhoods more widely.

The next section contextualises the research by first tracing how I came to study children's gender and sexual cultures. I then introduce the two primary schools, Tipton and Hirstwood, and present an overview of the methods and methodology used to access children's more private social worlds.

Tales of the un/expected: researching the gendered and sexual worlds of primary school children

I did not set out to explicitly research children's sexual cultures or relations. My original research focus centred upon gender and children's constructions of school-based masculinities and femininities. Like many ethnographic studies, the flexibility and reflexivity of the ethnographic process led to a shift in focus and the inevitable 'Pandora's box' indicative of qualitative research unfolded.[5] During the first term of the academic year in which the fieldwork was conducted (September 1995), I was increasingly witnessing quite a complex interactive and daily social and cultural network of (hetero)sexual performances by both girls and boys as they negotiated their gendered selves. An early excerpt from my research diary reveals one of several key analytic developments from which a series of research questions around the 'heterosexual presumption' (Epstein and Johnson 1994) evolved:

> Mrs Fryer tries to quieten the class down. She asks them to put their lips together. Adrian shouts out 'oo err, I'm not kissing everyone in this class'. Many of the boys and girls start laughing. Mrs Fryer looks at me, smiles, rolls her eyes and gives Adrian a long stare (of disapproval?). [Theoretical Note: Yet again Adrian entertains the class via sexual innuendo, with heterosexist overtones. Why are some boys more prone to interject (hetero)sexualised comments than others? Could it be something to do

with *not* having a girlfriend? (Adrian has never been a 'boyfriend') Are they under pressure to project their 'heterosexuality' in other ways? Is it part and parcel of the way boys 'do' their masculinity? Are they using sexual discourses to challenge/subvert teacher authority? Is it an attempt to display some sort of sexual power 'over' women/girls? Why is sexualised humour monopolised by particular boys? What about girls? To what extent are female teachers complicit in the (hetero)sexualisation of classroom discourse?]

(Tipton: fieldnotes)

From the more overt heterosexualised relationship cultures of girlfriends and boyfriends to more subtle forms of (hetero)sexualised talk and behaviour, I was beginning to tap into the ways in which gender and sexuality were inextricably connected and embedded in young children's schooling lives (Epstein 1997). Indeed, the development of the focus from children's gender relations to children's gender *and* sexual relations was, to some extent, an outcome of designing and conducting research in ways that created opportunities for children to shape and reshape the focus of the study. Before I explore some of the methods and methodology in more detail, I first want to provide some background information on the two primary schools, Tipton and Hirstwood, in which the fieldwork took place.

Introducing the schools

The locality: Market Tipton

Both schools are situated in Tipton St Peter's, a small semi-rural village, which backs on to Market Tipton, a small historic country town in East Anglia (England), within a 20-minute drive of an expanding cathedral city. The locality known as Tipton St Peter's is split straight down its centre by an arterial 'A' road and the River Dean. On the south side of the river lies Tipton Primary and on the north lies Hirstwood Primary.

Tipton and Hirstwood

Tipton is a mixed-sex Local Education Authority (LEA) controlled school with a declining pupil roll of 249, with SAT results below the national average at the time of the research (1996). Tipton's catchment area is white, predominantly 'working class'.[6] There are a few children from professional families who live in the older cottages and Victorian houses, and there are other children whose families work in agriculture and in local shops. Those who work in the nearby city in retail or factory work reside mainly in the adjacent 1940s council estate and the nearby 1960s housing estate.

Hirstwood is an LEA maintained mixed-sex primary school with a pupil roll of 392 and SAT results above the national average. The school has expanded and almost doubled in size over the past nine years. Hirstwood lies in the middle of a new and expanding 1980s housing estate of owner occupiers. Hirstwood's catchment area serves white, predominantly 'middle-class' families employed in professional occupations as teachers, lecturers, doctors, nurses and also on the managerial side of industry. One of the main differences between Hirstwood and Tipton is Hirstwood's popularity amongst the families living in Tipton St Peter's, (evidenced by its expanding pupil roll) and its strong academic record/ethos. The chief purpose in choosing two contrasting sites was not to set one school against the other in any simple compare-and-contrast formula, but to identify and analyse how key social practices, relationships and identities were constructed across both schools (see Renold 1999 for detailed discussion of these issues).

The 59 children who participated in the research were drawn from one Year 6 class in each school: Mrs Fryer's class of 29 (13 boys and 16 girls) at Tipton and Miss Wilson's class of 30 (13 boys and 17 girls) at Hirstwood. Each class reflects the mixed social intake of white working-class and white middle-class backgrounds (with more working-class children at Tipton and more middle-class children at Hirstwood). Eight of the children in Mrs Fryer's class at Tipton come from one-parent families and three live with their mothers and step-fathers. Three children live in one-parent families in Miss Wilson's class. In relation to academic ability, it was the children in Miss Wilson's class who at the end of the year achieved a far higher total of SAT scores, although the children in Mrs Fryer's class covered the full spectrum of academic ability, from two children (one girl, one boy) statemented with special educational needs to two very high-achieving boys. While it was always my intention to include an additional school situated within a multi-ethnic and inner-city locality, accessing children's more private social worlds and peer group cultures took longer than anticipated.[7]

Accessing children's social worlds: researching from the 'children's standpoint'

At the time of conducting the fieldwork (1995/6), very little had been written on the practicalities of doing research 'with' rather than 'on' children (Mayall 1994a). Children were still very much perceived almost as alien 'others' with their own and distinct 'alien' worlds that were somehow separated off from the 'adult' world. Much of this thinking has and continues to derive from developmental theories and their conceptual frameworks in which children are positioned as 'immature', 'culturally neutral' and 'passive bystanders' within processes of socialisation (see James et al. 1998; Woodhead and Montgomery 2003). Consequently, children's accounts of social reality and personal experience are rarely taken as competent portrayals of their experiences (Hutchby and Moran-Ellis 1998). At the time I was entering the field, Ann Oakley (1994) was writing about how developmental theories have only produced adult perceptions of children and perpetuated, if not created, the non-competency discourse that surrounds many psychological studies of children. Jens Qvortrup (1994: 2) was going one stage further suggesting that those who study children as persons in their own right, are almost considered 'improper' and 'unethical'. The neglect to focus solely on children as 'units of observation' highlights how little we value children's experiences and perceptions when taken as subjects of study in their own right (see Barrie Thorne's (1987) discussion of 'conceptual autonomy'). This was particularly the case in early educational research when a focus on infant schools almost entirely neglected the children in favour of the teachers and organisation of the school (Sharp and Green 1975; King 1978).[8]

I followed contemporary authors like Barrie Thorne, Bronwyn Davies, Paul Connolly and Becky Francis who have each conducted educational ethnographies with children as participants rather than the 'objects or subjects' of research (see Woodhead and Faulkner 2000). One of the most useful articles at the time was Leena Alanen's (1994) 'Gender and Generation: Feminism and the "Child Question"' in which she describes approaching research from the standpoint of the child (adapted from feminist-standpoint epistemology). Indeed, one of the central features of the study was its commitment to foregrounding children's own experiences and enabling them to wield some control over the direction of the research. Alanen (1994) has described this approach as research conducted from the 'children's standpoint', that is, giving voice and respecting children as knowledgeable and active subjects and using the research process as a vehicle through which children are enabled to communicate experiences that are important to them. Drawing from feminist research which re-centred women within malestream sociology, Alanen and others extend the feminist standpoint of knowing women and their social worlds through experience to knowing children, thus de-naturalising the phenomenon of childhood as the category of women was (and continues to be) de-naturalised and made complex. Rooted in experience, Oakley (1994), quoting Smith (1987) stresses how recovering children from the margins has many parallels to feminist methodologies:

> The sociology of women is a method that 'creates the space for an absent subject and an absent experience that is to be filled with the presence and spoken experience of actual women speaking of and in the actualities of their everyday worlds'.
>
> (Smith 1987: 107 quoted in Oakley 1994: 24)

Dorothy Smith argues that a feminist standpoint 'directs us to an embodied subject located in a particular actual/local historical setting' (Smith 1987: 107). In this way, characteristics of a feminist methodology which are derived from experience, rooted in practice and illuminative of multiple and different realities, can be adapted to research with children. This departs from those researchers who call for an entirely different process whereby the researcher has to put aside 'adult' preconceptions/views (see Corsaro 1981; Fine and Sandstrom 1988).

Unstructured friendship group interviews

From the outset, the research was specifically designed and carried out in ways that maximised and privileged children's subjective experiences. Alongside 'hanging out' and 'being with' children in a range of different contexts, one of the main methods employed to 'hear' children's own accounts and 'get close' to children's social worlds was through unstructured, in-depth group interviews, organised around children's friendship groups. As others have noted, conducting interviews with friendship groups often helps to create a non-threatening and comfortable atmosphere (see also Woods 1981; Davies 1982; Lewis 1992; Mauthner 1996; Hill 1997).[9] Being unstructured and being with their friends, many of the children could talk freely about a range of issues. As soon as the tape-recorder was switched on children would spontaneously launch into the latest significant event that week (often highly gendered). Others would set me aside before a group interview and tell me what they wanted to talk about that day. On a couple of occasions, when our time was up before the group felt that a particular debate or issue had been discussed thoroughly, they would request we pick up the topic in the next interview.

Encouraging children to raise their own issues and experiences also helped destabilise the adult-centrism embedded in many research projects carried out by adults with children, and went some way to promote participation and empowerment during the research process (Christensen and James 2000). Armed with the knowledge that no topics were 'off limit', combined with the creation (over the months) of a supportive and trusting environment (see Renold 2002a), previously unreported and private accounts of children's sexual cultures, described by Best (1983) as the 'third hidden curriculum', began to surface.[10] The exploratory nature of the group interviews often took off in some quite unexpected directions, including discussions and disclosures on more sensitive areas such as bullying, homophobia, sexual harassment, boyfriends and girlfriends, as well as talk about schoolwork, play, friendships, music, popular culture, fashion and appearance.

Over the course of the year, each child (59 in total) participated in at least six group interviews (82 group interviews in total). This longitudinal element enabled an exploration of how, individually and collectively, children's ideas, experiences and the group dynamic shifted and changed over time. Although children were free to talk about whatever they wanted, I would sometimes direct the focus of the discussion from a prior observation (e.g. gendering of playground space) or a key 'critical' moment (e.g. latest 'romantic' break-up). There were a number of occasions when some groups would raise the same 'critical' incident which offered multiple and contrasting perspectives (from boys' monopolisation of playground space to specific incidents of heterosexual harassment). As Stephen Frosh, Ann Phoenix and Rob Pattman (2002) found in their UK study of young masculinities, the group interviews became and were enthusiastically taken up as another key social site for 'performing' and 'doing identity'. As Jenny Kitzinger (1994: 159) stresses, the dynamic nature of the group interview 'enables the researcher to examine people's different perspectives as they operate within a social network and to explore how accounts are constructed, expressed, censured, opposed and changed through social interaction'. Furthermore, integrating the group interviews with participant observation enabled me to fully explore the performativity of children's gender/sexual identities from multiple perspectives and dimensions. For a more detailed and reflexive discussion on issues of informed consent and broader ethical issues around what it means to be a young adult women researcher listening to and talking with boys and girls about issues of gender and sexuality in the context of the primary school, see Renold (2002b).

Structuring the book

Children's own accounts and voices occupy centre stage in this book with five of the following seven chapters dedicated to the empirical data. Data presented in the chapters to come include excerpts from fieldnotes and analytic memos, but draw extensively upon the transcribed group interviews by way of foregrounding children's own observations, experiences and 'collective rememberings' (Kitzinger 1994). With the group interviews organised around friendship groups and thus either 'girls-only' or 'boys-only', combined with the tendency for many children to organise themselves into highly gender-differentiated groups (see Thorne 1993), Chapters 3 to 5 reflect yet simultaneously problematise this polarisation by focusing separately upon gender and sexual relations and identity-work primarily within, but also between girls' and boys' peer group cultures. Chapters 3 and 4 focus upon (the sexualisation of) normative, yet multiple and hierarchical, 'masculinities' and 'femininities'. Chapters 5 and 6 focus primarily on (the gendering of) normative, yet multiple and hierarchical, (hetero)sexualities through children's relationship cultures and the social and cultural world of 'boyfriends' and 'girlfriends'. Individually, each of these chapters tell four very different, yet related, stories about the powerful, constraining, pleasurable and painful ways in which (normative) gender is actively constructed and performed through an all-pervasive heterosexual matrix mediating children's everyday relations and relationships in expected and unexpected ways.

Chapter summaries

Chapter 3 explores the pushes and pulls of accessing, or being positioned by, 'older' (hetero)sexualised 'girlie' femininities. It illustrates how over two-thirds of the girls in the research were investing in a range of often contradictory discourses to produce their own and each others' bodies as heterosexually desirable commodities. A significant part of the chapter, however, also focuses upon those girls who actively construct their 'femininities' in opposition to sexualised 'girlie' femininities and thus directly challenge the ways in which girls are both objects, subjects and agents of a heterosexualised male gaze (through a critique of 'girlie' femininities and their access to dominant discourses of masculinity). The teening of girlhood, the (hetero)sexualisation of 'girl power' (and powerlessness) and the seduction of hegemonic masculinity for contemporary girls are key themes running throughout this chapter.

Boys' struggles to negotiate and embody an elusive range of hegemonic masculinities are the focus of Chapter 4. Here, I explore the experiences of what I have termed 'wannabe hegemonic boys' (just under two-thirds of boys in the research). I emphasise throughout how the fragility and ultimate unachievability of embodying an increasingly adult-centric hegemonic masculinity, and the costs and consequences of failing to pull-off convincing 'masculine' performances, negatively impact upon other boys and girls. I also explore how the appropriation and pressure to project 'older' gender/sexual identities differ significantly between and within the genders and across the two schools.

Chapter 5 returns to girls' peer group cultures and the (hetero)sexualisation of femininity. Here, I explore girls' preoccupations with heterosexual relations of desire and intimacy through an increasingly salient and girl-driven boyfriend/girlfriend culture and other heterosexualised performances and erotic attachments within and beyond the school gates. The chapter illustrates how all girls are actively negotiating an increasingly compulsory, yet multiple and hierarchical, heterosexual matrix which permeates and regulates their relations and relationships with each other and other boys. Continuing the theme of resistance and subversion of normative (hetero)sexualised femininities, this chapter explores a range of issues: from girls' struggles to strike up and sustain boy–girl friendships free from sexual innuendo, to girls as 'victims' and 'perpetrators' of gendered and sexualised harassment.

Chapter 6 explores how complex and contradictory heterosexual performances and in particular the role of 'boyfriend' can be to pre-teen boys and junior masculinities. I suggest in this chapter how the majority of boys in the study experienced the feminised boyfriend/girlfriend culture as one of fear (of being close to girls) and frustration (of failing to secure traditional sexual power relations) in 'real' relationship cultures (i.e. with girls in their class). The chapter pays particular attention to the ways in which boys reinvent themselves as sexually powerful (by drawing on a range of sexist and heterosexist discourses) while highlighting throughout how boys (particularly middle-class boys) can draw upon discourses of (sexual) innocence (e.g. sexual immaturity) in ways not readily available for girls. This chapter also explores the diverse ways in which the role of 'boyfriend' and discourses of love, desire and romance are deployed by a minority of boys (3 boys) who over the year achieve a celebrity-like status as the 'studs' of their class.

The final empirical chapter, Chapter 7, is dedicated to those girls and boys who were positioned by others and indeed positioned themselves as gendered and sexual fugitives or 'outsiders'. It explores the experiences of over a third of all children in the study who actively and persistently challenged or subverted the normalising and regulatory gender/sexual scripts, outlined in the four previous chapters. From reporting upon girls' and boys' own accounts of being routinely teased, physically bullied and excluded for choosing not to invest in the dominant and hegemonic forms of age-appropriate heteromasculinities, heterofeminities and heterosexualities, I consider the risky business of transgressing/queering gender and sexual boundaries and the real possibilities (and knock-on effects) of sustaining transgressive identities through collective resistance.

The concluding chapter draws together some of the salient 'findings' from the five empirical chapters. Each key finding is selected specifically to challenge the often heteronormative, highly gendered and ageist assumptions of young children's presumed sexual innocence in the wider media and current UK sex education policy and guidance. Each point aims to encourage a thinking Otherwise about the sexualisation of gender and the gendering of sexuality in the social worlds and identity-work of primary school children. It is not the intention of this book to offer specific suggestions and strategies to professionals and practitioners regarding anti-(hetero)sexist and anti-oppressive practice. However, the 'key findings' summaries do go some way to offering a number of 'starting points' (see Kenway *et al.* 1997) that might inform the development and delivery of a range of policies (from sex education to anti-bullying).

With the introductions to the research, my theoretical location and the overall structure of the book underway, the purpose of the next chapter is to contextualise and locate the five empirical chapters within a broader discussion of the ways in which discourses of childhood (sexual) innocence are deployed and manipulated in a range of socio-political contexts (from government to children's charities and the wider media). Particular attention is paid to the gendering of sexual innocence and the social construction of age and maturity. The rest of the chapter explores empirical research that has focused specifically upon issues of sexuality and primary schooling and the small cluster of school-based ethnographies which have begun to explore sexuality as embedded in the gendered worlds of children's childhoods.

Chapter 2

Presumed innocence

Young children, sexualities and schooling

Introduction

Childhood is a time of presumed sexual innocence. It is generally perceived as a space where children are untroubled and untouched by the cares of the (adult) sexual world to come. But sexual innocence is both a contested and gendered concept. This chapter aims to interrogate both the gendering and sexualisation of innocence within the generational cultures, 'boyhood' and 'girlhood'. The first third of the chapter is dedicated to mapping out some of the contradictory myths and moral panics that simultaneously deny and acknowledge the sexuality of children/childhood. In particular I explore how such panics are induced by the practices and policies of schools themselves and by the manipulation of dominant rhetoric and images of childhood from the media, government and non-government agencies. I also make visible and problematise the gendering of sexual innocence (particularly the feminisation of erotic innocence) and launch the concept, 'sexual generationing' to address the ways in which girls and boys draw upon and are differently positioned and policed by age-appropriate sexualised discourses.

The second half of the chapter introduces the reader to research that explicitly identifies the primary school as a key site for the production and regulation of sexuality. Here I focus specifically upon issues that stretch beyond the scope of the book, but in doing so, contextualise the study of children's sexualities more widely. Some of the issues include: exploring the (hetero)family ethos of the primary school and how it serves to police the boundaries of heteronormativity; teacher sexualities and the pressures to pass and perform as 'real' (hetero)men and women; the (hetero)sexualisation of teacher–pupil interactions; and the ways in which sexuality and childhood are discursively produced within recent DfEE (2000a) Sex and Relationship Education guidance.

This study is in dialogue and draws upon an expanding research literature which foregrounds the salience of sexuality in children's gender cultures and children as active agents in the construction of their gender and sexual identities. The chapter concludes with a brief overview of what I have identified as some of the key emerging themes from this literature. They include: the importance of time, place and context; the sexualisation of gender identities; the interaction of sexuality with Other differences; the construction of children's sexualities as 'immature'; and children's experiences of gendered and sexualised teasing and harassment. The very first section, however begins with a short historical overview of the construction of the 'primary school' as a key site for the nurturing and institutionalisation of childhood innocence.

'Signs' of childhood: schooling innocence

Since Phillipe Aries' (1962) landmark study, *Centuries of Childhood*, many social scientists, social historians and social anthropologists have been studying childhood as socially and historically constructed. It is now increasingly recognised that there is no essential or universal childhood. Rather, childhood is a transitory social and historical institution largely imposed and constructed by the practices of adults (Gittens 1998). Attitudes to Western children have changed rapidly over time, giving rise to a multiplicity of childhoods and ways of thinking about 'the child' (see Cunningham 1991; Jenks 1996; Hendrick 1998). However, the romantic notion of the 'innocent child' and discourses of childhood innocence endure (Cunningham 199l; Burman 1995; Gittens 1998; James *et al.* 1998). Developed first by Rousseau (1762) and reappropriated by Victorian sentimentalists, the representation of children as vulnerable and innocent brought about the birth of modern ideas of childhood. Erica Burman (1995) explains:

> Positioning children as standing outside worldly preoccupations, this romantic notion endows them with a unique, privileged perspective ... as more natural and more free from contamination by an alienated and alienating civilisation.
>
> (Burman 1995: 50)

Diana Gittens (1998) describes how the notion of children's innocence was essential to alleviate the fear, chaos and pollution of a rapidly changing world, hence the construction of childhood (and a revival of 'the family') as safe, protected and innocent.

The introduction of compulsory schooling in Britain in the 1870s and the mass removal and barring of children from adult spaces of work and the street relied heavily upon the notion of the innocent child (as dependent, vulnerable and powerless). The protection (and to some extent production) of childhood innocence was a central discourse fuelling many educational campaigns and guarded as *the* distinguishing feature separating adulthood and childhood (see Hendrick 1998). In many respects, the school, and specifically the British primary school, effectively institutionalised childhood innocence. Discussing the ways in which the post-war primary school was constituted on the basis of a fantasy of child protection, (safeguarding children's innocence), Valerie Walkerdine draws our attention to the 'greenhouse effect' of primary schooling:

It was centrally considered a safe space, a kind of greenhouse to which children would be removed from the squalor and degeneracy, the poverty and crime of cities in which implicit rebellion lurked, a 'natural' space where childhood could progress untrammelled.

(Walkerdine 1990: 117)

Many childhood commentators over the past quarter century have perceived a rapid reconceptualisation of modern childhood. Some focus upon the blurring of adult/child boundaries and the diminishing of childhood, as children intrude upon 'adult-defined' spaces (see Postman 1994). Others focus upon the extension of youth, as the uncertainty of 'adulthood' increases (see Lee 2001; Brannen and Nilsen 2002). In some ways, then, the primary school lives on as a greenhouse of protection and is perhaps one of the few social, cultural and psychological sites for producing and signifying childhood innocence. With the growing anxiety over children using and abusing public places (Matthews 2002) one could argue that the school 'playground', alongside the garden as the 'new outdoors' (see Valentine and McKendrick 1997; Valentine 1997), represents one of the few remaining social spaces for children to be childlike amongst their peers (albeit under the watchful gaze of adults). On the other hand, one could just as easily argue that there has always been and continues to be constant slippage between adulthood and childhood, and children have always been constrained by, yet strive for, adult knowledge and power (see Walkerdine 2004).

It is the construction of childhood as a time of innocence, and specifically sexual innocence as the ultimate signifier of childhood, that I want to explore in more detail below, primarily because much of the neglect surrounding children's sexualities stems from a historical (and current) preoccupation with the conceptualisation of children and childhood as innocent and innocence. Indeed, the historical separation of children from the adult world (or 'othering' of children) has hinged almost wholly on children's exclusion from (adult) realms of sexuality.

Children, childhood and sexuality: assumptions, myths and moral panics

In spite of Freud's insistence that children are sexual beings, they are still not regarded as such and there are now, more than ever, a plethora of rules and regulations that define sex as the exclusive realm of adults. Transgression of such rules [...] jeopardises a child's chance to even be considered a child.

(Gittens 1998: 174)

As the last section illustrated, it is often argued that the epitome of childhood lies in children's assumed sexual innocence and it is children's sexual innocence that marks them off from the adult world (Gittens 1998, Jenkins 1998a).[1] Although, as Stevi Jackson (1990) notes, piecing together the history of child-hood and sexuality is patchy and partial at best, many authors agree that the adult gaze on the sexuality of the child has come under close scrutiny and con-trol over the past two centuries (Weeks 1981). The Victorian era, for example, is widely recognised for its images and writings that connect the sexual with dominant concepts of childhood. Since then, the regulation of children's sexu-ality has been addressed in a number of areas, including: masturbation (Foucault 1978); school organisation (Fishman 1982); child sensuality in parenting manu-als (Jenkins 1998b); advertising and other sexualised images featuring children (Higonnet 1998; Holland 2004); ages of sexual consent (Walkowitz 1992) and most notably, child prostitution and adult/child sexual abuse (Kitzinger 1990; Kelly *et al.* 1995; Kincaid 1998; Jackson 1990). Although Freud drew our atten-tion to children as active sexual beings, 'it was concepts of repression and adult interference and intrusion rather than any notion of sexuality in children as a given or natural phenomenon' (Walkerdine 1999: 5) that have often assumed the focus of investigations into children, childhood and sex/uality.

Michele Foucault has written extensively on what he terms the 'peda-gogization of children's sex' and the ways in which children have (since Freud) come under close scrutiny and surveillance from the cradle to the classroom:

> Children were surrounded by an entire watch-crew of parents, nurses, ser-vants, educators and doctors, all attentive to the least manifestations of … sex.
>
> (Foucault 1978: 98)

The plethora of rules, regulations and taboos set up to cleanse children from sexuality created a paradox that constructed child sexuality as both natural (i.e. to be shielded and protected) and unnatural (i.e. to be controlled, restricted and educated). Writing on the current and historical sacredness of children, sex and sexuality, Joyce Bellous (2002), drawing on Foucault, summarises this double bind:

> Children were seen as preliminary sexual beings, on this side of sex, yet within its borders – astride a dangerous dividing line.
>
> (Bellous 2002: 80)

This dividing line between asexual child/sexual adult holds as much currency in today's censorious climate as in the past. Often the only option available when discussing children and sexuality is within the context of abuse and exploitation. In an article exploring the historical construction of childhood innocence and the progressive denial and removal of children's sexuality over time, Christine Piper (2000) suggests that little has changed. Whether engaged in consensual or abusive sexual acts children are often rendered non-children or as children who have been robbed of their 'childhoods' (Piper 2000). Using an example of a recent children's charity (National Children's Home) leaflet entitled 'Sexual Abuse and the Whole Child', a girl called Amy is described as being counselled to 'learn how to trust again' and helped by the children's charity to 'give back a little of the childhood her father stole from her'. Similar campaigns which conflate childhood innocence with sexual innocence, and sexual activity with adulthood, can be found in numerous children's charity fund/awareness raising advertisements, such as the poster campaign by Barnardo's in 2002 to combat child prostitution. Here 'ageing' (wrinkled) faces are transposed onto 'young' girl and boy bodies (dressed in their vests and pants) to graphically represent the juxtaposition of (sexual) innocence with (sexual) experience and (forbidden) knowledge (see also Holland 2004).

There are some writers who lament children's loss of innocence and call for a return of the 'innocent child' (see Postman 1994). Others, however, critique the romanticisation of childhood innocence (which is often depicted in opposition to an 'authentic childhood') and suggest how discourses of innocence profoundly endanger children (Kitzinger 1990; Kincaid 1994, 1998; Giroux 2000). Jenny Kitzinger, for example, describes how romanticised notions of the sexually innocent child stigmatise and exclude those who do not conform to this ideal, so that any child who sexually responds, or is sexually knowledgeable, is stained as 'damaged goods' and no longer justifies or warrants our protection (Kitzinger 1990: 160–1). Such is the denial of children's sexual awareness, that any child's early interest in sex can be interpreted as a warning sign that the child has been sexually abused.

The ways in which sexually 'knowing' children are read as sexually 'abused' children is highlighted by Scott et al., (1998) from an article in the *Sydney Morning Herald* on how parents should seek advice (and if necessary 'treatment') if their child displays inappropriate sexual knowledge or behaviour 'beyond their years'. As Piper (2000) succinctly illustrates, when it comes to discussing childhood and sexuality, there is usually one of two options: Child + Sex = Abuse or Child + Sex = Adult (non-child). What is rarely represented in the public imaginary is the equation, Child + Sex = OK.

There seems to be widespread belief that children do not know or should not know anything about sexuality. Moral panics and public concern that children are not innocent enough hinges primarily upon issues of 'early sexual maturation'. Diederik Janssen (2002) has termed this the 'hurried erotics discourse' which is viewed as 'a particular threat to cherished ideals of childhood' (Scott et al. 1998: 698). However, while some lament the 'too much too soon' mantra of the hurried child philosophy (i.e. children as sexually knowledgeable), others, particularly in relation to sex education and teenage pregnancy, suggest that children are receiving 'too little too late' (i.e. children as sexually ignorant).

This paradox has surfaced recently in the juxtaposition of the DfEE's (2000a) Sex and Relationships Education (SRE) guidance that encourages educators to draw on children's own knowledge and understanding (e.g. 'kissing'), and the

Sexual Offences Act (2003) which considers any sexual activity (including kissing) between children and teenagers under 16 as unlawful. This bill not only poses a challenge for sexuality educators of under-16s across the UK, but also to others (e.g. teenage magazine problem page columnists, ChildLine, etc.) who provide support and sexual advice to children already engaged in sexual activity (see Phillips 2003 and Children's Rights Alliance 2003). Once more, the 'child' and 'sex/uality' are presented as oppositional and incompatible. Sexuality is reinscribed as the property of the adult where adult power erases any notion of children's sexual agency in matters of consent and sexuality rights more widely.

By and large, children are assumed to either be 'immune' to, or passive recipients (if not victims) of, sexual representations within an increasingly sex-saturated entertainment and media industry: from 'kissing tips' in teenage magazines (*Bliss, Sugar, Cosmogirl*), young gay and lesbian british 'pop idols' (e.g. Will Young and Alex Parks), characters in soap opera story lines (e.g. *Coronation Street*) and other 'educational' programmes like ITV's pre-watershed *Love Bites*. However, as Kelley *et al.* (1999: 232) illustrate in their research on how children respond to representations of sexual behaviour on television, 'primary school children show considerable knowledge about personal and sexual issues … (and) soaps provide a platform for sharing and debating such knowledge' (see also Kehily *et al.* 2002; Buckingham and Bragg 2003). From my own recent observations of one Year 5 sex education class on 'making babies', one boy, reflecting upon an episode of Channel 4's *So Graham Norton* featuring two transgendered 'men', asked: 'can men that have had a sex change have babies?' (Ben, aged 9), thus confirming Debbie Epstein and Richard Johnson's (1998: 96) claim that 'it is ridiculous to assume that children don't draw conclusions from the visible, invisible and imagined sexual behaviour of the adults and children around them'. Sexual innocence, then, 'is something that adults wish upon children, not a natural feature of childhood itself' (Epstein and Johnson 1998: 97) – although I suggest in later chapters that children themselves also draw upon notions of childhood (sexual) innocence within their own sexual cultures and emerging sexual identities.

Simon Watney (1991) argues that we should not be debating whether or not children are sexual beings but concerning ourselves with the ways in which adults respond to children's sexualities. In addition to supporting the need to address the ways in which the adult world treats, recognises, regulates, punishes and ultimately creates children's sexualities, I suggest that we attend equally to the ways in which children are active in this process and produce their own sexual identities, cultures and relations within the constraints of the adult world (and their own peer group). Created within the gendering of sexual innocence, it is the eroticisation and sexualisation of young femininities which I discuss next.

All about Eve: sexuality … that's what little girls are made of

The eroticisation of innocence and the fascination with the erotic child is deeply gendered. From depictions of sexualised images of prepubertal girls in the Victorian era (Higonnet 1998) to the Lolita-like commodification of little girls as sexual consumers and performers in contemporary society (Jackson 1982; Walkerdine 1999; Giroux 2000), it is the girl-child, not the boy-child, whose innocence is eroticised. It is the eroticisation of little girls that provokes our (adult) concern for their protection. In March 2003 a tabloid campaign (the *Sun*) successfully halted the selling of 'sexy' underwear to pre-teen girls, from thongs and padded bras to T-shirts inscribed with 'Little Miss Naughty' motifs (see Brooks 2003). This is the same paper whose Page 3 'girls' use markers of childhood innocence to promote female sexuality by dressing women up as little girls. Indeed, as feminists have pointed out for decades, there is constant slippage and blurring between the categories 'woman' and 'girl', hence the term 'woman-child' (Burman 1995). Signs of childhood have been historically constructed as sexually alluring to the extent that women make great efforts to become more childlike and childlike symbols (school uniforms, sweets, toys, etc.) become sexually charged. *Guardian* columnist Libby Brooks highlights the infantilisation of women, or what I have termed the 'lollipop' approach to female sexuality, in her introduction to the children's underwear controversy:

> 'Opposite me on the tube sits a girl in a sex T-shirt. Her top is the design of a sweetie wrapper, but it says 'Man-teaser' instead of 'Malteasers' across her foam-boosted bosom'.
>
> (Brooks 2003: 15)

Societal anxieties over our girl-children as we enter the first decade of the twenty-first century centre around what Walkerdine (1999) has termed the 'proto-sexual' girl. That is, the pathologisation of any little girl who actively deploys dominant representations of 'older' female sexualities, whether it be padded bras and thongs, to erotic dancing and beauty pageant contests. In contrast to boys, where pathologisation centres predominantly upon violence, it is the sexual (precocious) girl that represents the Other to normal childhood – 'normal girls are well behaved, hard working and asexual' (Walkerdine 1999: 4).

What is implicit in many accounts of children and sexuality is that boys are rarely positioned outside the boundaries of 'normal childhood' for expressing themselves (hetero)sexually:

> Where girls forgo the child status if they are sexually active or even abused, violence and aggression (on the other hand) are the cultural norms that mark the boundaries for boys' exemption from childhood.
>
> (Burman 1995: 65)

I would argue that the feminisation of erotic innocence and sexuality more widely has resulted in an underdeveloped theorisation and neglect of boys' everyday sexual cultures beyond a discussion of 'dirty talk' or 'dirty play', usually framed within discourses of normative and maturing masculinities (Fine 1987). Indeed, discourses of pathologisation usually only surface in discussions of boys as sexual abusers or concern over boys' future (homo)sexual orientation if they deviate from (hetero)masculine norms. While it is possible to argue that (hetero)sexuality is much more a part of 'girlhood' than it is for 'boyhood', I would suggest otherwise. While the dominant discourse of the erotic girl-child certainly makes more visible the heterosexualising processes embedded in their constructions of femininity, boys are also subject to (and agents of) the heterosexual male gaze, although perhaps with a different set of pressures and consequences to girls. As shall be discussed throughout the following chapters, boy-ness and in particular boys' engagement with 'masculinity' and 'heterosexuality' throw up a number of contradictions. Boys are doubly feminised. They are locked into the 'feminine' side of the generational adult/child binary (when you consider the historical conflation of women with children, Burman 1995) and the 'feminine' side of the gendered masculinity/femininity binary (when you consider how hegemonic forms of masculinity are adult-centric and founded primarily upon employment, family, independence etc., see Haywood and Mac an Ghaill 2003: 72). Paying attention to the specificities of age and generation in girls' and boys' constructions of their gender and sexual identities is a central feature of this book and is expanded upon below.

Ageing childhood and 'sexual generationing'

The notion of generation and gendered generational relations is central to the ways childhood and the identity category 'child' has been and continues to be socially constructed. Childhood exists primarily in relation to its adult counterpart and is imbued with power relations where subordination of one group (female/child) is systematically structured in opposition to the other (male/adult) (see Alanen 1994, 2001). Furthermore, children, by virtue of their age, are variously positioned within the category 'child', and 'childhood' is designated as a particular temporal space within which the daily lives of children are regulated and interpreted.

Discourses of developmentalism continue to be widely influential in the ways in which children are tied to, and indeed tie themselves to, the transition of 'childhood' as a continual state of 'becoming' where all kinds of 'growth metaphors' abound. Chris Jenks (1996) illustrates:

> Childhood is spoken about as: a becoming; as a *tabula rasa*; as laying down the foundations; as shaping the individual; taking on; growing up; preparation; inadequacy; inexperience; immaturity and so on
>
> (Jenks 1996: 9)

I have already briefly discussed how 'growing up' and negotiating the generational adult/child binary is represented differently for girls and boys in relation to sexuality. These representations are further problematised and differentiated when the specificities within generational groups (e.g. between groups of 'children'), or what Bourdieu terms 'social generationing' (see Alanen 2001) are attended to. Allison James and Alan Prout (1998) have referred to this kind of social generationing as a two-fold process. Drawing on anthropological studies of 'age-class' and 'age grade' they explore how 'childhood' as a 'temporal duality' structures and constrains children's lives in formal and informal ways. *Age grade* refers to the fragmented and often unclear formal or informal groupings which have 'particular rights or duties which define the relationship of an age grade member to the social structure' (James and Prout 1998) such as the boundaries between the infant, child and teenager or the boundaries between adolescence and adulthood – concepts so blurred that new ones are regularly created (e.g. tweenager). *Age class* refers to groups of children who progress through the age class structure together, the most obvious example in Western societies being the schooling (Year 1, Year 2, Year 3 and so on) and daycare system (babies, younger toddlers, older toddlers, pre-school). And within each age-grade and age-class structure lies a set of normative expectations whether cognitive or behavioural that glue age, stage and phase together and by which children are judged and judge themselves. Those who fall short or exceed these norms can become the subject of concern (at best) and pathologisation (at worst). For example, children are often punished in school in terms of generational put-downs, such as 'you're behaving like infants'.

I would like to suggest that discourses of developmentalism also pathologise any deviation in the time-line of age-appropriate masculinities, femininities and sexualities. I have already outlined how girls' sexuality and the 'teening of girlhood' are subject to a 'hurried-child' discourse that usually spark only negative comments, such as 'she's growing up too quickly', 'she's a woman before her time' (see Chapters 3 and 5). While boys are rarely subject to the hurried-child discourse of accelerated gender identities, age-appropriate gender discourses can constrain boys in different ways. For example, a boy wearing nail varnish may be tolerated in pre-school but strongly discouraged in the junior years. Children themselves also invest in and draw upon developmental discourses and age-appropriate behaviours/activities to make sense of their emerging sexualities. One boy, Pete (see Chapter 6), describes his growing romantic interest in girls and sexual knowledge as 'the stage'. Other boys and girls would cast themselves as romantic players when they were 'older' informing me that as 10 year olds, they are 'too young' for boyfriends, girlfriends and kissing. As the subsequent chapters illustrate, girls and boys regularly take up and shake up childhood (sexual) innocent discourses and older 'adolescence/adult' discourses of sexuality. Indeed, given the increasing slippage and elision between social generations in relation to sexuality, the concept 'sexual generationing' (in addition to 'social generationing') is perhaps a useful one.

It addresses and scrutinises not only the social construction of chronological age and sexuality but also the patterning of time (e.g. individual and collective rhythms) as children negotiate issues and relations of gender and sexuality in different spaces (e.g. school, home, street) and social and cultural environments. It is the social, cultural and institutional space of the primary school, and research that has explicitly considered sexuality within this space, that I turn to in the next section.

Sexuality and the primary school: queering the field

Sexuality has only recently been explicitly addressed as a pervasive and normalising presence within the primary school (see Epstein and Johnson 1998). In one of the few articles focusing specifically on sexuality in the primary years, Amy Wallis and Jo VanEvery (2000) stress that the primary school is a sexual site just like any other institution. Sexuality, and in particular heterosexuality, is, they argue, 'not only present but crucial to the organisation of primary schools' (Wallis and VanEvery 2000: 411). The purpose of this section is to explore some of the less researched areas of sexuality and primary schooling: the familialisation of the primary school and the normalising gaze of hetero-patriarchal structures and practices; the construction of teacher sexualities (including teacher–teacher and teacher–pupil identity-work and relations) and official policies and practices of the taught curriculum. The literature regarding the 'informal' school or 'hidden curriculum' in terms of children's own sexual and romantic cultures, relations and identities concludes this chapter and provides a thematic backdrop to the subsequent chapters.

We are family: nurturing heteronormativity and primary schooling as the 'home corner'

There is a striking resemblance between the gendered division of labour and hierarchies of male power in primary schooling and the traditional patriarchal family (see Martin 1998). The predominantly all-female environment of the early and junior years sector and the higher ratio of male head teachers to female head teachers have led to many discussions regarding the feminisation and maternalisation of primary schooling (see Skelton 2001 for a brief, yet comprehensive historical overview).[2] This familial ethos in which female teachers represent the idealised position of the benevolent and nurturing bourgeoise mother and male head teachers represent the harsh authoritarian father is a parallel often drawn upon to expose and critique patriarchal child education philosophies (see Weems 1998). Indeed, 'being sent to the head' as the ultimate punishment bears an uncanny resemblance to the well-known phrase, 'wait till your father gets home'. Examples of similar kinds of authoritarian disciplinary practices can be found in a number of ethnographic studies of primary schooling, although head teachers do not need to be male to be the bearers of authoritarian masculinity (see

Skelton 2003). At Tipton, when the male head teacher retired, the acting head, Mrs Church, was feared and revered by most pupils in the school. In the first week of her new position, the supposedly 'toughest' and most frequently reprimanded (boy) pupil in the school was reduced to tears (after being sent down to her office earlier in the week) desperately pleading with his class teacher, 'please don't send me to Mrs Church, please please'.

Many authors have extended the familial analogy to the gendered role of pupils as children, where girls occupy themselves as 'workers' and 'helpers' within the domestic sphere/classroom and boys avoid anything perceived as 'girls' work' (be it washing up or studious behaviour). Given the connection between the notion of care with femininity, femininity with females and females as the proper and natural educators of young children, it is no surprise that primary education has been described (and repudiated) by some as a 'feminised' and 'masculine' free zone (see Skelton 2001; Ashley and Lee 2003). It is also no coincidence that the demise of traditional nuclear families and the rise of lone female headed households coincide with the promotion of male role models, 'not to care, love or nanny but as figures of authority and discipline' (Skelton 2001: 117).

Less reported is the relationship between the family as a normalised heteronormative institution and the primary school and specifically the intersection of gender essentialism (femininity is female), gender polarity (masculinity and femininity as binary opposites) and compulsory and gendered heterosexuality (heterofemininity and heteromasculinity). Lisa Weems (1998) takes up the themes of sex, gender and sexuality within early childhood education (USA) by tracing how the 'pedagogy of love' symbolised by the 'natural' relationship between mother and child, assumes and sets up a pathologised Other and serves to police the boundaries of heteronormativity:

> In the elementary classroom sexuality gets 'ordered' in the following way: Only the relations between (feminine) women and child can pass as the heteronormative mother and others become suspect and sometimes labelled perverse. Perversity is the term that is used to describe the relations of desire in elementary classrooms that exceed the boundaries of heteronormativity.[3]
>
> (Weems 1998: 32)

It is not only gay men teachers then that represent the Other and exceed heternormative boundaries (see King 1997; Silin 1995). Providing care becomes a risky business for all men teachers (see also Jones 2003, 2004). The feminisation of care constructs primary/elementary education as a no man's land where the (hetero)masculinity of men teachers becomes questionable and can result in displays of exaggerated or hyper-masculinities to demonstrate their masculine credentials to themselves and the public at large (see Francis and Skelton 2001b; Skelton 2001). This is the focus of the next section and the focus of more recent research reflecting upon the interrelationship between masculinity and heterosexuality of men teachers.

Teacher sexualities: from classrooms and staff rooms

Very little empirical research (my own included) has problematised or indeed rendered visible primary school teachers' constructions of their own gender and sexual identities. What little research there is has focused upon a much needed shake-up of men teachers' constructions of heterosexual masculinity (Francis and Skelton 2001b) and the experiences of gay and lesbian teachers (Letts and Sears 1999; Wallis and VanEvery 2000) – all of which involves negotiating some form of heterogendered 'passing' (as 'properly (hetero)masculine' or 'properly (hetero)feminine'). Drawing on their own individual research projects, Becky Francis and Christine Skelton (2001b) attend to the widely acknowledged dual process (in the secondary school at least) in which men teachers must prove their 'masculinity' by constructing themselves as authority figures and disciplinarians on the one hand and 'one of the lads' (by aligning themselves with dominant masculinities/heterosexualities and the policing and shaming of Other masculinities/sexualities) on the other. In doing so, they make explicit the heterosexist discourses underpinning such performances and the pressure to perform as 'properly masculine' within the 'feminised' environment of the primary school:

> [...] heterosexist discourses (reflecting homophobia and misogyny) are drawn on by men teachers in the classroom to construct their own masculinity in opposition to the boys that they are 'other' ... [T]his positioning by men teachers of themselves as 'real men' and thereby different to females and dismissive of 'the feminine' ... can be seen as one way of establishing their masculine credentials in a female profession.
>
> (Francis and Skelton 2001b: 15)

Passing and performing as 'real men' or indeed 'real women' can involve hiding aspects of identity that are Other to dominant gendered and (hetero)sexual scripts. Wallis and VanEvery (2000) highlight how gay, lesbian and bisexual teachers who do not conform to normative gender performances (e.g. 'soft' men or 'butch' women) are targeted by pupils and teachers alike through sexual/gender jibes and speculation as to their non-heterosexual orientation (see also Caspar et al. 1996; King 1997; Letts and Sears 1999). The limited research on gay and lesbian teachers working within the primary and early years suggests unsurprisingly that in many ways identifying as lesbian or gay is either experienced or reported more widely (particularly in tabloid press) as being incompatible with being a teacher. The notion that gay and lesbian teachers are inherently and inevitably dangerous to children insofar as they represent a corrupting influence upon children's presumed (heterosexual) innocence is nowhere better exemplified than in the tabloid reporting of Hackney head teacher Jane Brown's decision to turn down tickets for the ballet *Romeo and Juliet* on the grounds that she supposedly considered it 'a blatantly heterosexual love story' (*Daily Mail* 20 January 1994, see Epstein 1997),[4] as Epstein notes:

> It is clear, from this coverage, that the very possibility that children might learn to consider non-heterosexuality as a thinkable (if not viable) option through the example of lesbian and gay teachers is regarded as a cause for extreme concern.
>
> (Epstein 1997: 190)

It is no wonder then, given the recent political climate and 'discourses of derision' (Ball 1990) facing teachers more widely, that non-heterosexual teachers keep their sexuality private and normative heterosexual performances are limited to the straightest of straight. Given the ways in which the staff room can operate as a prohibitive space policing non-normative gender, race and sexual identities, Wallis and VanEvery (2000) conclude that for many primary school teachers, the classroom is the one remaining space where they have a certain degree of flexibility in the way they present themselves to children. However, as Epstein and Johnson (1998) highlight, for many 'out' gay teachers who seek to challenge the normalisation of heterosexuality and carve out a space from which to over-write children's own heteronormative expectations within the primary classroom, this becomes a difficult if not impossible task. They describe how one gay teacher's account of coming out to his class was met with disbelief and denial (see also Danish 1999). Again, the analogy of the primary school as 'home corner', and its hetero-familial ethos, partly helps explain how 'even out gay teachers are read as heterosexual' (Epstein *et al.* 2003: 30), such is the pervasiveness of children's own heteronormative assumptions and imagined futures. Research investigating the ways in which teachers and students police each other's gender and sexual identities is explored further below.

(Hetero)sexualising teacher–pupil relations

When research has addressed inter-generational (e.g. teacher student) sexual interactions, much of the reporting has centred upon the abusive adult-sexual gaze. Problematising some of these accounts, Francis and Skelton (2001b) draw attention to the ways in which men teachers perform and construct their gender and sexual identities (i.e. their 'heterosexual masculinities') with their female students. The following example is an extract from Skelton's field notes of one primary school teacher's flirtatious behaviour in which he positions himself as a 'sex object':

> The children are told to meet up in the hall for PE after they have got changed. Phillip Norris (the teacher) adds, 'You'll want to be quick girls because I've got my sexy shorts with me today' and he wiggles his hips (Skelton, fieldnotes).
>
> (Francis and Skelton 2001: 15)

In their interpretation of this extract Francis and Skelton (2001b) move beyond conceptualising the interaction between Phillip Norris and 'the girls' as wholly oppressive. Rather they invite a reading which highlights how some sexual behaviours can be interpreted as simultaneously harassing and seductive, by drawing attention to the 'mixed emotions' many girls experience in feeling 'gratified by male objectification' yet also 'experiencing such behaviour as harassing' (see also Hey 1997; Walkerdine 1997, 1999) – a theme that is just as prevalent in girls' interactions with same-aged (boy) peers, as subsequent chapters illustrate.

While the ways in which teachers police children's gender and sexual identities is well established in school-based research, much less is known about how children themselves actively regulate teachers' gender/sexualities and how sexuality can overturn expected power relations between teachers and pupils. The most often cited example of the latter is Walkerdine's (1981) depiction of two 4-year-old boys' interaction with their nursery teacher. Walkerdine interprets their manipulation of sexist and sexualised language as their way to position their female class teacher as 'the powerless object of male sexual discourse' and to seize control for themselves (see also Chapter 6). Even less researched is the 'missing discourse of desire' (Fine 1988; Tobin 1997) on the part of the student (e.g. romantic 'crushes' and flirting with teachers) and the interrelationship between the desire for education and desire for the teacher as educator (see Epstein and Johnson 1998; Skelton 2001). Although not the focus of this book, I witnessed a number of occasions where pupils positioned their teachers or teaching assistants either as (hetero)sex objects or objects of (hetero)romance. At Tipton, two groups of Year 3 girls doted on a Year 10 boy on work experience from the local secondary school, treating him like a psuedo pop-idol by running up to him screaming his name and following him around the playground. There was also a group of Year 6 girls at Tipton who would 'wolf whistle' at Mr Thomson, their PE teacher, when he took off his tracksuit bottoms to play football. More recently, on another school-based project (Coffey et al. 2003), a Year 2 boy declared that he was in love with his old nursery teacher and that he had bought her flowers and would like to marry her when he was old enough.

Promoting (hetero)sexuality: from wedding projects to sex education

The forces of heteronormativity regulating teacher–pupil relations, staff cultures and school organisation also underpin official 'sex and relationship' education guidance and the everyday formal curriculum in primary schools. Queering elementary education, Sears (1999) writes:

> As cultural cops of the ancient regime, elementary school teachers unmindfully enforce 'compulsory heterosexuality' through stories of nuclear animal families and questions of mommies and daddies.
>
> (Sears 1999: 11)

In an article exploring the sexual learning cultures of 5 to 7 year olds, Debbie Epstein comments upon how teachers complicitly reinforce children's heteronormative values and imagined futures. Observing a class project in which children were asked to draw a picture of themselves as grown ups (as part of a broader topic on 'work') over half of the girls (but none of the boys) drew themselves as 'brides' or 'mothers with small children'. However, rather than questioning or problematising girls' choices (e.g. by encouraging them to focus upon their 'careers'), the class teacher responded with: 'what a lovely picture – so you're going to be a bride when you grow up are you' (Epstein 1997: 39).

Such (hetero)familial discourses (e.g. marriage and babies) are explicitly prescribed within the DfEE's (2000) own Sex and Relationship Education (SRE) guidance in which 'children should be taught about the nature of marriage and its importance for family life and for bringing up children' (DfEE 2000, p. 11, para. 1.21). Throughout the guidance there are numerous references which unofficially promote 'heterosexuality' despite the DfEE's specific claim that the guidance 'is not about the promotion of sexual orientation' (DfEE 2000: p. 5, para. 9). The 'orientation' and 'relationship' promoted throughout is specifically that of 'heterosexuality'. Other sexual orientations are not only invisible (e.g. there is no reference to gay, lesbian or bisexual identities) but addressed in the guidance solely in relation to (homophobic) 'bullying' or 'harassment'.

Commenting on the construction of children's childhoods, Berry Mayall (1994a: 4) states that 'in most spheres, modern childhood in Western European countries is characterised by protection and exclusion'. Dominant discourses of 'protection' (e.g. of children's sexual innocence and from harm and disease) and 'exclusion' (e.g. of sexual relationships outside of a heteronormative context and of any notion that sex might be fun or pleasurable) predominate throughout the SRE guidance. Unfortunately the myth of the (sexually) innocent child and the fear and anxiety of promoting anything other than a delayed (hetero)sexual relationship (singular!) prevents many teachers (and government officials) from recognising and thus effectively supporting the pleasures, pains and power relations embedded in children's own relationship cultures. As the next section and indeed subsequent chapters illustrate, children's own sexual behaviour and knowledge blur and problematise many of the boundaries set up in the 'official' SRE guidance around what children should or should not know, learn and experience.

Encountering the 'third' hidden curriculum: children's own sexual cultures, practices and subjectivities

Writing over 20 years ago, Raphaela Best's educational ethnography of boys and girls in their first four years at junior school is one of the first published accounts of the primary school as a curricularising agency for the production of children's sexuality.[5] Best (1983) describes children's sexual learning as the 'third hidden curriculum' (the former two being the official 'academic' and hidden 'gender' curriculum) – a curriculum that usually takes place away from the gaze of the watchful adult:

> So, while the adults hemmed and hawed, the children went about learning and experimenting on their own, careful to protect the frightened adult world's need for ignorance, all the while garnering what they could from whatever source they could to expand on their personal observations. They found ways to circumvent adult scrutiny and allay suspicion. [...] they found ways to hide them (sexual activities) from surveillance.
>
> (Best 1983: 109)

Children talked to Best about playing 'house' in the early years, where girls and boys coupled up as mothers and fathers and sat around kissing, to engaging in more public 'kissing' and 'dating' games in later years which could involve more private genital touching and watching games of 'look and see' and 'show and tell'.[6] Such rich ethnographic research which recognises the school arena as a central erotic and sexual playground for children (in industrialised societies) is rare in studies of the junior years, possibly because of the myths that prevail in relation to 'adolescence' as the psychological, social and biological trigger for sexual feelings, relations and identity constructions.

Primary school ethnographies of children's gender relations in the 1980s and early 1990s seldom centralised sexuality as part of the ways in which boys and girls negotiate their gender identities (although see Walkerdine 1981). Only relatively recently, have studies of pre-teenage gender relations/identity-work begun to explore how sexuality shapes and is shaped by gender in a myriad of ways, from clothes and sport to friendship and play. Few studies have examined children's sexual relations, cultures and discourses with the same theoretical complexity and attention to detail that studies of gender relations have enjoyed. This is particularly true of the (hetero)sexualisation of school-based gender identities (see Redman 1996; Epstein 1997; Renold 2000; Wallis and VanEvery 2000; Epstein et al. 2001a, 2003; Redman et al. 2002). Cumulatively, this expanding body of research is beginning to address a number of research questions central to exploring children's sexual cultures, relations and identities as they are experienced and produced within the school context. Below is a brief synopsis of some of the key emerging themes from this literature as I have identified them. They include: the significance of time and space; the sexualisation of gender identities; the intersection of sexuality with other differences (e.g. social class, ethnicity and disability); sexual teasing and harassment; and the discursive construction of children's sexuality as 'play'. Many of these themes will run throughout the subsequent chapters and will be developed further in the concluding chapter.

Locating sexualities: the importance of time and space

Since Best's groundbreaking ethnography of the 'third hidden curriculum' a number of researchers have begun to identify primary schools as 'significant cultural sites in which sexualities are produced, reproduced and contested' and how pupils are actively engaged 'from a very early age, in the production of sexual meanings, practices, power relations and identities' within these sites (Redman 1996: 175). How children create, appropriate and redefine spaces within the school arena to negotiate and explore sexual relations and identities is a cross-cutting theme in much of the published research on young pupils' sexual cultures. And it is the 'playground' and other areas officially designated as 'play' spaces within the school that are most commonly reported as sites for sexual learning and displays of sexual knowledge and awareness. Research suggests that 'playground sexualities' abound in a number of social and cultural forms, from the traditional games of 'kiss chase' and 'mummies and daddies' in the early years to more contemporary games (e.g. 'Blind Date') and rhymes and songs drawn from popular culture (see Clarke 1990; Davies 1993; Thorne 1993; Epstein 1997; Epstein *et al.* 2001a; Reay 2001).

The spatiality of 'playground sexualities' is a central feature in my own research. For example, I witnessed in the later junior years (Years 5 and 6) how established boyfriends and girlfriends graduate to a particular space at the far end of the sports field near the trees (and thus away from staff surveillance) to 'hang out' and 'snog' (see Chapter 5). This particular space was well known to other pupils as 'couples' corner'. Other 'public-made-private' spaces have been documented in Kehily *et al.*'s (2002) depiction of the 'diary group girls' who marked out their own personal and private territory in the public arena of the playground to discuss 'puberty/periods', 'erotic attachments' and 'imagined (predominantly heteronormative) futures'. My own and others' research also illustrates how those boys and girls subject to sexual teasing and harassment appropriate private spaces (e.g. bushes or 'wildlife' area) to circumvent and directly avoid the often cruel scrutiny of 'the public' (peer) gaze. The playground is thus a multiple territorial site in which children hide, share or display sexuality and sexual relations.

While the playground is deemed the 'official' designated space for children to 'do play' and thus unofficially 'do sexuality', other public and private 'inside' spaces (such as the assembly hall, the classrooms, the toilets, the corridors and the cloakrooms) are just as suffused with an underground sexual economy and a cast of covert and overt sexual performances. For example, Kehily *et al.*'s

(2002:16) description of the 'paraphernalia of contemporary girlhood' permeates both classroom and playground pupil cultures. Here, a range of cultural commodities such as 'badges, stickers, posters, pencil cases, T-shirts and pictures from magazines' collectively act as a barometer of normative heterosexual femininity alongside the cosmetic culture of lip-balms, nail-varnish and the re-fashioning of school uniforms to mirror the local high-street 'look' (see also Thorne 1993; Renold 2000).[7] In relation to the sexualisation of classroom interaction Davies (1993: 27) gives an example of how even borrowing a pen or pencil from the opposite sex can be strewn with sexual overtone and meaning. I explore in Chapters 3 and 5 how heterosexuality, heterosexual hierarchies and sexual stigma operate to police everything from group project work to seating arrangements.

Finally, the ways in which girls and boys define their own spaces to perform and negotiate their gender/sexuality will change and shift between and within schools and year groups, and over time. In their study of children's relationship cultures across four schools, Epstein *et al.* (2001b) found differences both within and between pupils' romantic cultures. Practices such as 'going out' and 'dating' were more prevalent in two of the four schools, and the meanings attached to boyfriends and girlfriends varied significantly from context to context and within and between schools.

The heterosexualisation of gender: gender norming and gender bending

As discussed earlier, children and childhood are profoundly gendered in diverse and often contradictory ways: from the feminisation of childhood (where women and children function together as the 'other' of men) to the sexualisation of girls/femininity and the masculinisation of the 'developing child' in educational discourses (where maturity is equated with masculinity). The eroticisation of (feminised) innocence and the ways in which being a 'normal' or 'proper' girl involves investing in cultural markers that signify dominant notions of heterosexual femininity has been explored in a number of educational ethnographies of gender relations and feminine subjectivities. Early years studies have explored young girls' 'dressing up' culture and their rapidly developing knowledge of gendered cosmetics (Connolly 1998; Walkerdine 1999; Oschner 2000). Studies of the later junior years have highlighted a more sophisticated embodiment of 'older' sexualised femininities (see Davies 1993; Thorne 1993; Francis 1998; Renold 2000; Reay 2001). However, there is still a tendency to theorise older primary school girls' investment in the production of their bodies as heterosexually desirable commodities as an effect of developmental 'maturation' discourses (i.e. their transition into 'adolescence' signified by their changing pubertal bodies, see Thorne and Luria 1986; Thorne 1993) as opposed to girls' performing and negotiating 'compulsory heterosexuality'. By contrast, boys' sexual cultures and identity constructions and the role of sexuality in the production of multiple masculinities have been overlooked (perhaps because boys' puberty is experienced relatively later than girls').

A central theme throughout the empirical chapters in this book is how girls and boys experience this sexualisation in different ways. While I make much of the multiple ways in which girls and boys 'do' sexuality and gender, a pervasive theme running throughout is how girls are always already (hetero)sexualised as part of 'normal' femininity and girlhood and how boys on the other hand are (homo)sexualised when they deviate from 'normal' masculinity and boyhood. Whether it is the gender-norming of (hetero)sexualised femininities or the gender-bending of (homo)sexualised masculinities, all gendered subject positions (e.g. 'tomboys', 'squares' or 'sissies') are to some extent subject to the heterosexual male gaze and all are produced within a heteronormative framework of 'compulsory heterosexuality'.

Romancing sexualities, intimacy and relationship cultures

There is a growing body of research which highlights the salience of children's own romantic cultures and relations especially through the subject positions 'girlfriend' and 'boyfriend'. Children as young as four and five are actively engaged in the boyfriend and girlfriend culture (see Connolly 1998). Epstein *et al*.'s (2001a) research in junior schools supports earlier studies of how six year olds 'date', 'dump' and 'two-time' (Best 1983; Thorne and Luria 1986). Debunking the myth that heterosexual relations symbolise entry into 'adolescence', research into children's own romantic cultures continues to highlight the multiple ways in which children interpret their local boyfriend/girlfriend culture and discourses of love and romance. For example, I explore how girls and boys position their classmates, neighbours and media stars as 'potential' boyfriends/girlfriends and engage in a range of sexualised practices from kissing and touching to holding hands. The range of derogatory (e.g. 'slag', 'bastard', 'tarty') and complementary (e.g. 'sexy', 'fit', 'gorgeous', etc.) heterosexualised evaluations of boy/girl classmates' attractiveness and romantic desirability is also explored and problematised. I argue that not only are girls objectified by the (hetero)sexual male gaze, but boys are increasingly feeling the scrutiny of a (peer-based) sexual female gaze (see also Epstein *et al*. 2001a).

To varying degrees and emphasis most of the research on children's sexual and romantic cultures has highlighted the gendered power relations at play in the production of heterosexual hierarchies. US researchers Adler and Adler (1998) suggest that popular girls and boys (usually those who came closest to the gendered 'ideal') are the most romantically desirable (see also Thorne 1993; Epstein *et al*. 2001a). Thorne and Luria (1986) explore how sexual and romantic teasing creates and maintains social, gendered and sexual hierarchies. The production and reproduction of heterosexual hierarchies is an enduring theme in subsequent chapters, as are the ways in which children's friendships are mediated by pupil's sexual cultures and relations (Kehily *et al.* 2002). For example, Walton *et al.* (2002), in their analysis of 552 stories by children aged 9–10 years, of interpersonal conflict in relation to issues of sexuality and romance, identify contradictory dominant discourses. These include: 'romantic norms violate friendships norms', 'romance as trivial', 'romance as important', and 'romance and sexual behaviour as grown up'. The power and inherent contradictions in the discourses of romance and (hetero)sexuality in the production of children's gendered peer cultures and friendship circles is particularly undertheorised in the literature (see Gagnon and Simon 1973; Plummer 1990) beyond stating that young boys shy away from inter-personal intimacies and are more interested in (hetero)sex acts or that young girls are more interested in romantic and emotional intimacies than sexual activity (see Plummer's critique). Much less researched are homoerotic and same-sex intimacies and desires (although see Redman *et al.* 2002) and resistances or challenges to dominant heterosexual storylines (Davies 1993; Rossiter 1994; Epstein *et al.* 2001a).

Sexuality and Other 'differences that make a difference'

Epstein *et al.* (2003) argue in their chapter on the 'normalisation of heterosexuality in the primary school' that sexuality and children's sexual cultures cannot be separated off from other social and cultural differences 'that make a difference' to patterns of inequality and power relations. Different cultural and social backgrounds make available not only different versions of masculinity and femininity, but different versions of sexuality. Connolly (1995), for example, explores how a group of infant boys (mixed-parentage, white and African-Caribbean) fashioned a collective identity as the Bad Boys. Drawing upon the hyper-sexualised image of the black African-Caribbean male they positioned themselves within discourses of gender, childhood, adulthood, 'race' and sexuality as both heterosexually powerful and desirable (amongst their peers) and simultaneously as aggressive, troublesome and problematic (for teachers and peers alike). Connolly also illustrates the ways in which South Asian boys are effeminised and rendered romantically undesirable and how South Asian girls are positioned as sexual rejects where 'to be associated with an Asian girlfriend is definitely a term of abuse' (1994: 181). But where the Bad Boys were constructed as under-achieving in educational discourse, South Asian girls as 'helpful, quiet and hardworking' were produced both as 'ideal pupil' and located within a discursive position that defined them as both feminine and Other in relations of heterosexual femininity (see also Ali 2002; Bhana 2002; Allan 2003).

Epstein *et al.* (2002: 27) argue that it is not just black boys or working-class girls who 'carry' sexuality and thus represent 'sexuality' for an entire class or year group; any child who performs sexuality with confidence and knowledge can 'carry' sexuality in this way (see also Davies 1993 and Chapter 5). Power relations in constructions of difference are thus central to our understanding of how sexuality is produced within children's cultures and social relations, as Epstein *et al.* emphasise:

> Difference is also about power, and the ways that sexualities are read, experienced and produced takes place within contexts that are structured through power and resistance in complicated patterns of inequality.
>
> (Epstein *et al.* 2003: 27).

However, while research is paying closer attention to how ethnicity, gender and sexuality intersect and make available a range of identities and social positionings for children to take up, other differences 'that make a difference' such as physical disability, learning difficulties (see Benjamin 2003) or children who are 'looked after' by the state (see Barter *et al.* 2004) are relatively absent in the research of children's negotiations of 'everyday' gender/sexual relations. This study is unfortunately no exception.

'Playing at' and 'preparatory' sexualities: becoming and being sexual

As discussed earlier in the chapter, a distinguishing feature of research into children's sexual cultures is the developmental reference to children's active engagement with their sexual selves and worlds as a transition to an older, usually 'adolescent' sexual identity. Terms that commonly crop up include references to children's sexuality as: 'induction', 'graduation', 'preparation', 'emergent', etc . While locating children's sexuality as 'emergent' enables us to account and explore how children are positioned and take-up available sexual discourses as young children, there is also a tendency to view children as just 'playing at', 'practising', 'trying on' or 'mimicking' older sexualities. This positioning tends to treat children solely as sexual becomings rather than exploring and taking seriously the tensions and contradictions of children as sexual beings and becomings (see Epstein 1993a). Because of the supposedly unnatural association of sexuality with children, it is often only through the discursive representation of children's sexuality as 'play' that it becomes possible to speak and write in a legitimate and socially acceptable way.

When children's active engagement with sexuality looks less like 'play' and takes on a more polished sophisticated (and serious) performance, where the lines between adult/child or young child/older child become blurred, adult anxieties are raised. As subsequent chapters will address, there is a need to recognise the place of play as a defining feature of children's 'emerging' sexualities, while registering the importance and seriousness in the 'here and now' of these 'emerging sexualities' – that is recognising children as both sexual becomings and sexual beings. In the same way that researchers (e.g. Rossiter 1994) have attempted to rescue the trivialisation of pain and shame of adolescence as just a normal and natural part of growing up, so there is a need to take seriously the pain, pleasure and power of children as they negotiate and construct their sexual identities, relations and cultures. This is about taking seriously the consequences of sexualised bullying and harassment and perhaps taking seriously on a more abstract level the limitations of some forms of sexual play, produced as they are within a constraining heteronormative framework.

Punishing sexualities: teasing and harassment

When sexual harassment and schooling has been the focus of research, the site of investigation has been the secondary school and subsequently the lives of adolescents. Early feminist research explored young women's experiences of heterosexual harassment (Davies 1984; Jones 1985; Mahony 1985; Lees 1986, 1993; Wolpe 1988; Halson 1989; Herbert 1989; Mahony and Jones 1989). Later research in the 1990s and 2000s, which began exploring young people's constructions of school-based femininities, masculinities and sexualities, exposed the relationship between gender-based and sexualised forms of violence and harassment, particularly its role in the production of hegemonic heterosexual masculinities (Mac an Ghaill 1994; Kehily and Nayak 1996; Kenway and Fitzclarence 1997; Duncan 1999; Sunnari et al. 2002; Martino and Pallotta-Chiarolli 2003) and in the policing of queer sexualities (Friend 1993; Epstein 1994; Laskey and Beavis 1996; Epstein and Johnson 1998; Epstein et al. 2003).

Despite isolated incidents within the media and references within broader projects on the gendered worlds of primary school children (Best 1983; Evans 1987; Clark 1990; Davies 1993; Thorne 1993; Adler and Adler 1998; Francis 1998; Connolly 1998, 2004; Skelton 2001; Swain 2000, 2002a, 2002b, 2003; Bhana 2002; Ali 2002), there are very few detailed accounts that centre the experience of pre-teenagers (although see Clark 1990 and Stein 1996) – possibly due to the fact that very few ethnographic studies locate the primary school as a key arena for the production of sexual identities (Renold 2000; Epstein et al. 2002). In the chapters that follow, I explore how the practices of physical and verbal forms of heterosexual, homophobic/anti-gay and heterosexist bullying and harassment are the means by which many children define, create and consolidate dominant masculinities and femininities, (hetero)sexual identities and heterosexual hierarchies. The implications for policy and practice to address and support the more damaging side of children's gender/sexual cutlures and relationships are discussed in the concluding chapter.

Concluding notes

Throughout this chapter I have located the primary school as one of the key institutional spaces, protecting, promoting and nurturing the sexual innocence of young children. In doing so I have explored some of the ways in which the adult world recognises, regulates, punishes and ultimately creates children's sexualities.

The idea that sex/sexuality is something peculiar to adults and adulthood or even 'older' teenage childhood is both short-sighted and dangerous. Discourses of 'denial' and 'delay' in much of the sex education guidance sits uncomfortably with research which demonstrates (pre-teenage) children's knowledge and curiosity on a wide and diverse range of sexual matters. In sum, children seemed to be denied yet simultaneously acknowledged as both sexual beings and becomings.

Much of the chapter was aimed at making visible the heteronormativity of the primary school and the regulation and policing of both teacher and pupil sexualities as well as problematising the gendering and generationing of young children's sexualities. In particular, I have addressed the widely recognised (hetero)sexualisation of young femininities and the less acknowledged pathologisation of boys that deviate from age-appropriate (hetero)gendered norms. Finally, research literature which has foregrounded, and informed, my own research into children's own sexual cultures was discussed in relation to six key themes, all of which interweave and shape the analysis of the following five empirical chapters. Central to all of this research is an exploration of how young children are both active and agentic in their gender and sexual identity-work, and often acutely aware and have internalised the many (hetero)normalising discourses that operate to shape and police their gender and sexual relations. The first empirical chapter concentrates upon girls' peer group cultures and girls' individual and collective negotiation of increasingly (hetero)sexualised femininities.

Chapter 3

To be or not to be 'girlie'

Negotiating (hetero)sexualised femininities

Introduction

Recent research on upper junior girls and femininities suggests that one of the most popular and dominant ways of 'doing girl' is by accessing and projecting a heterosexualised femininity (see Ali 2000, 2003; Reay 2001).[1] While confirming this finding, this chapter also explores the ways in which all of the girls in the research constructed their femininities by either aligning themselves with (and thus desiring) or against (and thus in opposition to) dominant sexualised feminine discourses, or what Miss Wilson (Hirstwood's class teacher) termed, 'girlie' femininities.[2] Individually and collectively, the girls in this research study seemed to have one of two choices: to be 'girlie' or 'not-girlie'. The latter included everything from rejecting or critiquing the heterosexualisation of femininity to ditching femininity altogether and crossing the gender divide to become an honorary boy.

One of the most pervasive themes in this chapter is how discourses of compulsory (hetero)sexuality both empower, constrain and punish girls in multiple and contradictory ways. Part of this analysis involves paying close attention to the relational nature of gender identities, as being co-constructed between (boy–girl) and within (girl–girl) the genders. Thus, I will be exploring how girls are multiply and hierarchically positioned and actively position themselves in relation to other girls/femininities, especially heterosexualised 'girlie' femininities. I will also be examining how girls construct different versions of femininity in relation to boys and hegemonic heterosexual masculinity.

Given the status and desirability of the 'girlie-girl' subject position, the first two sections are dedicated to exploring normative (hetero)sexualised femininities. 'Embodying girlie' and 'Tarty but not too tarty' explore girls' investments in producing their own and others' bodies as heterosexually desirable commodities. Each section traces how girls' pleasures, pressures and anxieties of desiring and performing young 'sexy' femininities are regulated within 'official' and 'unofficial' school contexts. This leads to an exploration of how the sexual double standard (Cowie and Lees 1981) is alive and well patrolling the border-work of 'appropriate' and 'inappropriate' (hetero)sexuality for *all* girls and how the construction of each is contingent upon context, time, social class and girls' own individual histories of engaging with an increasingly 'girlie' culture.

'I'm Not a Girlie' tells the stories of two groups of girls: a popular group of girls of varying academic ability and social backgrounds at Tipton, a relatively unpopular group of high-achieving girls from professional and fairly affluent middle-class backgrounds at Hirstwood and Erica, a self-identified 'tomboy' (middle-class, high-achiever at Hirstwood). I explore how these girls consistently constructed their gender and sexual identities by socially and culturally distancing themselves from 'girlie' femininities but in distinct and contrasting ways. All had some success in being able to call upon critical frameworks that enabled them to challenge and critique dominant notions of the (hetero)erotic girl. The final section, 'You're Sexist ' explores the Tipton girls' (aka the 'top-girls') construction of a more powerful femininity by strategically infiltrating the (usually) all-boys game of football via a range of anti-sexist and equal rights discourses which they then use to overturn other sexist and heterosexist injustices beyond the sports field. Their story, however, highlights their privileged position as ex-girlfriends and the heteronormative base required for such negotiations and transformations.

Embodying 'girlie': fashioning hyper-femininities

From my earliest days in the field, I soon became aware of how girls were quickly learning to desire and create the 'perfect body' and how fashion (being 'in', being 'out') became a heuristic device through which they culturally coded their own and each other's bodies as representing (or not!) the bodily ideal. Of special concern was their desire for 'thinness' and 'beauty'. Arms, legs, hips and thighs were regularly checked, prodded and poked as girls positioned their own and other girls' bodies as 'too fat' or 'too thin' while struggling with the often impossible task of assigning each other's faces in a continuum of attractiveness. 'Bodily' dissatisfaction was a recurring theme in many group interviews as girls subjected themselves and were subject to what Chernin (1983, 2004) terms, 'the tyranny of slenderness' (see also Bordo 1990, 1993, 2004 and Grogan 1998). The following extracts are taken from a focused interview in which I asked the question, 'how do you feel about the way you look?'

SCHOOL: TIPTON

Alison: When you're in erm, I've got some tight tops and there's this one that I really like but I don't dare to wear it because when you're in tight tops it makes you look fat and shows it, shows it out.

[…]

Alison: Sophie thinks that she's perfect and she doesn't like me because er she thinks I'm fat and horrible and everything.

ER: She's said this to you?

Alison: No, but I know she does because of the way she looks …
ER: And how does that make you feel?
Jenna: It makes, it just makes me feel angry that erm coz they keep picking
           on you saying, some people keep pick, they keep picking on you say-
           ing you're fat and not thin and/
[…]
Alison: If everybody was like like Sophie then they'd like you, but otherwise
           they wouldn't.

SCHOOL: HIRSTWOOD

Sally: People say that Debbie's fat but she's not/
Danni: She's not she's just got a bit of/it
Sally: Well built/
Tina: Yeah, she's just well built
Danni: Yeah
ER: And how/does Debbie feel do you think
Hannah: I think I'm fat but/

Positioned at the margins of popular peer groups, Debbie, Jenna and Alison
were only too aware of how 'corporeal capital' (gained by girls like Sophie
'doing what they want') could be transformed into 'social' and 'sexual capital',
resonating in Alison's words, 'they'd like you otherwise'.[3] Although the girls
were seduced by the notion that inhabiting the ideal body would put a stop to
being called 'fat', they also sought alternative discourses, such as 'well built', to
console each other and counter being positioned in this way. By way of contrasting narratives, there were also some girls (usually 'popular', 'pre-pubescent'
and 'stick-thin') who used the discourse of 'not being thin enough' in playful
and pleasurable ways (see Nilan 1998). Identified by others as 'the thinnest girl
in the class', Mandy, for example, admitted privately to me following one interview, that she quite enjoyed the attention and concern from others when she
used to worry about her arms being 'too flabby', because she knew she 'did not
need to diet'. Mandy's skinny, pre-pubescent body did indeed represent the
'bodily ideal' that not only her peers, but many older girls and women strive to
emulate (see Bordo 1990).
    Regardless of body shape or size, a recurrent theme in girls' body talk was
how their 'body projects' (Bartky 1988) were produced almost wholly within a
heterosexual framework of desirability. Jacobus et al. (1990: 4) suggest that 'perceptions and interpretations for the body are mediated through language and
the surrounding culture'. For girls, the somatic ideal that many of them were
investing in was embedded within a dominant heterosexual/sexist culture that
positions the female body as a heterosexual object. From the girls' own
accounts, it seemed that their bodies were only desirable when, through the
validation of others (boys and girls), they were heterosexualised. Sophie, for

example, reveals how she was only deemed 'attractive' by her boyfriend when she was 'going out' with him and Mandy and Kirsty pinpoint 'boys' as the sole reason for their 'worrying' leg-size:

SCHOOL: TIPTON

ER:	Does Todd (Sophie's ex-boyfriend) ever say anything about the way you look?
Harriet:	Yeah he does he calls her/
Sophie:	Yeah he says that I'm ugly when I'm not going out with him.
ER:	Does he?
Harriet:	Yeah but he says that she's really/
Sophie:	He thought I had nice legs when I was going out with him (laughs).
Harriet:	And now he says that she's really ugly and everything so …
[…]	
Mandy:	We're just worried about our legs particularly.
Kirsty:	Yeah.
ER:	Because of fashion or/
Mandy:	Boys.
Kirsty and Mandy:	Boys.

Frustratingly, the bodily ideals that the girls worked with were also routinely contradicted and often bore no relation to 'real' body size. Sophie, for example, was positioned as 'ugly', 'perfect', 'fat', 'thin', 'pretty' and 'sexy' within just one school term. 'Attractiveness' it seemed, was not only a culturally and socially shifting concept, but contingent on being heterosexually desirable or involved in a heterosexual relationship (see Chapter 5). There was also a temporal dimension to this process. Girls shifted back and forth from 'gazing upon' their own or other 'bodies' as sexual objects (whether it be childhood toys such as 'Barbie', female peers like Sophie or international supermodels like Kate Moss) to being 'gazed upon' and thus becoming the object of heterosexual desire. Interestingly, girls who invested the most in producing their bodies as hetero-sexual commodities were those girls who viewed playing with Barbies at age 11 as a sign of immaturity (most reported to having given them up at age 7). These girls were now regulating and inscribing their own bodies and drawing upon 'older' (their words) more mature femininities.

Flirty-fashion and dirty dancing: tales of power and pleasure

Clothes were a central source of social and sexual capital and one of the most visible social and cultural markers of differentiated femininities and differenti-ated friendship groups as Anna (Hirstwood) illustrates in her comment below:

Anna: Danni and Melissa would never be friends … Melissa wears sporty stuff like Umbro shorts and Danni is like, high-heeled shoes and mini-skirts.

Danni, like many 'girlie-girls', was producing a particular hyper-sexualised femininity through a popular sartorial and cosmetic culture – practices embedded within what I have termed the 'flirty-fashion' discourse. Using various techniques, from rolling up the waist-band of school-skirts to applying lip-gloss and mascara, being part of the 'girlie' culture was all about flirting with the sexual boundaries of asexual/sexual child and the gendered generational boundaries of adult or teenage woman/girl-child. The following three extracts go some way to exploring these discursive practices and bodily performances. I have specifically chosen extracts from Hirstwood to counter some of the assumptions that only working-class girls invest heavily in popular ('flirty') fashion and 'older' femininities (see Hey 1997). The first extract reveals an underground cosmetic economy that girls shared, swapped and applied in secret under their desks, or in cloakrooms and playgrounds. The second extract details the specialised knowledge of popular fashion and economic capital required to access the 'flirty-fashion' discourse (the contradictions of which are explored in the next section). The third extract brings together the ways in which this discourse (and girls as agents of the discourse) produces girls' bodies as objects and subjects of heterosexual desire within the informal school. The impact of the 'flirty-fashion' discourse upon the 'official' or formal school is unpacked later.

I Cosmetic culture

SCHOOL: HIRSTWOOD

Sally: I've got seven lipsticks I've got millions of eye shadows/
Danni: I haven't I/
Sally: I've got this box, yeah, it's full of eye shadows, this Tammy Girl one (popular female fashion store for ages 7–14).
ER: And do you wear it when you go out?
Tina: I've got all different shades, have you got all different shades?
All: Yeah.
ER: So do you/
Sally: I've got one mascara.
Danni: Yeah but she got her mascara from *Shout* (teenage magazine) she doesn't buy it.
Tina: And you know I only wear a lipstick coz I think that eye shadow is a bit too over the top. Sometimes/I put really light colours just a little bit and you can't hardly see it but you feel good.
Danni: I know/

[…]
Sally: I put that peach and that white together, Tina I put that peach and that white together.
Tina: Mmm (nodding approvingly).
ER: So why do you like wearing it then?
Tina: Coz you like feel fashionable and/
Sally: You just sort of look prettier.

2 Popular fashion

SCHOOL: HIRSTWOOD

ER: OK, so what do you like to look like then?
Sally: Nice.
ER: And what's nice?
Tina: Nice is trendy, fashionable, everything/

★★★

ER: How do you know what's in fashion and what isn't?
Anna: Everyone/wears it.
Kate: Magazines and you see it in shops.
ER: So when you see it in magazines are they your age or a bit older or/
Kate: A bit older/
Anna: Yeah, but we wear it anyway.
ER: So do you try to look like they look in the magazines or/
Debbie: You just get what you want like, I wouldn't go and get this really/ sad jumper or something but I don't know, it depends on whether you like the fashion or not.
ER: So if you didn't like it would you still wear it?
Anna: Yeah I would probably because everyone else wears it/
[…]
ER: Who are the 'in' people? (asked in response to their positioning a group as 'in')
Anna: The trendy people.
Annabel: The ones that wear 'Fruit of the Loom' jumpers … don't wear school uniform and wear shoes that/
ER: What sort of shoes?
Anna: Like a three inch thick sole, well heels. Debbie's got shoes that are about that big heel and that sort of 'in' thing.
ER: So does that make you 'in' then?
Anna: Yeah, Tina's quite 'in' and her heels are about that big (shows me).

3 (Hetero)sexual desirability

SCHOOL: HIRSTWOOD

ER: So what is fashionable?
Sally: You just wear what you/like.
Danni: You just wear what you're comfortable in.
ER: What you're comfortable in yeah?
Danni: I wear jeans and/
Sally: Well it depends really, because it depends where there are most boys.
Danni: If Mikey (a boy that Sally fancies) was walking down the street/ and she looked really horrible she'd probably hide.
[...]
Sally: (discussing an ex-boyfriend) And Debbie fancies him and she's wearing short skirts up to/here.
Danni: She rolls her skirt so/it's really short.
Tina: She rolls her skirt up and if you look at her now she's pulled it right up to there and she's rolled it all over yeah like that and it's up here and you can see all the pleats going in like that and its all tucked up and all/the backs tucked up.
Danni: It doesn't hang straight (pulls a face of disgust).
ER: So she's made her skirt shorter?
All: Yeah.
ER: Why, why has she made it shorter?
Danni: Dunno.
Hannah: She fancies Sean, she says she doesn't but/
Tina: She does.
ER: So is she rolling it up for him or?
All: Yeah.
Hannah: Yeah I think so.

Many girls took delight and pleasure in the projection of their heterosexual desirability. Group interviews were interlaced with 'make-over' talk, particularly discussions over what girls could or could not wear inside and outside of school (and even inside or outside the classroom, see below). Popular teenage magazines such as Shout, Sugar, Bliss and J-17 acted as a pretty good guide to contemporary 'barometers of girlhood' (McRobbie 1997) and the official school uniform could easily be transformed to reflect dominant high street fashion, producing a range of unofficial school uniforms. Offering 'free' gifts, from necklaces to lip-balm also enabled girls to participate in a cosmetic world they may or may not have access to for a number of economic or geographical reasons.

A typical lunchtime routine involved spending ten minutes or so in the toilets getting 'made-up' and re-fashioning their uniforms before they exited out onto the playground en masse, linking arms and walking with an identifiable strut. Younger girls and boys would stare and sometimes mimic the walk of the girlie-girls. At Hirstwood they used the narrow passages between the main playground and school building as a mock-catwalk and would often stand on the sidelines of the football pitch, watching the boys (who were also watching them). At Tipton, a regular core group of girlie-girls would invade the boys' games of football by parading 'catwalk' style diagonally in a line across the centre of the pitch. Other sources of power and pleasure involved stylised dance routines. Not confined to the school toilets (see Walkerdine 1981), dance routines to current chart hits (e.g. Steps, Kylie or S Club 7) were performed almost daily, most of them faithfully copied from BBC1's *Top of the Pops* and many involving quite sophisticated and erotically charged movements, which the older girls practised to perfection. Almost celebrities in their own right, popular girls at the 'top of the school' often generated a small crowd of younger wannabe 'girlies' (and the odd younger boy) who would swing and sway and sometimes join in with the lyrics and/or try out dance sequences.

'Looking pretty' by investing in a sexualised cosmetic culture and re-fashioning their official school uniform could be interpreted as girls' internalising the sexual 'male gaze' (see Holland *et al.* 1998). Regulating and producing their femininities within normative and constraining scripts of heterosexual desirability, as others have noted, could work against them as they get older (see McRobbie and Nava 1984; Lees 1993; Hey 1997; Kenway *et al.* 1997; McRobbie 1997). For example, the 'male gaze' was omnipresent throughout Sally's interview, confirming and re-confirming her heterosexual desirability as she tailored her 'look', 'depending upon where there are most boys'. To this end, 'femininity becomes the ultimate legitimator of masculinity … it offers to masculinity the power to impose standards, make evaluations and confirm validity' (Skeggs 1997: 113). However, like Carol in Valerie Hey's chapter of working-class teenage hyper-heterosexual femininities, Sally (along with other girls) also achieved a real sense of power and agency in her new-found 'sexy' body, particularly when being 'sexy' contradicted 'innocent school girl' discourses (Walkerdine 1996).

Anxiety, regulation and surveillance

While there were many pleasures to be had in consuming, embodying and projecting sexualised femininities, sometimes these feelings were undermined by the pressures and anxieties of 'keeping up appearances' (see Skeggs 1997). One girl, Claire, for example, admitted that she wouldn't go to school, or would arrive late, if, in her eyes, her hair 'didn't go right'. Claire would sometimes wash, dry and style her hair up to three times before school until satisfied with the desired outcome. Such concern over her appearance nearly prevented her from going on the summer school trip when she found out that she could not bring her hair dryer and there were none supplied at the hostel.

The high status generated from these social and cultural practices also provided a means of policing and regulating the boundaries of the 'girlie-girl' subject position. Only girls who had access to the specific knowledge and capital (economic, cultural and social) could participate in the 'girlie' culture. Some girls were pushed out of dance circles with comments such as 'go away, you don't know this one' or for wearing 'sad skirts' or 'official' school uniform skirts or jumpers. Ironically, even those girls who did consume and don high-street fashion admitted to compromising on what they really wanted to wear 'because everyone else wears it' (see Anna's comment above). In some ways they were sacrificing their own personal taste for a collective taste (usually dictated by media, magazines and high-street fashion stores) that enabled them to fit 'in' with the hope of making them 'feel good' and 'look pretty'. As Valerie Hey (1997: 65) notes, 'the desire to become and the fear of being displaced as a girl's significant other' was strongly felt by girls who were positioned as 'outsiders' in the 'private talks' of the more popular girls who had access to this cultural hegemony. Moreover, the difficulty of accessing these dominant discourses led many girls to exclude and position some of their 'best friends' in a continual hierarchical struggle to be most 'popular'. Some of the daily feuds and 'falling out' did at times seem to be indicative of each girl's struggle to be 'in'.

Being 'girlie' and thus the production of the (hetero)sexual or erotic girl-child was also 'officially' regulated by the schools themselves and in a number of contradictory ways. On one level, the cosmetic culture, flirty-fashion and dirty-dancing were implicitly sanctioned (and almost expected) by staff within the context of the 'school disco' and within the child-centered spaces of the playground. However, there were always times when the informal school (in the form of peer group cultures) collided and threatened the authority of the 'official school'. An example of the latter was a withdrawal of a recent school policy at Hirstwood in the changing routine for swimming and its interpretation by children themselves (girls in particular). Mr Brady, the head teacher, thought that it would be more expedient if pupils brought tracksuits to change into after their swimming lesson. However, tracksuits were interpreted as a legitimate licence to bring in any clothing from home and many girls brought in their mini-skirts, cropped tops, jewellery and make-up (and thus spent much more time in the changing rooms than previously). Following a 'lecture' on how the school was not an arena for 'fashion parades', the new dress code was withdrawn. Children's gendered/sexualised sartorial selves were once again 'officially' regulated and the division between acceptable/unacceptable girl-child/girl pupil maintained (although re-fashioning of the official school uniform continued unabated).

The next section explores further the ways in which some girls are inscribed by (hetero)sexualised discourses and practices more indicative of research on adolescent girls and women, and how girls' take-up of sexualised discourses and erotic bodily performances can provoke mixed feelings amongst staff and pupils depending on 'who' is doing the performing and the competency of the performance.

'Tarty but not too tarty': contradictions in the production of the (hetero)sexual school 'girl'

Flirting with 'older' sexualities and negotiating the subject position of child-woman is a precarious occupation for primary school girls. Not necessarily because of the adult-centric anxiety surrounding the corruption of childhood (female) innocence (a point of view rarely expressed by children), but because very few girls despite their desire to be 'sexy' and 'fashionable' could agree on how to achieve that end. Rossiter (1994: 6) similarly argues how girls in her study were trying to 'obey the rules of discourse that are themselves contradictory'. In this study the contradictions were manifest in the borderland space between 'tarty' and 'tart'. The ultimate goal was to avoid the latter whilst trying to secure the former in a continuous daily battle to project a heterosexually desirable body. The extract below is taken from an interview in which a popular clique of girls are discussing what is fashionable and what is not:

SCHOOL: HIRSTWOOD

Claire:	I don't like being left out.
ER:	No?
Trudy:	You don't want to like erm go too far looking like out of the/(ordinary?)
Annabel:	*I don't want to look too/tarty.*
Trudy:	*But/you want to look a bit tarty.*
ER:	So you want to look attractive but not too tarty?
All:	Yeah yeah/
Annabel:	Yeah that's it.
ER:	So how do you look attractive, what sort of things would you wear, do you wear make-up?
Trudy:	I've got a bag, my mum gave it to me, I've got lipstick, eye makeup, eyeliner, mascara/
Annabel:	Yeah but you don't too much otherwise it looks really tarty.
Trudy:	Yeah, I only/wear a little bit.
Claire:	I don't need mascara/
Trudy:	No I don't need that
Annabel:	*It's tarty.*

SCHOOL: HIRSTWOOD

Carrie:	I'm not being horrible, but have you seen Trudy's skirt, it's her five year old sister's! ... and it's like up here (draws an invisible line well above her knee).
ER:	And you think that's too short?
Carrie:	Yeah.

ER:	Why have girls started wearing short skirts?
Hannah:	Because one person does/then everybody else does.
Carrie:	They like to show off their legs.
ER:	Why?
Carrie:	Coz they want to impress the boys I suppose, like Trudy when she bends down you can see her bum.
Hannah:	People really dress up.
Carrie:	Yeah Trudy does, she puts blusher and makeup and eye shadow and lipstick.
Janine:	She gets carried away with makeup.
ER:	Do people think she goes over the top? (they nod)
Carrie:	Some people say she's a tart.
ER:	Is she?
Carrie:	No.
Hannah:	Like it happened to Debbie but it blew over.
ER:	What happened to Debbie?
Hannah:	People calling her a tart/because she wore her skirt up there.
Carrie:	Did they? Did they?
ER:	So who would? Other girls /or boys as well?
Carrie and Hannah:	Girls.
Janine:	Girls are bitchy.
ER:	How do you know which length skirt to wear/without being called a tart?
Carrie:	I think it's just above your knee.
Janine:	Or just below.
Carrie:	Just above, coz if it's like that it's too/
Hannah:	Yeah – not like that (hitches her skirt up well above the knee).
Carla:	Well, I roll my skirt up (looks confused).

These extracts resonate with the sexual double standard identified by Cowie and Lees (1981) when teenage girls talked about their sexual reputations and the ways in which 'slag' (or 'tart' in this case) was used by girls as a form of social control over other girls (see also Lees 1993; Hey 1997). Just as Sue Lees noted (1993: 36), meanings attached to 'tart' and 'tarty' did not necessarily refer to sexual activity but to sexual identities and performances.

The extracts above capture the difficulties girls encountered as they negotiated a discourse that at one moment rendered them attractive and at another labelled them a tart, not only by their friends but also by their parents.[4] While it seemed impossible for the girls to define for me the length of skirt appropriate for a disco or for school, there did seem to be a theme of sexual excess running throughout their narrative as they attempted to collectively construct an (imaginary) dividing line between legitimate and illegitimate sexual displays. Talk about those Other 'tarty' girls who 'get carried away', 'go over the top' or go 'too far' and reveal 'too much' seemed to be transgressing a symbolic dividing line in which sexual excess (whether it was having a skirt that was too short or wearing too much make-up for school) aligned girls too closely with 'older' and forbidden sexualities, thus placing them outside childhood and the discourse of 'nice' girl. At the same time, the girls took a lot of pleasure and excitement in flirting with the very forbidden sexualities that they were policing on a daily basis. On a more sober note, however, while their male classmates used the terms 'slag' or 'tart' as terms of general abuse, it did seem, as Rossiter (1994) and other studies of girls relationships have found (Hey 1997), that the girls themselves were their own harshest critics both through self-surveillance and surveillance of others. Thus, central to the production of hyper-femininity and the sexual girl-child was this ambivalent notion of 'tart/y' – a discourse accessed and produced by girls as a source of both pleasure and pain. A discourse that not only confused those learning to emulate their celebrity peers (note Carla's final comment) but also the very girls positioned as *the* 'fashionable' and 'in' girls.

Girls and their peers were not the only ones regulating the boundaries of sexual excess and childhood (sexual) innocence within the school. Teachers were also complicit, if not central to these evaluations. One girl, Kirsty, was referred to me (privately) by her class teacher as a 'tart' for openly displaying and enjoying her sexuality with other girls and boys (see Chapter 5). Barrie Thorne, in her discussion of girls and sexuality, draws attention to the ways in which girls' pubescent bodies pollute notions of childhood innocence:

> In our culture we draw sharp distinctions between 'child' and 'adult', defining child as relatively asexual … and the adult as sexual … charged with sexual meaning, fully developed breasts seem uncomfortably out of place on the body of individuals who are still defined as children … a sense of pollution derives … from the violation of basic lines of social structure.
>
> (Thorne 1993: 143)

While some teachers did draw attention to the changing and developing bodies of primary school girls in the upper junior years, their comments tended to centre on the ways in which puberty seemed to 'be happening earlier and earlier' (Year 2 female teacher). Anxiety over the ways in which girls were symbolically violating the boundaries between adulthood and childhood were not projected onto those girls who possessed pubescent/'adult' bodies, but those who enjoyed using and dressing their bodies in sexualised ways, 'developed' or not. Teachers were confronted on a daily basis with the myth of the asexual sanitised school girl as clusters of girls (young and old) accessed the flirty-fashion 'girlie' culture promoted by media and magazines, but also, as suggested earlier, by schools themselves in the form of the school disco.

Regulatory practices by teachers towards girls using and dressing their bodies in sexualised ways was not only contingent upon context but also upon girls' own histories within the 'girlie' culture. For example, over half of all the Year 6 girls at Tipton transformed their school uniforms on a daily basis to comply with what they thought to be fashionable and were generally not prevented from doing so by the teaching staff. However, when one girl, Julia (not part of the 'girlie' clique), transformed her usual image (cardigan, knee-length skirt, neat pony-tail, ankle socks and 'sensible' shoes) for the flirty-fashion of the 'girlie' culture, she was quickly stopped in her tracks. Following a heated staffroom debate, she was asked at morning break to 'roll down your skirt, sort your hair out and wipe that stuff (make-up) off your face'. Julia's 'new look' was almost a mirror image (right down to the colour of her lip-gloss) of one of the most popular ('girlie') Year 6 girls in the school. Her skirt was hitched up so high that it was uneven at the back and she had changed her shoes for a pair of luminescent pink 'jelly-bean' (plastic) sandals. She had carefully applied a glossy 'peach' lip-balm, rouged her cheeks and moved her pony tail from the base to the top of her head so that her hair fell about her face. Although she looked no different from many of the other girls in her class, her make-over was deemed inappropriate not only by the teachers but by other pupils too.

The ways in which Julia's transformation is constructed as 'inappropriate' gives rise to a number of interpretations. Firstly, Julia was a 'middle-class' girl attempting to access a predominantly working-class subject position (at Tipton at least, see below). As Davies (1993: 137) notes, class differences are often read by both adults and children as sexual differences, where transgression of one signifies transgression of the other. The teaching staff's intervention at Tipton could thus be seen as regulating and limiting Julia's mobility and transgression between both gender, sexual and class subject positions. However, it is important to note that the majority of 'girlie-girls' at Hirstwood were from professional 'middle-class' backgrounds. In addition, while Julia was at ease trying on different gender/sexual identities (see Chapter 7), staff were not so comfortable in her swift and sudden transformation. They might also have been concerned at the uneasy fit between Julia's heterosexual agency projected by her new sexualised make-over and her non-participation within the boyfriend/girlfriend culture and all that that entailed. Perhaps Julia's assumed 'inexperience' was thought to be 'corrupting of an innocent state' (Walkerdine 1996: 326). Certainly, and on a wider note, Julia's performance renders visible the ways in which young (in this case) working-class girls' (hetero)sexualised 'girlie' femininities are produced as normal and natural (and thus not intervened in) and how only sexual excess in its most visible and parodic form is deemed 'inappropriate'.

'I'm not a girlie': challenging hyper-femininity and the male (sexual) gaze

Not all girls invested in the heterosexualised hyper-femininty of the 'girlie-girl' subject position/culture. There were two friendship groups, one in each class at

Tipton and Hirstwood, and one self-identified 'tomboy', Erica (in the parallel Year 6 class at Hirstwood), who consistently constructed their gender identities by overtly differentiating themselves from 'girlie' femininities, although as we shall see, in contrasting ways. The group at Hirstwood (Penny, Alicia, Dana, Liz and Kelly) were a bunch of high-achieving girls from predominantly professional 'middle-class' backgrounds. They were collectively and derisively known as the 'square-girls' mainly because of their intense preoccupation with academic success and rejection of the 'girlie' culture, boys and masculinity more widely (see Renold 2001a). In contrast, the girls at Tipton (Harriet, Amanda, Hayley, Jane and Jo) were a popular close-knit friendship group of mixed academic ability and social backgrounds (although headed by a vocal 'middle-class' leader, Harriet). They were labelled by some of their peers as the 'top-girls' – a term which I have also drawn upon to highlight their hierarchical status and, like Reay's (2001) 'spice girls', their collective 'girl power'.

Creating social and cultural distance from their 'girlie' peers, these girls seemed to be taking part in a wider practice of what Hey calls 'deficit dumping'. This was a practice in which they displaced and disassociated themselves from some of the more overt practices of heterosexualisation. From a discussion which centred around body image, the extract below illustrates how through a sophisticated critique of the 'tyranny of slenderness' they each drew upon counter-discourses of difference ('I like to be different'), non-conformity ('I don't like to be the same'), individuality ('I don't like to be part of the wallpaper' and 'you should be your own person really') and agency ('I wear what I wanna wear'). This collectively enabled them to challenge the dominant sartorial and somatic ideals that preoccupied many of their female classmates:

SCHOOL: TIPTON

Hayley: (referring to supermodels) I wouldn't do that, I wouldn't want to look like that coz they're so skinny and I wouldn't want to be anorexic or anything/

Jo: No, coz a lot of people go anorexic just to look like the models.

ER: So you're quite wary of that are you?

All: Yeah.

Harriet: I don't care what they/look like, I look like I wanna look like.

Jo: I don't care what they look like.

[...]

Jane: Yeah well if someone doesn't like what I'm wearing then it's their problem not mine.

Jo: Yeah that's what I do, I wear/what I wanna wear.

[...]

Jo: I like, I like to be different, I/don't like to be the same

Jane: I like to be different as well.

Jo: I don't like to be part of the wallpaper.

[...]

Jane:	I don't like looking like other people/
Jo:	I don't like being like part/of the wallpaper.
Jane:	I don't like being like anyone else.
Jo:	I mean you should be your own person really.

Central to their refusal to be seduced by popular fashion and the current media obsession with body size and weight was a firm rejection of the heterosexualisation of girls' bodies. In a conversation about what the girlie-girls in their class are going to wear to the school disco, Harriet and Amanda critique the notion that girls' bodies are purely commodities for the attraction of boys and men:

SCHOOL: TIPTON

Harriet:	Yeah, they all wear like mini-skirts to discos, but I don't want to, I'm wearing my shorts-dungarees to the discos (laughs) ... and they're all wearing these mini-skirts.
[...]	
Amanda:	I'm just wearing my check T-shirt/and shorts.
Harriet:	Yeah.
ER:	So/
Amanda:	They wear, they wear like mini-skirts to impress the boys.
ER:	Do you think so?
Amanda:	Yeah and we, I'm just going in something that is comfortable, not so that boys'll go out with me.
[...]	
Harriet:	She (Kirsty) likes to impress the boys, but me and Amanda aren't, don't really care.
[...]	
Amanda:	Some people like something that's comfy and then some people think 'oh I've got to look like tarty/
Harriet:	Yeah going around and getting all the boys around you.
ER:	So you don't feel like that at all?
Harriet:	No, if boys like you then they like you for the way you are not coz of how you look or how fashionable you are.
ER:	What about you Amanda, do you feel the same or not?
Amanda:	Yeah the same because you can't, I mean the boys can't fancy you like just coz you've got good clothes on/
Harriet:	Yeah, they fancy you just ... they should go out with the clothes not you (laughs).

As the extract above illustrates, differentiating themselves from 'girlie' femininities was most apparent in the girls' projection of their sartorial self. While Penny and her friends radically rejected any conformity to an identifiable fashion (see

Renold 2001a), both the 'top-girls' and Erica (the self-identified tomboy) replaced the flirty-fashion of the 'girlie' culture for a sporty look. Favouring, in their words, 'comfy' over 'tarty', they swapped high heels for trainers, tight-fitting tops/blouses for baggy T-shirts and sweatshirts and wore cycling shorts under their skirts or trousers rather than mini-skirts. Adopting a sporting fashion that emphasised fitness, activity and comfort was one of the ways in which they signalled their flight from sexualised 'girlie' femininities. Rejecting the notion that girls' bodies exist only as heterosexual objects of desire (e.g. 'I'm going in something that's comfortable, not so that boys'll go out with me') and critiquing the ways in which girls 'dress to impress the boys', Harriet directly challenges dominant heterosexual discourses as much as she rejects dominant scripts of body and fashion.[5]

Back at Hirstwood, Penny and her friends (the 'square-girls'), while not directly critiquing the ways in which the girlie-girls at Hirstwood 'just dress to impress the boys', nevertheless continued to distance themselves by positioning those that did participate in the flirty-fashion culture as immature in a premature desire for older sexualities (Penny: 'they act as if they're three years older than they actually are'). In many ways, their critique drew upon the more adult-centric hurried-erotics discourse (see Chapter 2) of girls 'growing up too quickly' and doing 'too much too soon'. Whether drawing upon developmental/childhood innocence discourses, liberal feminist or humanist discourses of individualism, both groups of girls were having some success in being able to call upon critical frameworks that enabled them to disassociate themselves from, resist and to some extent challenge dominant notions of the (hetero)erotic girl.

Asserting difference and independence from dominant 'girlie' femininities involved, in the girls' own words, seeking 'change' rather than 'fitting in'. And, like any minority group struggling to carve out a discursive space to inhabit, the strength of the group collective was a vital component in creating and accessing alternative ways of 'doing girl'. Like the teenage girls in Sue Lees' (1993) research and the junior girls in Becky Francis' (1998) ethnography, one of the most successful forms of resistance and subversion to gender norms and practices was the solidarity of a strong friendship group or what Lees terms, 'collective resistance' (see also Kehily *et al.*'s (2002) 'diary group girls'). For example, at Hirstwood, the majority of girls accessed or desired 'girlie' femininities, perhaps because the only other femininity being produced within the school was an academic 'square-girl' femininity (see Renold 2001a). Maybe, given the academic ethos of the school, coupled with its predominantly 'middle-class' catchment area, being 'girlie' was a powerful and seductive signifier of a more transgressive and radical femininity(?). While there were girls, similar to Diane Reay's (2001) 'Spice Girls' who drew upon discourses of difference, individualism, sexual independence and non-conformity, these would exist alongside dominant heterosexualised femininities. Girls, like Sally below, engaged simultaneously with non-girlie and girlie femininities:

SCHOOL: HIRSTWOOD

ER:	So what is fashionable?
Sally:	*You just wear what you/like.*
Danni:	You just wear what you're comfortable in.
ER:	What you're comfortable in yeah?
Danni:	I wear jeans and/
Sally:	Well it depends really, because it *depends where there are most boys.*
Danni:	If Mikey was walking down the street/and she looked really horrible she'd probably hide.
Sally:	*I'd get mega dressed up.*
ER:	You'd get mega dressed up?
Sally:	Yeah.
ER:	What would you wear then?
Sally:	Don't know/
Danni:	She'd probably wear her 'love' top.
Sally:	Would I ... oh *that* top/
Tina:	And your jeans/
Sally:	No I wouldn't I'd wear my 'Woa' top/
Danni:	Oh yeah this 'Woa' top that she's/got
Sally:	And my white skirt thing/
Hannah:	I'm not really bothered.
Sally:	*I'm not bothered if I see boys really but I am if I see Mikey/*
Tina:	I like to look, I like to look like I like to feel comfortable yeah, but I like to also be fashionable as well/
Sally:	Yeah.
Tina:	And wear trendy stuff.
ER:	So not just for boys but for you.
All:	Yeah.
Sally:	*I don't care really/*I just wear what I like

In the extract above, Sally manages to access and maintain contradictory subject positions insofar as she wants to be fashionable and gets 'mega dressed up' for boys (thus investing in the prevalent 'for the boys' discourse of heterosexualied girlie femininities). But simultaneously, she doesn't care what she looks like and wears what she likes (thus accessing discourses of non-conformity, individualism and difference of the 'top-girl' subject position). As other research on young girls' femininities has suggested (see Bradby 1994), alternative discourses of female sexual independence can co-exist and compete with dominant 'acceptable' heterosexual ones, where traditional storylines merge with new ones (see also Davies 1993). However, Sally was one of the few girls who could jump between competing femininities. As one of the most popular and romantically desirable girlie-girls in Year 6, Sally is perhaps already in a privileged position to try on and feel comfortable accessing ostensibly competing discourses. For less popular and marginalised others (see Chapter 7) the transition to and mobility between subject positions (whether daring to be 'different' or struggling to conform) seemed almost impossible either without this (hetero)normative base, or without the collectivity of a like-minded friendship group which seemed vital in being able to carve out and sustain a social and cultural space in which to perform non-hegemonic femininities.

You're sexist: traces of girl power (?)

The perceived inactivity of the girlie-girls who 'just sit around and chat' (Penny, Hirstwood) or 'stand there and gossip about clothes and boys' (Amanda, Tipton) was a further defining feature with which the self-defined 'non-girlies' differentiated themselves from 'girlie' femininities. However, where Penny and her friends continued to play fantasy playground games such as 'Ponies' (activities which other girls had dropped in earlier years), Amanda and the other 'top-girls' sought to penetrate and join the sporting male hegemony, which in both schools was football. However, like many girls before them they were routinely excluded from the game (see Renold 1997; Skelton 2000; Swain 2000). Indeed, it was often reported as one of the girls' first experiences of overt gender discrimination and their understanding of sexism and patriarchy more generally (see Holly 1985). As the extract below highlights, girls were not necessarily prevented from participating in the game 'officially' (for example, Hirstwood had set up a girls-only team). Rather, it was their unofficial exclusion from the game at 'playtime' and the monopolisation of football and other ball games contracting the playing spaces of most girls and younger junior pupils (see Chapter 4).

Girls don't do football ...

Most of the girls in the study were aware of the exclusionary techniques and overt sexism inherent in the game and the attitudes of many of the boys who played football (whether they were interested in playing football or not). What set the 'top-girls' and Erica ('tomboy') apart from the rest of their female classmates was their determination to access and challenge the existing discursive practices that had excluded them for most of their schooling lives. Quite simply, sport became a form of resistance to 'girlie' femininities (Hargreaves 1982). However, while Erica (Hirstwood), as an honorary boy, had been playing football with the boys, as one of the boys, for many years, Harriet and her friends faced multiple layers of discrimination, as the following extract from my first interview with the girls about 'playtime' illustrates:

SCHOOL: TIPTON

ER: Mandy, you said earlier that football isn't really a girl's game/
Mandy: Yeah, I dunno/
Harriet: Everything should be girls and boys ... coz we're all the same, just, but just kind of different.
Sophie: Different sexes.
ER: Do you all think like that?
All: Yeah.
Harriet: It's not fair coz some people push you out, just because you are a girl or just because you're different/
Mandy: That's sexist.
ER: Do you experience this in school?
Mandy: Yes.
Harriet: All the boys think .../
Mandy: You can't play football/
Harriet: I nearly always say to these boys 'you're sexist' because they like go, 'oh you shouldn't do this coz you're a girl, you shouldn't do this coz you're a girl and it's not fair/
Mandy: Yeah.
ER: Do you ever do the same to them and want to keep something that only girls can do?
Hayley: No we don't do that to them ... it's like they've got this tennis ball and we just watch ... they won't let us play.
ER: Is that always the case?
All: Yeah.
Harriet: Unless you're going out with one of them.
All: Yeah (big sighs all round).

This interview extract highlights a number of competing discourses as Harriet and her friends make sense of a range of gendered discriminations and injustices. Many of the girls are recognising that exclusion from football is embedded in discourses of a sexist patriarchal culture ('you shouldn't do this/that coz you're a girl') and draw upon discourses of equality of opportunity ('everything should be girls and boys') and feminist discourse ('you're sexist') to attack that culture. However, they are also acutely aware of more specific heterosexist discourses in which mixed-gender interaction only seems possible through their heterosexualisation ('they won't let us play ... unless you're going out with one of them'). Or, one could add, in the light of Erica's full acceptance at Hirstwood, the abandonment of the category girl entirely. Nevertheless, they were still bent upon exercising their right to negotiate equal access 'with the boys' which involved countering both sexist and heterosexist discourses and practices. And it was the former that the girls tried first.

Challenging sporting male hegemonic practices through anti-sexist discourses was a challenging and often futile practice. Girls were confronted daily with assumptions that they were somehow lacking in competence and skill by the mere biological fact that they were 'girls' (see Wright 1996: 77). Hannah explains how such discourses had the effect of producing a circular argument where exclusion from the game ('no, you're a girl') or within a game ('they never pass to you') prevented the girls from developing their skills or proving their competence ('they won't let you try'):

SCHOOL: TIPTON

Hannah:	Like in the summer on the field I like playing football but the boys never let you ... and like in games if you play, they never pass the football to you.
Kate:	No, in football in games we just like stay in there.
ER:	Why do you think that they are stopping you from playing sometimes?
Hannah:	Well sometimes if you go up to them and say 'can I play football?' they say, 'No you're a girl, you're not good enough' or something like that.
ER:	But the fact that you do score goals and that you can play/
Hannah:	Yeah but they won't let you try.

In the second term at Tipton, the girls' resistance took the form of invading and sabotaging the boys' games by running diagonally across the pitch, stealing the ball, and sunbathing in the goal area to: 'get in the way so they can't play' and 'really annoy them'. Disruptive practices such as these, however, only served to strengthen and reinforce the boys' attitude that 'girls never take the game seriously' and only 'muck up the game' when they do participate. The only strategy which was identified by the girls as successful was developing friendships with the boys which as Chapter 5 sets out in detail, only seemed to be achieved by being a girlfriend or ex-girlfriend of one of the players. Other girls who wanted to play football but who were routinely excluded were more than aware of this heterosexualised access. Jenna and Georgina put their exclusion down to being the wrong 'type' of girls:

SCHOOL: TIPTON

ER:	So, do you ever play football with the boys?
All:	Nooooo.
ER:	Never/?
Jenna:	Hayley does and Harriet and Amanda.
Rachel:	I sit on the field and meditate.
ER:	So how come they do and you don't?

Rachel:	It's just so/boring, football.
Georgina:	I want to, they just won't let us join in.
Jenna:	Yeah, us sort of girls,/coz we're not
Rachel:	I'm allowed to join in.
ER:	Because you're not what?
Jenna:	We're not like the gooder (sic) type that boys like.

Girls (like Harriet and Amanda) who did manage to sustain access to the game reported how they were no longer labelled as 'rubbish' and while many of the boys and the girls themselves considered that they were 'still learning', there was a marked departure from earlier discourses of access which revolved around notions of 'allowing', 'privilege' and 'favour' (Francis 1997: 528). And although Davies (1993: 132) notes that 'access to boy-ish things is undermined by the policing of heterosexual boundaries', positioning themselves as 'more than girlfriends' (although still ex-girlfriends) and thus solely as heterosexual subjects and objects of desire seemed to impact upon the ways in which boys treated and perceived them. As the following extract illustrates, boys were beginning to re-assess their own beliefs about 'girls' and heterosexualised girlie gender identities more widely. Indeed, both girls and boys at Tipton were entertaining new ways of 'doing girl' (although see Chapter 4 and 5). Little by little girls were countering some of the sexist and heterosexist discourses in which they were positioned as 'tomboys' or 'potential girlfriends' for wanting to play football:

SCHOOL: TIPTON

ER:	Do you think your relationship with the boys has changed since you first started (playing football)?
Kirsty and Hayley:	Yeah.
Jane:	You never used to talk to them, unless you were going out with them and then you just used to say, hi or bye (laughs).
All:	Yeah.
Hayley:	We have some boys as friends now don't we?
Jane:	Yeah, we can have conversations with them.
Kirsty:	Be with them as friends.
Hayley:	Yeah.
Jane:	Yeah, like before, if you just talked to a boy it'd be 'oh, you fancy him' (in a sing song way).
Hayley:	Yeah as soon as you talk to a boy, people are like 'oooh' sort of like 'Haley for someone' or/
Kirsty:	They don't do that anymore.
Jane:	I know, but they used to.
[...]	
ER:	So do they include you in the game totally now?

Hayley and Jane:	Yeah.
Kirsty:	Yeah.
Jane:	Well sort of.
Hayley:	Yeah they, we just ask them if we can play football and they say, 'yeah sure, we're shooting that way'
Kirsty:	When we used to try and play they used to call us tomboys and all that didn't they?
Hayley:	Yeah.
ER:	Do you think it's because you've become more friendly with them, that/ you're beginning to play with them.
Hayley and Kirsty:	Yeah, yeah.

The significance of developing mixed-gender friendships free from (hetero)sexualised innuendo and teasing is discussed in detail in Chapter 5.

From the field and into the classroom

By the end of Year 6, anti-sexist and equal rights discourses became an everyday part of the 'top-girls' vocabulary and didn't stop on the football pitch. Active, vocal and angry (see also Singh 1993: 56), they continued to refuse to be treated differently on the grounds of their gender and persisted in resisting and rejecting gendered stereotypes and expectations within the classroom and other formal pedagogic spaces:

SCHOOL: TIPTON

Amanda:	Boys get to do all the painting/
Harriet:	Yeah they get to take down all the paintings and projects from the wall and that coz they think they're big and strong and everything/ and
Amanda:	It's not like we're weaklings or anything
Harriet:	And we have to sit there and do drawings or something while they're doing that.
Amanda:	Yeah and they're allowed to lift heavy things and we're not coz we're just weak (sarcastically)
[...]	
ER:	So when the boys did take the projects down, did you do anything about it or try to/
Amanda:	Yeah, we just say, I don't care if I'm not allowed to do it, we just went ahead and did it anyway.

While Harriet and Amanda's decision to 'go ahead' and stand on the tables to take the project work down from the walls may appear insignificant, there were very few girls who would act upon what they saw as sexist injustices. Many girls would complain either to each other or to myself but few would take direct action. For example, Harriet would strive to get her voice and ideas heard in a mixed-sex project group, comfortable and practised in her challenges with boys in the classroom as on the football pitch. In contrast, Penny, Dana and Alicia (whose femininities seemed to be constructed 'against the boys' and thus less comfortable in mixed–gender interactions) struggle to achieve a similar task and often give up:

> Dana, Jake, Stu and Simon have been put in a team together to work on their design ... Dana walks over to Jake and Stu, as she is seated opposite them, and says to them 'now we've finished (our designs) we can compare them'. Dana shows Jake her design by putting it in front of him. He looks at it briefly but does not say anything and continues with his design. Simon also ignores Dana's designs and even when she puts them in front of his face, he continues talking about his ideas ... Dana passes Simon's designs to Jake voluntarily, to which Simon shouts 'get off'. Dana corrects one of Simon's instructions before she gives Jake Simon's designs. She is not thanked and her designs are disregarded by the other two boys.
>
> (Hirstwood: fieldnotes)

Being 'with the boys' (rather than 'for the boys' or 'one of the boys') and working within existing symbolic systems by taking and subverting male dominance for themselves enabled Harriet and her friends to mobilise a collective agency with which to challenge and transform gendered discriminatory practices and maintain a version of femininity and feminism across playground and classroom cultures. As a collective project, all 'members' of this friendship group benefited in some way over the course of the year as Amanda's recollection of no longer being the 'quiet little girl in the corner' testifies:

SCHOOL: TIPTON

Amanda:	I seem to have grown up a bit more, like I couldn't stick up for myself before coz coz whenever someone used to say something to Harriet she always used to go at them and I used to stay back.
ER:	Girls or boys or anybody?
Amanda:	Anybody ...
Harriet:	If they said something horrible to me, I'd say something horrible to them.
ER:	Yeah, so now you maybe have learnt something from Harriet?
Amanda:	Yeah.
Harriet:	I think that you can't just go and hide everywhere and let everyone push you about because if they can say that to you why can't you say that to them?

[...]

Amanda: ... I used to be the quiet little girl in the corner
ER: So how would you describe yourself now?
Amanda: Erm erm, it was, it was the Year Sixes, I dunno, they just used to bully you in a way, everyone would pretend I wasn't there, if you know what I mean, well I felt like it anyway ... and now I feel like I'm more I'm more, friends with everyone in the class.

Over the year, the girls' collective critique of 'girlie' femininities, their manipulation of heterosexual capital in their drive for equality (symbolised by their penetration into the all-boys footballing culture), their sustained critique of the ways in which they (and other girls) were positioned as object and subjects of the male gaze, all point to a kind of girl power and feminist resistance. However, it was a resistance which involved a whole lot of Othering and various techniques of exclusion towards non-hegemonic masculinities and aggressive or hyper-sexualised femininities (see Renold 1999). Moreover, empowerment involved not only literally being 'with the boys' but taking on and embodying hegemonic forms of masculinity. But while I recognise the ways in which 'girls' subversions and transgressions are nearly always contained within, and rarely challenge existing structures' (Reay 2001: 164), the girls' infiltration and assimilation of masculine discourses and practices did support and enable them to overturn many day-to-day gender and sexual inequities, albeit from their privileged heterosexualised position as 'ex-girlfriends'.

Concluding notes

This chapter has been concerned with exploring the ways in which girls in this research were constructing their femininities in relation to a heterosexualised 'girlie' femininity and how all girls were to some extent positioned in relation to a heteronormative male gaze. The most subscribed to femininity was the (hetero)sexualised 'girlie' femininity attracting over two-thirds of all the girls in the study (almost regardless of, yet mediated by, social class, academic ability, body shape, etc.). Drawing on the widely available popular culture (TV and teen-magazines), these girls were each investing in and policing their own and others' bodies as heterosexually desirable commodities. While girls accrued a sense of excitement and power by blurring the boundaries of the sexual-adult-woman/asexual-girl-child and tapping into 'older' sexualities, such feelings were often overcast by the shadow of a highly contradictory sexual double standard triggered by an ambivalent discourse of sexual excess (e.g. 'too tarty' or 'over the top'). I describe girls investing in 'girlie' femininities as co-constructing a femininity 'for the boys', insofar as they were routinely subject to, and policing agents of, a heterosexual male gaze and thus doing a good job of underwriting hegemonic heteromasculinity (Kenway *et al.* 1997). I also briefly explored how the school was complicit yet uneven in the policing and regulating of 'girlie' femininities both 'officially' (via the school disco) and 'unofficially' (via school uniforms) – protecting some children (e.g. Julia) and pathologising others (e.g. Kirsty).

The chapter also explored how some girls were constructing their femininity in opposition to (hetero)sexualised femininities and actively challenging the ways in which girls are simultaneously objects, subjects and agents of a heterosexualised male gaze (and thus attacking the very essence of what it means to be 'girlie'). Two main subject positions were identified: the 'square-girls' at Hirstwood and the 'top-girls' at Tipton. Like Reay's 'nice-girls', the 'square-girls' were high-achieving, hard-working, rule-following and lacked any interest in popular fashion or 'boys' either as friends or boyfriends. However, their intense preoccupation with academic success and rejection of 'girlie' culture left them open to verbal abuse and they were routinely subject to various techniques of exclusion. Constructing their femininity as 'non-girlie', refusing to have anything to do with boys whilst maintaining a 'clever' academic identity to some extent resulted in their defeminisation and, as Chapter 5 goes on to illustrate, their 'desexualisation'. As a tight-knit friendship group, however, they withstood and maintained their 'academic' femininity over the course of the year using a mixture of strategies from avoidance to in-house ridicule (see Reay 2001). They also drew upon classed and generational discourses, within the safety of their own peer group, to position themselves as 'superior' and other girls and boys as 'silly' and 'immature' (see Francis 1998). Actively critiquing and challenging gender and heterosexist injustices, however, was only consistently maintained by one peer group – the 'top-girls'.

Almost an amalgamation of 'tomboy' and 'girlie', the 'top-girls' engaged in a powerful critique of dominant heteroseuxalised femininities. Unlike many girls, they developed relationships with boys as friends as well as boyfriends which placed them in a unique and powerful position to infiltrate the boys' football games and combat not only their long-running exclusion from the game but also other forms of sexist discrimination in the classroom. While other individual girls (from Hirstwood and Tipton) did, from time to time, draw upon similar discourses of equity and anti-sexism, their impact was minimal by comparison. Mobilising a 'collective agency' was a key strength to accessing and sustaining a counter-discourse. Like Penny and her friends, the 'top-girls' were an exclusive, high-status and tightly-knit friendship group. However, like the 'tomboy' subject position, their 'girl-power' seemed only possible by taking up and drawing upon masculinist discourses and a number of Othering practices which denigrated subordinate masculinities and femininities that did not mirror their own! The question of whether infiltration and assimilation of masculinised discourses and practices, whilst transgressing conventional regimes of (hetero)sexualised femininity, can be conceptualised as 'girl power' is something that is open to debate.

With the exception of the academic femininity of the 'square-girls' at Hirstwood, all the other femininities served to entrench and valorise a particular version of masculinity – a hegemonic (heterosexual) masculinity. Whether it was by 'joining the boys' and raiding boy-culture to empower and rally against sexism, cultivating a femininity to sexually attract and 'impress the boys' or ditching femininity and girlhood altogether to be and become a 'boy', (hegemonic) masculinity was being constructed as both desirable and desiring. I make this point, albeit crudely, not only to highlight the ways in which young girls are constructing their femininities in relation to and integrated with hegemonic masculine discourses, but also to explicitly contrast the seduction of masculinity for contemporary girls/girlhood with the repulsion of femininity for contemporary boys/boyhood.

Chapter 4

Boys 'doing' masculinity

Mission impossible?

Introduction

Boys' experiences of 'doing boy' and achieving 'masculinity' in this chapter resonate with many other ethnographic accounts of primary boys, masculinities and schooling (Davies 1993; Thorne 1993; Connolly 1998, 2003; Gilbert and Gilbert 1998; Francis 1998; Swain 2000, 2002a, 2002b, 2003; Martino and Beyenn 2001; Skelton 2001). Hierarchical masculinities and feminine disassociations (see Connell 1995) are recurring themes in boys' narratives. Sport (e.g. football) and violence (e.g. fighting) also persist as key discourses and embodied practices through which many primary-aged boys define and construct what Carrigan *et al.* (1987) conceptualised over 15 years ago as 'hegemonic masculinity'. Developing Gramsci's notion of 'hegemony', Bob Connell (1995: 76), has defined and explored hegemonic masculinity as a contested and elusive ideal that generally fails to empower specific individuals but nevertheless operates to produce 'culturally exalted' forms of (heterosexual) masculinity via the domination of other men and the subordination of women, femininity and Other (non-hetero)sexualities. Since the late 1980s 'hegemonic masculinity' has become one of the key analytic concepts through which masculinities in school-based research have been theorised (see Mac an Ghaill 1994; Parry 1996; Dixon 1997; Kenway and Fitzclarence 1997; Connolly 1998; Skelton 2001; Frosh *et al.* 2002; Swain 2003).

The usefulness of drawing upon the concept of 'hegemonic masculinity' as a way of theorising the dominance and power of particular masculinities has, however, come under close and critical scrutiny of late. Becky Francis (2000: 14), in particular, has argued that it can potentially serve to 'reify gender as something more fixed than is the case' and overlook the ways in which boys can occupy multiple and contradictory masculinities. I would suggest, as does Skelton (2001: 52) that this is most likely an effect of the ways in which it is 'loosely used' rather than a problem with the notion of 'hegemonic masculinity' per se.

Others, such as Haywood and Mac an Ghaill (2003), have problematised the ways in which the deployment of 'hegemonic masculinity', as an adult-centric term, has been less than effective in capturing the generational dynamic of masculinities in many studies of masculinities and schooling. For example, in school-based research, sexuality has traditionally rarely been considered a constitutive element of 'boy-ness' (in contrast to the sexualisation of femininity) because of the taken-for-granted norms at work in the construction of boyhood as a time of (non-sexual) activity, discovery and 'play' – away from girls and (hetero)sex! Only recently have studies begun to explore the relationship between gender and sexuality in the making of pre-teen (hetero)masculinities and the relationship between anti-girl/femininity behaviours (misogyny) and anti-gay or homophobic sentiments. This chapter, then, will not only pay attention to the specificities and interaction of age, gender and (hetero)sexuality in young boys' struggles to achieve 'hegemonic' masculinity, but also the contextual contingency of hegemonic masculinity (e.g. what is hegemonic in one school or location or moment may not be hegemonic in another) and how this creates the conditions for differential power relations across space and time (Connolly 2003).

This chapter focuses primarily on wannabe 'hegemonic' boys. That is, boys who actively construct their masculinities or sense of 'boy-ness' through what they consider to be culturally exalted forms of masculinity. An emerging theme throughout the chapter is boys' frustrations in desiring and achieving 'older' teenage masculinities as 10- and 11-year-old boys within the child-centered context of the primary school. While boys' negotiation between immature/mature masculinities is more pervasive and visible in the following chapter on boys' interpellation into the world of romance and sexuality, it is also central to the ways in which these Year 6 boys were doing and talking about doing 'boy'. As the title for this chapter illustrates, I have found the elusive (Connell 1995) and adult-centric (Haywood and Mac an Ghaill 1996) conceptualisation of 'hegemonic masculinity' especially productive in theorising young boys' struggles and aspirations to embrace and embody 'older' masculinities as an impossible practice – as 'mission impossible'.

I first begin by exploring the masculinisation of sport and the gendering and generationing of playground space through one of the most dominant subject positions – 'footballer'. I examine the extent to which success at sports (in this case football) translates to success at being 'masculine', and explore how school policies and cultures can produce and reinforce hierarchies of masculinities and heterosexualities.

Football, football, football: the masculinisation of sport and playground space

Sport, as an organising institution for the embodiment of hegemonic masculinities, has been well documented as a language and practice of domination in school-based research (Corrigan 1979; Kessler *et al.* 1985; Hargreaves 1987; Fine 1987; Walker 1988; Mac an Ghaill 1994; Connell 1995; White *et al.* 1995; Parker

1996a, 1996b; Connolly 1998). It is therefore not surprising to discover that the playground is the most commonly cited example of overt gendered segregation, and football the most commonly cited activity of the monopolisation of outside space (Delamont 1990; Ross and Ryan 1990; Thorne 1993; Renold 1997; Swain 2000, 2003; Skelton 2001; Connolly 2003). This study is no exception (although see Connolly (2003, 2004) and Swain (2000) for schools that have banned 'football'). Football dominated playground space, relations and activity in gendered and age specific ways in both schools.

At Hirstwood the school field was officially divided (by school policy) between 'football' and 'other', or 'anything else' as one girl put it. This resulted in the majority of girls, who did not play football, being crammed into one half of the playing field with the infants and younger juniors. Not only did this policy legitimate a 'boys-only' zone (with most pupils and staff equating football exclusively with boys) but sanctioned a particular type of 'sporting' masculinity and gendered age-hierarchy. For the Year 6 boys who did not want to play football, their absence reinforced their Otherness in both gendered and generational ways. Their location alongside girls and infants aligned them with 'femininity' and 'immaturity', often indicated by the name-calling they received which included the terms: 'babies', 'girlie', 'silly' and 'sad'. Connolly (2003) also notes, in his ethnography of an inner-city, multi-ethnic primary school, how the feminisation of 'non-footballers' can produce racial and gendered segregation:

> To be seen playing football with children who were regarded as weaker and/or less skilled would certainly undermine the masculine identities that the boys had so carefully constructed. For these boys, this meant that not only were girls routinely excluded from football games but also South Asian boys who had generally been constructed through racist discourses as inferior and effeminate.
>
> (Connolly 2003: 119)

Boys (at both Tipton and Hirstwood) who were regular 'competent' footballers could gain power and kudos amongst their peers (especially younger boys): kudos that was enhanced by the game's status and visibility within the 'official' school as the only regular after-school team sport. It was the only sport to be oversubscribed with an 'A' team and a 'B' team and a waiting list of wannabe footballers which produced and reinforced a hierarchy of masculinities and (hetero)sexualities. Boys from the 'A' team were also considered (by both girls and other boys) to be the most romantically desirable. They were 'players' on the football pitch and 'players' in the field of romance (see Chapter 6).

Although nearly a third of all boys refused to engage with the footballing culture (see below), a significant majority, almost regardless of technical skill, positioned themselves firmly within dominant football practices and discourses. For example, Stuart took on the role of 'ball catcher' and 'human goal post', while Martin, who avoided the ball for fear of being hurt, always placed himself in the vicinity of the pitch/football crowd. Being a 'footballer' extended well beyond being a member of the 'official' school team or the physical game itself. Besides the embodiment of 'footballer' fashion, which involved wearing local, regional or national scarves, hats, stickers and bags, boys regularly practised stylised manoeuvres associated with the game (e.g. sliding tackles, shoulder barges and diving 'headers'). These took place both on and off the pitch. There were many occasions when during my classroom observations boys were compiling a team for next playtime, or creating a fantasy football league that was secretly passed under the tables from boy to boy. For some boys, being a 'footballer' meant exactly that. Eight boys chose 'professional footballer' for their future occupation and 14 subscribed or regularly accessed the magazines *Match* and *Shoot* (see also Hall and Coles 1997). It was thus no surprise to find football 'talk' infiltrating classroom life and the curriculum more widely. The following example follows a discussion of why some of the boys did not participate in the class magazine organised to raise money for 'Children in Need':

SCHOOL: TIPTON PRIMARY

Rachel:	Martin and Aaron right, when we were doing our magazine, they go, 'well we're not going to be in it unless you do, unless you let us do something about football'.
ER:	What did you say to that?
Rachel:	We said that we don't want football things in it so they go 'right we're not going to be in it', but now they're back in it again.
[...]	
Rachel:	And you see that all the time, that boys want to do something they say 'we're going to do football otherwise we won't be in it ... coz they're always doing football, cricket or something like that .../
Georgina:	Rugby.
Rachel:	It's always got to be something like/
Georgina:	Like sport/
Rachel:	Got something in it for boys' sports, about boys' sports.
ER:	Are girls not like that then?
Rachel:	No.
Kirsty and Claire:	Yes (laughs)
Georgina:	Well I am sometimes a bit like that/
Rachel:	Well, sometimes, but not all the time, boys, that's all they ever think about ... all they've got on their/
Kirsty:	When I did a magazine last time I wanted football things in/
Rachel:	All they've got on their brains is football ...

The ways in which 'sports success is success at being masculine' (Willis 1977: 122) was a discourse internalised by many boys, most notably in their daily commentaries of how many goals they had scored or saved, or in their endless critical appraisal of their own or other boys' sporting skill and mastery. As other researchers exploring the interconnection of sport and masculinity have noted, at the core of this hegemonic masculine ideal were repeated physical displays of skill, aggression, competition, domination, stoicism and strength (see Messner and Sabo 1994: 38). The intensity, commitment and investment in the production of their bodies as 'sporting' bodies and the intimate relationship between sporting prowess and hegemonic masculinity became markedly visible when football at Hirstwood was banned in the late autumn and winter months because of 'dangerous' playing conditions (i.e. a 'wet and muddy' field). Flouting school rules, a core group of the 'A' team replaced the football with a tennis ball and continued to dominate playground space and construct their own version of football. At Tipton, the normalisation of football and boys' monopolisation of playground space and activity was so naturalised as 'what boys do' that when football was banned here (because it was considered 'too rough' and a number of younger children were increasingly injured by the ball) one boy, Colin, cried out in despair: 'I mean, what else are we supposed to do?'[1]. What they did, in fact, was take-up other embodied practices that projected all the physical displays of an athletic masculinity, including the domination of playground space and the social exclusion of girls and 'non-footballer' boys.

At Tipton, running competitions and displays of stamina and muscular athleticism predominated to the extent that some of the 'A' team used the newly erected play equipment for 'chin-ups' and 'leg lifts' and even established a mock fitness circuit. With the boundaries between 'football' (boys)/'non-football' (girls) less clearly defined, more of the Year 6 girls joined in with some of the boys' running games. However, in the activities where girls began 'beating' or displaying greater skill or competence than the boys, such as in a jumping game (in which girls consistently jumped higher), they were quickly superseded by games of less interest to the girls. In contrast to Tipton, the seasonal banning of football at Hirstwood, where there was no play equipment, made more visible the relationship between sport, masculinity and violence. Here, the frequency of fighting games (discussed in the next section) increased to the extent that a number of boys were formally reprimanded in a school assembly and told that the 'rough games' had to cease 'otherwise playtimes would be abandoned'. This 'masculinization of violence' (see Mills 2001) and the social construction and normalisation of 'play-fighting' as 'boys being boys' is explored further below.

Doing 'tough', being 'hard': fighting masculinities and compulsory violence

> Sam and James are wrestling each other on the left-hand side of the playground. Sean, Sam, David and Ryan form a semi circle around them. They

are cheering, but it seems to be more for Sam than for James. The boys have told me that their fighting games are fun, but James looks as though he is fighting for his life. Both boys are sweating and have very red pained faces. The only boys enjoying this seem to be their 'friends', watching. There are no girls watching this 'game'.

(Hirstwood: fieldnotes)

From Best's (1983) 'warrior band', to Connolly's (1995) 'bad boys' and Jordan's (1995) 'fighting boys', engaging in fighting behaviours and other performances of physical 'violence' seemed to be a compulsory component of 'doing boy' (see also Evans 1987; Clark 1990; Thorne 1993; Skelton 1996; Adler and Adler 1998; Francis 1998; Holland 2003). Adler and Adler's (1998: 41) US research describes a regime of toughness marked by 'displays of physical prowess'. Best (1983) similarly identifies a group of 8-year-old boys who formed a club ('the tent club') whose macho codes called specifically for a range of 'fighting abilities' that 'meant playing rough' … and 'meant being able to take it' (Best 1983: 23). Explicitly or implicitly, many of these studies point to the connection between fighting and violent aggressive behaviour in the making of young hegemonic masculinities. As I will go on to argue, fighting practices as a pedagogy of violent masculinities was one of the few performances in which boys could legitimately access 'older' masculinities, naturalised as an expected, although frowned upon, feature of playground activity within a discourse of 'boys will be boys' (see Holland 2003).

The playground as 'battlefield' was one of the main sites in which young boys became little 'warriors' (Jordan 1995). A range of fighting masculinities were produced through games in which they were the arbiters and co-ordinators of physical power and domination. This could be physical domination over each other (e.g. the 'tripping up game') or over imaginary vulnerable groups (e.g. 'granny-bashing game'):

SCHOOL: HIRSTWOOD

The 'trip 'em up' and 'granny bashing' games
ER: So what sort of things are you playing?
Ryan: Lift 'em up or trip em up.
ER: Lift them up or trip 'em up?
Jake: Right, it's like squint and you've got to run across and there's two people there and you've got to lift them up and most people trip them / up.
Sean: Ryan got me yesterday and he stuck his foot out
ER: So you literally lift people up or you trip them over?
All: Yeah.

(Later, that year ....)

ER: What about in the playground, do you still play that tripping up game?
All: Yeah.
Jake: I got this massive black eye and it was all swollen.
ER: With that game?
David: No, / we were playing 'granny bashers'.
Ryan: I wasn't there, I wasn't there right and/
David: You link arms/there's these ...
Ryan: I was doing it the day before.
David: There are these big fights that we have, and me and Jake went in and someone tripped Jake up and their knee smacked his eye.
ER: Is that why the game was stopped?
All: Yeah.

In contrast to research which suggests that aggression and physical fighting are behaviours generally engaged in by low-achieving boys from 'working-class' backgrounds (see Connolly 2004), the normalisation of young boys' violent behaviour seemed to cut across class and academic ability. High-achieving boys from professional backgrounds (Ryan, Hirstwood) and low-achieving boys from 'working-class' backgrounds (Liam, Tipton) were the two 'trouble-makers' and 'bullies' of their school year in their respective schools. It seemed that 'fighting' and other forms of physical violence as signifiers of hegemonic masculinity were more easily assimilated and accessed by boys of all ages and thus transcended social-generational boundaries in ways that the embodiment of sexuality and other signifiers of adult masculinities (e.g. man as 'big and strong' or as 'provider') do not. On the other hand, there were clear differences between the 'fantasy play' and make-believe 'super-hero' games of the early primary years to the 'fighting play' and the more overt gaming of violence such as the 'granny-bashing' games of the later primary years. The feminisation of 'immature' masculinities is explored later in the chapter and more fully in Chapter 7.

Violent playground behaviours, or what Skelton (1996) refers to as 'outside behaviours', also permeated classroom interactions and other contexts in the school such as the stairs and corridors leading into the classroom:

This is the third occasion in two weeks when the boys, on their way down to the assembly hall, have punched the cardboard box full of old school projects. This is a very battered box. After punching the box, they then push and trip each other up along the corridor and perform quite daring feats as they swing and slide down the banister to the lower floor. I am yet to witness girls doing this.

(Tipton: fieldnotes)

Fighting, and other forms of physical violence, emerged as a recurrent theme in boys' talk throughout the school day. Fighting tactics, congratulatory comments on physical endurance (discussed later), showing each other their marked and scarred bodies (see Best 1983) and recalling and mythologising past fights with openers like, 'did you *see* that fight…', were all ways in which discourses of 'being tough' were produced and maintained. Interviews rarely concluded without some recourse to the latest fight or risky adventure (just as many girls' conversations turned to who was 'going out' with whom). When there were no new personal stories to recount, many boys drew upon and switched between their experiences 'out of school' with each other or of older brothers, uncles and fathers with an overall aim to produce a story more violent than the last:

School: Hirstwood

'Going mental'

Sean:	Can I just tell you one more story?
ER:	OK
Sean:	My brother last er last Friday, he came home about one 'o' clock in the morning from The Stage (pub) … yeah and he comes back, like he comes back in my room and then, and then I was like asleep and he fell on me, and then he starts telling me this story that there was a punch up and everything. And he said that he kicked in five people (laughs) and he said that they are coming back next Friday and how he wants to have another fight (interruption as two pupils go to the toilet). He said er it was better when you're drunk coz you can't feel it and his mate mouthed off and ran away (laughs).
ER:	So what do you think about this? Just funny or/
Sean:	No it's good.
ER:	It's good? Is that how you want to be when you're older?
Sean:	Well yeah I like boxing/
ER:	What about you Ryan do you like fighting?
Sean and Ryan:	Yeah.
Ryan:	And these people in the Nirvana concert they get out of their heads and go up on the stage and jump into the crowd head first/and they can't feel it because they're so out of it.
Jake:	And you know the Manic Street Preachers?
ER:	Yes.
Jake:	Right erm they have to have fences around them right coz it's not coz of the fans you see it's because of them, they're completely mental right, they jump into the crowd and start smacking people in the head with their guitars and that and

they're not allowed to do it so they have to have a fence around them/

Ryan: Yeah I'm going to see them in concert.

[...]

'Going more mentaller'

(Sean so far has avoided answering questions on concern over his appearance)

Sean: I've got this BMX yeah and erm once, there's this place called Treeden, and you've got all these car doors and we make ramps but I never wear a helmet coz I do more mentaller (sic) stuff then he does.

ER: So/

Sean: I fell off like, when er I'd just come back from the leisure centre, and I had to ride my bike up and there were these steps and I put my bike up and I go really fast and jump off it ... cool.

Ryan: Yeah and er once there was this caravan site and it's got this one way ramp. So me and my brother had races and time trials round it and there was this place with loads of gravel and erm you're meant to like slide down there and I forgot to and I come off and my hand skids across and I had loads of gravel in it but erm and I took my helmet off and there were loads of dents in it.

ER: Good job you had your helmet on.

Ryan: Yeah/

Jake: Oh/ yeah.

David: Right right.

ER: Go on Jake,

Jake: Oh yeah right I was at my uncle's for a week and and my uncle he's a bit, a bit mad really and er and erm so I went down the pub right and there were these people and they had this ramp going into the river and they got their bikes and they were jumping and going into the river and my uncle said, 'right oh, why don't we have a go?' and I said, 'no' and then erm and my little cousin who's about two months old got stung on the lip by a wasp so we had to go to a little casualty place and there was this man who was doing the jumping on the bike and all his head, split open it was disgusting,

Ryan: Right/

David: We were, me, Jamie, Ryan and my brother were jumping in the river and stuff and my brother wasn't wearing shoes and he got a big cut. He had to go to casualty.

While many boys would relay tales of risk and danger, some boys more than others used the interview as a forum to re-create themselves as 'rough-boys' and 'tough-guys', particularly if their 'hard' masculinities were under threat or exposed as vulnerable or fragile by other boys (e.g. if I attempted to follow up an incident in which they were the ones being 'pushed' or 'tripped up').

Recounting stories associated with physical violence may have been one of the ways in which boys attempted to shock me as an 'adult' researcher by demonstrating their knowledge of a range of violences which they think I might consider as taboo (see Connolly 1995). This could also have been one of the ways in which boys were projecting a hyper-masculine performance in the face of a dominant adult femininity (Walkerdine 1981; Skelton 1997). Interestingly, boys who drew upon the more familiar and often humorous territory of the warrior narratives tended to do so just after or during conversations that shifted into the personal or emotional. This was particularly the case in some of the earlier interviews when the boys were interviewed in larger groups (more than four) and more so with boys from professional backgrounds. However, I would also stress that once the novelty value of the initial interviews wore thin then the majority of boys used the group interviews to explore the anxiety and pressures of having to maintain a stoic front and negotiate the fine line between feeling pain and showing emotion.

Embedded in the fighting discourses of being 'hard', 'rough', 'tough' and 'macho' was a discourse of endurance (see Fine 1987). Many boys worked hard at maintaining their bodies as 'pain free' zones. Signs of emotion and pain, particularly in the release of tears, were constantly struggled against and avoided, unless as one boy pointed out, 'you are really really hurt'. Many of the girls in the study were also acutely aware of the performance of endurance by boys as a means to maintain a particular 'macho' look:

SCHOOL: HIRSTWOOD

Trudy:	I think it's because now they have to show off, they always have to put on an act.
ER:	Do they?
Annabel and Trudy:	Yeah.
Trudy:	And when they fall over and they really hurt themselves they just laugh/it off and you think
Annabel:	They put on an act/ and
Carla:	And David David really hurt himself when Kevin was hurting him and he just laughed, he don't dare to cry.
Annabel:	Yeah, they just laugh, they don't dare to cry because it doesn't add up to their macho look.
Carla:	Yeah and everyone would laugh at them.

'Crying' could call a boy's gender and (hetero)sexual identity into question because of the ways in which crying and emotion were perceived by the majority of boys as 'weak' and a signifier of 'girlie' femininity. However, there were many contexts in which crying was an acceptable behaviour and many boys supported and comforted each other in times of emotional stress. For example, at the beginning of one group interview (Tipton), Martin unexpectedly burst into tears. The other boys looked shocked and confused and I immediately took him outside and asked him if he was okay and wanted to talk about it. He told me how his dad had been rushed to hospital that morning and he was concerned about his welfare. Although none of the other boys knew about Martin's dad, they were both supportive and sensitive and did not once ridicule him for crying in ways that I have seen in the playground for falling over or sustaining minor physical injuries. Emotional control, release and support were heavily context dependent. And over the year I noticed how issues relating to boys' wider families, close homosocial friendships or their relationships with girls were legitimate triggers in ways that minor physical injuries or subtle forms of 'bullying' were often not. The fine line and ambiguity between fighting with and without consent and the harmful consequences of producing rough and tough masculinities are discussed further below.

'It doesn't hurt, it's just a game, isn't it?': the naturalisation and masculinisation of physical violence

The blurred boundary between what constitutes a 'game' and what constitutes harmful and abusive behaviour, or 'bullying', are issues that many primary school researchers on boys and masculinities have been grappling with (Best 1983; Evans 1987; Thorne 1993; Skelton 2001). Both extracts below highlight the ambiguity surrounding issues of consent in play and the often unequal power relationships embedded in much of the 'play-fighting' in which one boy's harmless fun is another boy's oppression and abuse (see Edley and Weatherall 1996: 109).

SCHOOL: HIRSTWOOD

(Discussing the 'tripping up' game)

Ryan: It's quite fun if you don't get hurt
ER: So who /
Ryan: It's not like really mad violence you just trip em up/
Sean: Like Ryan you were going after James because and then me and Chris like jumped up and pushed and smacked him right /
Jake: Yeah yeah and we were standing there and Sean and Sam comes in and goes 'stop fighting' and kicked him right at the same time and they go, 'aaaagah' (they all laugh)
ER: How do you get away with all this fighting in the playground, don't the dinner ladies stop you?
Sean: Yeah, but if they do, if they see you and if they're like looking and someone says stop it, you like walk to another place, like you walk over to the other side and start again.

(Rick confronts Ryan on how he used to 'beat' him up in Year 5)

Rick: You used to beat me up
Ryan: No I didn't/
Rick: Yes you did, you did body slams on me
Ryan: That was because we were *playing* fights
Rick: Were we? (sounds unsure)
Ryan: Yeah.

The fusing of violence with play underpinned much of boys' talk on 'play-fighting'. 'It's just a joke' or 'it's just a game' were indeed among the most common justifications of fighting practices (Blackmore 1995). Weaving and lacing violent behaviours with humour was one of the means by which boys either disguised or avoided the overt charge of being a 'bully'. Laughter was often synonymous with pain in the production of 'hard' masculinities as we have already seen in the telling of violent stories as a form of entertainment and in the game-play of fighting and other 'punch and run' practices in the extracts above (see also Nayak and Kehily 1997). Although some overtly violent games were expertly carried out away from teaching staff on playground duty (see Sean's last comment), for most boys, play-fighting was a tolerated semi-legitimate expression of violence/masculinity.

Over the past few years increasing attention has been paid to the role of the bully, the bullied and bullying practices within primary and secondary schools. While recent definitions over the past ten years have begun to identify bullying as patterns of dominance embedded in relations of power and control which directly affect everyone in the school (see Smith and Sharpe 1994), much of the bullying literature remains gender-blind (Mac an Ghaill 1994; see also Chapter 7). Askew and Ross (1988) conducted one of the few early studies which specifically addressed how the physicality of boys, with their rigid and stylised forms of strength, competition and aggression, signifies what it means to be 'masculine' (for more recent work on the masculinisation of violence in schools see Mills 2001). As this study and many other studies focusing on gender relations and schooling have revealed, so pervasive and naturalised is the discourse 'boys will be boys' (i.e. boys will be violent) that violent behaviours are tolerated, legitimised and reproduced as 'play', as 'not serious', as just 'boys being boys'.

Fights and fighting games involving some form of physical violence were unlikely to come to the attention of staff and be interpreted as 'bullying' or as 'problematic' thus warranting intervention unless there was a clear unequal power relationship (older/bigger and younger/smaller pupils). Or, as the extract below reveals, when a fight drew in a crowd. Even the most alert and perceptive teacher could not always determine when to intervene given how many children were highly adept in disguising violence through humour, role-play and even sporting tactics. Other more overt strategies included alerting other children to teacher proximity by 'standing watch' or simply 'finding another place' (above) where they could carry on:

As I look round the playground, I suddenly see what looks like a severe form of physical violence. One boy is down on the floor, on his side using his arms to defend himself from a boy standing over him, kicking him in the head and stomach. Two other boys are joining in. I look round to see where the teacher on playground duty is and she is facing the other way. There are two to three boys keeping a watch on where she is looking. After a minute or so I can no longer passively watch this behaviour and run to tell the teacher on duty.[2] The head teacher is informed and I am needed as a witness when the two boys refuse being positioned as 'bullies', deny kicking the boy and instead try to pass off their behaviour as a game.

(Hirstwood: fieldnotes)

The two boys above were unsuccessful in re-framing their actions as 'just a game'. With an obvious 'victim' and 'perpetrator' it was a recognisable form of physical violence in which the two protagonists fitted neatly into the subject position, 'bully'. However, to be positioned as a 'bully' was neither desirable nor powerful, in fact, the very opposite. There were clear developmental, social and cultural boundaries in which physical violence within games, or as self-defence or through humour was a legitimate and often compulsory component of a 'tough masculinity'. Whenever I suggested the possibility that some of the boys' games looked like bullying to me, they were, as we have seen, very careful to re-state that they were 'just playing'. They associated bullies with boys who continually and repeatedly 'picked-on' the same child over a substantial period of time or when fighting went 'over the top' – what Ryan refers to as irrational 'mad violence'. Indeed, as Joyce Canaan (1996) outlined in her deconstruction of what it means for young men (aged 16–24) to be 'hard', 'not fighting' and 'not acting hard' as a form of disciplined self-control was more effective in expressing a hegemonic (adult) 'masculinity' than getting into fights, and thus being out of control. Thus, perhaps, the gaming of violence through 'play-fighting' and 'humour' was not just about trying on 'older' masculinities (e.g. boxing and wrestling) or disguising violent practices so as not to get caught. It also reflects boys' own recognition that 'fighting' or 'violence' per se is socially unacceptable and not at all 'manly'.

Bodies do matter: inflated masculinities and the problematics of self-grooming

Being 'hard' but not acting 'too hard', playing fighting games which involve inflicting and enduring 'controlled' rather than 'mad' violence and presenting a stoic truculent self in the face of physical and emotional pain were just some of the ways a number of young boys were doing 'masculinity' and producing their bodies as 'boys' bodies (see Swain 2003). The fine line between being 'hard' and being a 'bully' and showing emotion without being called 'weak' or a 'sissy' were hegemonic practices few boys reported much success at achieving. Very few boys were able to cash in their much practised physical capital for social capital and status, particularly when their embodied performances of hardened masculinities were perceived as just that, 'an act', as something 'less than real'. And it was the wannabe 'tough-guys', the boys who seemed least 'tough' or 'hard', who put in by far the most spectacular performances – performances which, as Jo and Marie recount (below) betrayed them at every turn:

SCHOOL: TIPTON

Jo: [...] Martin goes round thumping people
ER: Does he?
Jo: Yeah, but he's not hard, he likes to think he's hard, he goes round thumping people and we just stand there going, 'Martin this doesn't hurt', and it's sort of like, he punches you twenty times and we're still standing there going, "Martin this doesn't hurt" (Laughs)
ER: So then what does he do?
Jo: He gets in a right mood, kicks something and chucks the chairs around the class.
ER: So why do you think he's started thumping more?
Marie: To look cool.
Jo: Yeah to look cool, but it doesn't work/, not with Martin
ER: It's not working?
Jo: No.
Marie: (We) just thump him back.
ER: Why not with Martin?
Jo: Well with Martin, he's just a bit of a softy really.
ER: Is he?
Jo: Yeah ... you can go up to him and tap him and he goes 'oh don't do that, that hurt' .
ER: But he still tries to be cool and look hard?
Jo: Yeah, but it doesn't work.
ER: The fact that he has no effect on you probably makes it look worse does it?
Jo: Yeah (laughs) he wants to look hard, and the only way to look hard is to beat people/ up and Martin.
ER: Is it?
Jo: Yeah, well that's what works for the boys anyway ... and Martin tries to beat a girl, because there's no way he could beat up a boy and he can't even beat up a girl!

'Looking hard' to 'look cool' is easily parodied by the girls here and Martin's actions only serve to reinforce the fact that 'he's a bit of a softy really'. Like many boys, Martin's pre-pubertal body fell so significantly short of the much sought after 'older' muscular macho body that demonstrations of physical and material violence produced comedy rather than fear in recipients and onlookers. Other strategies deployed by the majority of wannabe 'tough-guys' included aligning themselves with the physical size and dominance of 'older' masculinities by re-fashioning their uniforms in ways that made them 'look bigger' (than their 'real' size and perhaps girls and younger boys). 'Chunky' masculinities could be created (and inflated) by wearing over-sized clothing. The popular 'baggy' iconography at the time of the research (reflected in the boy bands of popular music and culture) included wearing trousers so baggy that excess material would gather around their ankles. Sweatshirts would hang and flap around their knees, sleeves would often have to be rolled up to hold a pen or pencil and belts securely fastened so that their trousers stayed up! Physical size could be overcome and the baggier the better to secure an 'older' look:

SCHOOL: TIPTON

Pete: Emma, Emma, I've got, I, I even wear baggy trousers to school/ (not all of the boys' parents allow them to wear 'baggy trousers' to school)

Darren: Yeah look at them, look at that (he points and shows me Pete's baggy trousers)

Darren: Well these aren't very but/ (points to his own)

Colin: These were very baggy when I was in Year 5 (says grumpily).

Darren: I wore these since I was a Year 5 and they're still quite/ baggy

Timothy: I'm quite tall so I have to have twelve-year-old's trousers (says proudly)

ER: So you've all got quite baggy trousers?

All: Yeah.

Pete: Mine are the baggiest.

Darren: Look look these are really, I've got baggy ones at the bottom, look (shows me)

ER: So they have to be baggy at the bottom, not just long?

Darren: Yeah.

Pete: My my 'Eclipse' (high-street brand) jeans come down to the floor/

Darren: So do mine/ my jeans come down low.

★★★

ER: Do you wear baggy jeans the same as Martin?

Aaron: Well not really baggy jeans/

Liam: They're not baggy are they …

Aaron: Not yet, I'm a bit too young for that/

Liam: You're what?/

Martin: I love baggy jeans.

ER: So you like baggy jeans Martin but you feel you're a bit too young for that Aaron?

Aaron:	Well well I'm older than him.
Martin:	He's not young, but he just doesn't like 'em probably/
Aaron:	I like 'em, but they don't suit me just yet.
Michael:	I don't like baggy jeans, but I like baggy T-shirts/
[...]	
ER:	Martin what were you going to say?
Martin:	I've got four pairs of baggy jeans but hardly any of them fit me, still, I just wear 'em anyway (Liam is hitting Michael with a pencil)
ER:	None of them fit you?
Martin:	No, but I just wear them/
ER:	Even if they're too big?
Martin:	I put a belt round them.

Creating the illusion of an 'older' muscular masculinity by puffing up their bodies with over-sized clothing (see Klein 1993) provides an interesting contrast between the tight and skimpy fashion that aligned the 'girlie-girls' with 'older' femininities. With a number of Year 6 girls taller and often stronger than the Year 6 boys, the illusion of size and strength was a constant battle and the tension between the 'ideal' and 'lived experience' of doing 'manly' masculinity confronted boys daily, both in their failure to meet 'hegemonic' standards of 'older' masculinities and in their inability to convincingly demonstrate their difference from passive and 'weak' femininities.

Clothes and footwear weren't the only signifiers of a 'cool' and 'fashionable' masculinity. Many boys talked about sporting the 'right' haircut (which at the time of research was an 'under-cut' – spiky top and fringe, clipped sides and shaved at the back of the neck). This style was high maintenance and involved regular visits to the hairdressers and daily applications of hair-gel. Investing and self-styling their bodies to achieve and represent the 'right look', however, involved some tricky negotiation. First, admitting to the range of practices and time and care invested to produce a 'cool' masculinity was in itself not very 'cool'. Being 'cool' involved conforming to the latest fashion but not admitting to doing so. As Ali (2000: 126) noted amongst upper primary boys, there was a 'fine line between being good-looking without being vain' especially when vanity 'could align them with gayness'. Second, boys who shied away from or resisted engaging in the local boyfriend/girlfriend culture considered boys' incessant talk about grooming and styling as 'too old' (just as they would view wearing 'baggy trousers' as indicative of an 'older' fashion). Having the choice to be able to draw upon developmental discourses of a non-sexualised 'boyhood', however, provided a further contrast to the ways in which many girls were almost expected to project heterosexualised femininities.

The struggle for boys to engage with an 'older' heterosexual economy of body-beautiful products became highly transparent in the teasing (by teachers and pupils alike) of boys who admitted to wearing branded deodorants and aftershave – especially boys who were not interested in, or making the transition to relating to, girls as potential girlfriends. There were many failed 'make-overs' by those boys who dared to 'do cool'. Darren's bleached brown hair turned bright orange rather than white-blond. Pete's over-zealous use of his dad's aftershave one playtime resulted in a group of younger children evacuating the boys' toilets coughing and spluttering. Because of the ultimate mismatch between young boys and mature masculinities, boys who did attempt the tenuous transition to become mini-men were frequently ridiculed and negatively labelled as 'too cool' for 'going over the top' (see Chapter 6). They were not, however, positioned within derogatively sexualised discourses in the way that girls who exceeded sexual-generational boundaries of age-appropriate heterofemininity were (see Chapter 5). While some boys could draw upon romanticised discourses of a non-sexualised 'boy-hood' to resist and critique other boys' anxiety over 'fashion', there were a number of boys who were reporting concerns over their embodied masculinities and struggling to achieve the 'right look' in similar ways to the girls.

The social acceptability and take-up of dominant somatic and sartorial grooming discourses and practices, however, differed markedly between the two schools. At Hirstwood, for example, subscribing to the fighting cultures and the production of a 'tough-guy' masculinity far outweighed concern over appearance and the presentation of a 'cool' masculinity. The significance of social class, given the Tipton boys' greater investment in 'older' sexualised masculinities, is discussed further in Chapter 6. It is the rocky transition of boys' attempts to masculinise their boy-child bodies by drawing upon adult hegemonic masculinising discourses and practices that I want to emphasise. Well over two-thirds of boys openly expressed their feelings of powerlessness and anxiety in their struggle to embody the impossible fiction of an adult-defined hegemonic masculinity with many a performance pulled apart and ridiculed as poor imitations of what popular culture and wider society defines as a 'manly'. No wonder then that one of the main routes through which boys defined their sense of boy-ness and masculinity was in opposition to 'femininity'.

'Girls', 'geeks' and 'gays': making masculinities through feminine and Other disassociations

I'm not a girl

In the second week of my research at Tipton one of the ancillary staff, Mrs Croft, brought in some freshly cut roses from her garden and passed them round the girls in the class to smell and admire. As she collected in the flowers, Pete suddenly stood up and announced to the class, 'I don't like roses, I like mud' and sat back down again. The stark contrast between something so historically and traditionally 'feminine' (roses) and 'masculine' (mud), and the need for Pete to firmly locate himself in the 'masculine' quite astounded me, particularly as this declaration was so overt, so public. A few people chuckled and went quietly back to their work. As a researcher, however, this was a critical moment insofar as it symbolised one of the many performances I was to witness in relation to the ways boys actively construct their masculinities as 'not female', 'not feminine'. Given that very few boys sustained any comfortable security in producing their young masculinities within 'older' hegemonic discourses, is it so surprising that boys take to defining their boy-hood and masculinity in opposition and difference to 'girl-hood' and 'femininity' as many other primary school studies of children's gender relations have found? (Best 1983; Jordan 1995; Francis 1998; Skelton 2001; Swain 2002b).

The 'borderwork' (Thorne 1993) practised by boys to police the 'boundary maintenance' between boys (masculinity) and girls (femininity) was most transparent in boys' active segregation and detachment from the company of girls. As illustrated earlier, most of the Year 6 boys regularly excluded most girls from the majority of their playground activities and rarely did boys talk about or strike up relations with girls as friends (although see Chapter 6). As the following three extracts highlight, gendered segregations, in which boys actively evaded being physically close to girls, infiltrated classroom relations and were deployed by both Miss Wilson and Mrs Fryer as a strategy for classroom management and discipline:

> Boys and girls are lining up to go down to assembly. I notice how the majority of boys wait on the other side of the room for the girls to finish queuing before they line up. Liam is asked to close the gap between himself and a group of girls. He refuses and pushes Murray behind him instead.
>
> (Tipton: fieldnotes)

★★★

> The class has become very noisy (boys seem more noisy than girls) and Mrs Fryer is trying to quieten them down so that the test she is about to give them is conducted in silence. After a few minutes she threatens them that she'll 'sit the girls next to the boys'. There is an immediate outcry from most of the boys and some of the girls. They rapidly quieten down.
>
> (Tipton: fieldnotes)

★★★

> (The two Year 6 classes merge for maths)
> Miss Wilson's maths group have found themselves seats. Harry arrives a little late and is the last to find a seat. Other boys have all found seats next other boys. The only place left is next to Anna. Miss Wilson sees this and directs him to the seat and apologises to him, 'sorry about that Harry'.
>
> (Hirstwood: fieldnotes)

Lining up and seating arrangements were, in addition to the gender differentiation within the playground, key organisational features in which the spatiality
of boy/girl dichotomies became most visible. Children invariably segregated
themselves into same-gender groups (and within gender groups, see section
below). Children's fear of opposite-gender proximity was also drawn upon as a
form of behavioural management (Mrs Fryer) or apologised for (Miss Wilson).

The teasing and ridicule of boys who fraternised too closely and spent too
much time 'with the girls' is discussed in the following chapter (see also Swain
2003). I am not suggesting that boys and girls occupied distinct and separate
social worlds and that there were not other ways besides gender in which
pupils were organised and organised themselves (particularly through dimensions of age, class, ethnicity and academic ability, see Connolly 1998; Ali 2002;
Benjamin 2003). There were also girls in both schools who enjoyed the company of boys and felt empowered by participating in boys' pursuits (football, in
particular) and were, in the main, embraced by the majority of boys (see
Chapter 3). However, all the boys in the study engaged in some form of 'anti-
girl' talk in which femininity and the category 'girl' were synonymous with
weakness, incompetency, lack, inferiority and disease (see Walkerdine 1990). In
particular, these anti-feminine tropes and stereotypes were drawn upon by boys
in situations where they wanted to assert their rights to power as hegemonic
'boys' over girls. This could occur by excluding girls from playground games
(e.g. football), by asserting their intellectual superiority (e.g. by undermining
girls' academic work) or by positioning girls as generally inferior (e.g. boys are
better than girls). Each of these themes is illustrated below:

Power in the playground

In the extract below, exclusionary discourses are drawn upon to prevent girls
from playing football. They position girls in a number of ways: from lacking
skill ('cos they're rubbish' and 'they muck up the game') to girls' lack in general
('girls are rubbish' and 'because they're girls').

SCHOOL: TIPTON

(The comments below are from four boys placed at the middle to lower end of
the school's B-team)

ER: Sometimes I see you playing football with the tennis ball in the cor-
          ner?
All: Yeah.
ER: And that's where you play football?
All: Yeah.
ER: But I've never seen any girls play that, why not?
Martin: Coz they're rubbish/
Aaron: They don't want to play, they're /rubbish.

Martin:	Girls are rubb-ish (says this loudly into the tape recorder).
Liam:	We wouldn't let 'em play any/way.
Michael:	They don't want to play, they don't like it.
Aaron:	Yeah.
ER:	Well I've been talking to a few and they said they did want to play to begin with, but you wouldn't let them play?
Liam:	Yeah that's true.
ER:	Is that right? (to the other boys)
Liam:	Yeah.
Michael:	Yeah.
Aaron:	Yeah, that is true (they all look at each other and laugh)
ER:	So why do you want to keep the game to yourself?
Martin:	Because they're girls/
Aaron:	And they tackle/
Martin:	And they muck the game up ... and they chuck it every where (the others laugh and nod in agreement)

Power in the classroom

In the following extract, gendered competitiveness is both overt and covert as boys undermine girls' academic efforts by depicting their achievements as 'failures', belittling their serious commitment to schoolwork and mocking their contributions in whole-class discussions (see also Mahony 1985; Francis 2000; Skelton and Francis 2003).

SCHOOL: HIRSTWOOD

Tina:	It's just sometimes, the boys laugh at you if you get a question wrong/
Carrie:	Yeah/
Tina:	And when we were doing our recorders, they were laughing and putting us off and everything.
ER:	Does that happen in class?
Tina:	It did in our three minute talk, they were laughing.
ER:	But did you laugh at them then they were doing theirs?
Tina:	No ... they sort of giggle at ours and everything.

★★★

Everybody is working in groups of three or four. Each group is drawing and writing about a recent visit to a local historic town. Tom looks over at Kimberly's table. He then gets up and walks up to them, peering at their work and sneers; 'What is that? – My dog could do better than that ... my dogs bum could do better than that' and walks off.

(Tipton: fieldnotes)

★★★

> Julia is engrossed in a very long (400 pages) novel that Mrs Fryer (class teacher) has handed her to read. Two of the boys opposite tell her that she is 'mad' to read a book like that and start laughing. Julia responds with, 'so, I like reading' and continues to read.
>
> (Tipton: fieldnotes)

Boys (masculinity) are better than girls (femininity)

This short extract symbolises the ways in which boys draw upon traditional discourses of femininity as physically weak ('wimpy') and emotional ('crying') to conclude that 'boys are better than girls' by constructing violence (as a property of boys) rather than emotional outburst (as a property of girls) as a more superior ('better') response to conflict:

SCHOOL: HIRSTWOOD

James: They're (girls) wimps.
ER: Well there are some quite big girls in your class/
James: No they're all wimpy.
[...]
David: The boys are better than the girls, the girls are always, they always start crying, crying and stuff, but the boys if they get in an argument they just beat each other up and that's it.

In contexts in which boys' performances of hegemonic masculinity were most vulnerable and under threat (e.g. being 'beaten by a girl' at a class test or being 'beaten up' physically), anti-girl gestures and anti-girl talk were a common reaction. It was also at these times when 'masculinity-making' performances were more pronounced, and thus only served to draw attention to and reinforce a failing masculinity.

I'm not a geek

Many studies have illustrated how boys who dare to deviate, stray or repeatedly struggle to live up to the hegemonic masculine ideal (which can vary between schools and communities, see Connolly 2003 and Swain 2003) can incur high social and emotional costs and be subjected to a number of Othering practices in which deviation from hegemonic norms is subordinated and pathologised. As we have discussed so far, not only do boys actively construct and define their 'boy-ness' in relation and opposition to girls and hyper-femininities, but they do so in relation to non-hegemonic masculinities (Connell 1995; Frosh *et al.* 2002) by creating a hierarchy and continuum of masculinities crudely built around a dichotomy of 'proper'/'not proper' masculinities (Boldt 1996).

All of the boys in the research were subject to a number of gender-jabs and gender-ridicule. Boys who were routinely targeted, however, were those boys who were positioned by their peers as Other to the normative scripts of hegemonic masculinity – a practice that affected over a third of all boys in the study and one which enabled other boys to re-position and produce their ways of 'doing boy' as normal and dominant. Behaviours that contravened hegemonic scripts included boys who were studious and pro-school (not necessarily high achievers), rule-followers rather than rule-breakers, preferred fantasy games over football, cars over computer games, romantic ballads (e.g. Boyzone) over nu-metal (e.g. Green Day) and did not adopt the popular modes of fashion or 'hard' body postures. How those boys managed to sustain non-hegemonic masculinities within the primary school is discussed in detail in Chapter 7. What I want to highlight here, in the following extracts, are the ways in which hierarchical masculinities were created and maintained in a number of sites and contexts by boys who blurred gender and generational boundaries and how these boys identified and experienced their difference within a bounded and constraining gendered dichotomy of 'us' (Other) and 'them' (Normal).

The following extract highlights how embodied notions of 'soft' (feminine) and 'hard' (masculine) were equally applied to music as they were to risk-taking behaviours or displays of toughness:

SCHOOL: HIRSTWOOD

Toby: Yeah, there's all the er rough people and then there's all the soft people.
Simon: And they always try, all the normal people/
ER: Do you /see yourself as different to them?
Simon: We're not exactly tough ... we just don't want to get involved in any fighting or anything.
Toby: Yeah.
ER: Why not?
Simon: Well, we don't /want to get told off.
[...]
Toby: Well everybody, all the sort of like rough guys like all this Nirvana and stuff/
ER: OK what do you /like then?
Toby: But I'm scared to say what what I like its like/
ER: What do you like then?
Toby: Yeah we like soft music, we don't like all this 'heavy metal'.

This gendered mapping of the body and popular culture into categories of 'soft' (feminine) and 'hard' (masculine) also extended to the ways in which the physical spaces within the school were gendered, thus revealing how institutional structures and discourses make available particular (normative) gender subject positions. We have already discussed how Year 6 boys at Hirstwood who did not play football were squashed into one half of the playing field alongside Year 6 girls and all the infants and younger juniors, thus aligning them with 'femininity' and 'immaturity'. While being excluded or absent from a particular masculinised space could reinforce a boy's Otherness (or non-hegemonic status), so could inhabiting a space traditionally associated with girls/femininity. At Tipton, choosing to 'stay in class' (and 'do work') rather than 'play outside' at designated break times was one such feminised space:

SCHOOL: TIPTON

Colin: He's (Damien) a geek, he just stays in (class) all the time and does Maths.[3]

[...]

Colin: And Damien, he never, at PE he goes on the apparatus we got outside, he doesn't dare do any flips off or something over the ladder thing/

Adrian: Yeah, they're not adventurous, they're not adventurous/ they are not adventurous.

Colin: They just like sitting at/ home.

Darren: Maths maths maths maths/

Pete: And they don't dare to go on top of the climbing frame or anything like that.

Darren: Yeah, they just get on one line and go 'oh that's high enough thank you'.

As the interview progresses, the boys' polarisation between 'inside' and 'outside' extends to encompass the boys' perceived inactivity beyond the school gates ('they just like sitting at home') and their lack of adventure and risk-taking behaviour when they do engage in 'outside'/'play' activities.

Girls study, boys mess around: hegemonic masculinity in the classroom

Bringing 'outside' behaviours into the classroom and presenting a more active, masculinised self was another key strategy deployed by over two-thirds of boys ('working' and 'middle' class) to avoid the many labels associated with the feminisation of 'working hard' and 'studiousness' (e.g. 'nerd', 'geek', 'girl'). Being 'studious' could involve quiet, settled study, visibly 'working hard' at a task, silent reading, publicly adopting a pro-school attitude and taking test results seriously. By engaging or being perceived to be engaging in any of these activities/body postures, boys could potentially leave themselves open to verbal abuse and ridicule. In contrast, play-fighting in the classroom, rocking on chairs or sitting on them backwards, throwing 'academic' equipment around (such as rulers, erasers, paper) and generally 'mucking' and 'messing about' could position boys in opposition to girls (who 'chat') and the feminisation of passive learning (Walkerdine 1990):

> Alicia and I walk back to the classroom following an interview. She tells me how she thinks 'the boys mess about and the girls chat'. She explains to me (which confirms my observations) that the boys and some of the girls will avoid work if they can. She tells me how she can't work with Jake and his friends because they are always 'messing around' when they work [Methodological note: I have noticed over the past 8 months how many of the boys at Hirstwood are continually 'joking around' when they are supposed to be 'on task' and how they seem to try hard not to look like they are 'working'].
>
> (Hirstwood: fieldnotes)

In the main, 'messing about' has often been theorised as a 'coping strategy' (Mealyea 1989) and/or an 'antidote' to the 'boredom', 'ritual', 'routine', 'regulation' and 'oppressive authority' of schooling (Woods 1976: 185). In particular, parody and subversion of 'official' classroom rules have been conceptualised as a product of class tensions and deployed by 'oppressed groups' as a form of 'resistance' to the pressures of a middle-class school ethos (Willis 1977; Dubberly 1988). However, the majority of pupils found 'messing about' were the middle-class boys at Hirstwood with SAT results above the national average. Like Pollard's (1985: 206) middle-class 'jokers', these boys combined 'having a laugh' with an eager, although disguised, willingness to learn. They seemed to be injecting humour into classroom life as a way of securing an academic identity that did not equate academic success or studiousness with 'square' or 'geek'. 'Having a laugh', thus went some way to dislocate academic effort from academic success (see Mac an Ghaill 1994; Renold 2001b).

It is important to stress, however, that being called a 'geek' was not simply a matter of engaging in non-hegemonic activities such as preferring to play 'Power Rangers' over football or enjoying 'quiet study' over 'messing about' and 'having a laugh'. There were boys who could blur gender boundaries, so long as they engaged in some masculinity-making activity. For example, boys could regularly opt out of football and fighting if they invested in 'heterosexual' discourses and 'being a boyfriend' (see Chapter 6). Boys could also locate themselves as 'studious' and 'pro-school' if they were also 'high flyers' on the football pitch. The pressures to conform and perform as 'properly masculine', however, seemed to increase over the academic year, leading a number of boys to detach themselves from previous 'non-hegemonic' behaviours and more marginalised friendship networks and take up more socially acceptable ways of 'doing boy'.

From geek to goalie

Approximately two-thirds of boys were involved in daily performances that differentiated them from 'Other' subordinate masculinities in an attempt to maintain their status, albeit fragile, as dominant hegemonic boys. There was, however, an increasing number of studious and high-achieving 'subordinate' boys in both schools, towards the onset of the SATS, who were strategically disassociating themselves from the activities of their non-hegemonic peers. These boys began investing heavily in dominant masculine practices, such as fighting, messing about in class, and football. It seemed that they were aware that by engaging in other status-enhancing behaviour (such as sport), the labels of 'goody-goody' could be nullified. Consequently, and possibly due to the constant teasing and bullying they received, they were making a conscious and noticeable effort to change their ways and, as one boy put it, 'join the opposition'. 'Stuart's story' (below) traces, in detail, the transformative processes and identity-work of a white, middle-class high-achieving (Levels 5 and 6 in SATS) boy's effort to smooth out the contradictory 'layers' within the hierarchy of masculinities that produced him as 'geeky' and 'square', and negotiate a more acceptable masculinity as a star goalie:

Stuart's story

The first term, as the following extract illustrates, saw Stuart (Tipton) being teased, ridiculed and ostracised by dominant peer groups:

> Classroom: Timothy and Aaron tease Stuart about his football and train drawings. They take his book from him and laugh at his pictures. Pete walks over to the group and asks Aaron and Timothy to cross their fingers. Stuart does too even though he is not asked. Pete then sees this and says to Stuart, 'not you, not you'. Stuart uncrosses his fingers and looks quite upset.

However, from expressing and exhibiting no real interest in football or sport prior to Year 6, the following extract marks Stuart's overt if tentative interest in becoming part of the dominant playground culture:

> Playground: The Year 6 boys are playing football with a tennis ball (bar Damien, William and Murray). Once more, Stuart is hanging around the edges and collecting the ball if it strays from the game's boundaries. He is not thanked, but almost expected to be a ball fetcher now.

In the second term Stuart joins one of the school's football teams (B-squad) and there is a noticeable difference regarding his classroom behaviour. He now completes set schoolwork in half the time and devotes the latter half to reading football magazines and creating fantasy football leagues. These activities are greatly admired by his (male) peers.

Classroom: While consistently maintaining high academic results, Stuart only does the bare minimum regarding set class work. He seems to finish the set work as quickly as he can and then spends the rest of the lesson reading football magazines hidden behind his text book. Many of the boys are aware that he does this and think it is 'cool'.

From 'ball catcher' and 'goal post' in the first term to revered football star as 'goalie', towards the end of the middle term, Stuart's acceptance and assimilation into the hegemonic footballers' culture seems to directly correlate with the fact that Stuart is no longer bullied or ostracised by his male peers:

Playground: Stuart is now fully integrated into the Year 6 games of football as a goalie. He walks in and out (from playground to classroom) with them and is no longer ostracised or bullied by `the majority of the 'sporting' boys. He seems to have developed quite a heroic status as a goalie.

While Stuart's 'star' status confirms Gilbert and Gilbert's (1998) findings that what distinguishes the 'nerds' from the 'pro-school' boys is sport, it was difficult to get a sense of how far Stuart consciously and strategically developed an interest and skill in football to achieve a more dominant masculinity and re-position his subordinate status with the sole intention of staving off the bullying and teasing. His male peers were, however, clearly aware of the relation between 'fitting in', 'playing football' and becoming an acceptable, hegemonic male:

SCHOOL: TIPTON

ER:	So who gets it the most in your class? (bullying)
Martin:	It's always the square bears, but Stuart isn't a square/ bear anymore?
Michael:	Stuart, everyone likes Stuart, apart from Liam, Damien/ and
Colin:	Yeah, Stuart's got a lot better/ hasn't he?
Martin:	Last year Stuart was, we didn't like him that much/
Michael:	No not at all.
ER:	What was he like in Year 6 (all talk at once, then Colin talks)?
Colin:	It was like, here's dick head lets go and beat him in and stuff like that.
[...]	
ER:	Do you think Stuart has actually changed?
Colin:	Yeah a lot.
Martin:	He's brilliant in goal.
ER:	Is he?
Colin:	He used to be rubbish, but now he's class/
[...]	
ER:	Do you like him better as a person now?
Colin:	Yeah definitely.
Darren:	Yeah

Darren:	He's changed a bit as well
Colin:	Yeah, he doesn't play with Damien anymore, coz coz we don't like people like Damien.
Colin:	Yeah, he's really changed, he's just come on to our table and has just fitted in.
Darren:	He's quite funny, sometimes as well.
ER:	So do you think he has fitted in Colin because of the football?
Colin:	Yeah, yeah.
Darren:	Yeah.

However, while the majority of boys readily accepted and to some extent created Stuart's transformation from 'geek' to 'goalie' (thus simultaneously reinforcing and confirming their hegemonic status), his identity management was publicly rejected by his female contemporaries. Through a weekly, exclusionary ritual of verbal taunts and jibes aimed at both his gender ('gay', 'geek') and learner ('square') identity, the girls in his class continued to expose the contradictory layers that Stuart was trying so hard to suppress (see Chapter 7). While he may have 'made it' in the popularity stakes amongst his male peers, his star status as goalie did not transform his pariah-like status among the girls.

Concluding notes

This chapter has been concerned with foregrounding boys' struggles, fantasies and failures in negotiating and embodying an elusive and ultimately unachievable range of hegemonic masculinities. As I argued in the introduction to this chapter, I have found Connell's concept of 'hegemonic masculinity' especially useful in two main ways. First, in its ability to capture boys' lack of comfortable security or sustained feeling of power in investing in and taking up dominant masculine discourses and practices (e.g. fighting and football). Second, and almost as a consequence, the ways in which all of the boys in the study engaged in some form of anti-girl talk/behaviour when hegemonic masculinities were under threat (especially by boys positioned lower down the gender/sexual hierarchies). A persistent theme in this study (and others, see Skelton and Francis 2003) is the ways in which girls, as perceived bearers of 'femininity', and boys who refuse or fail to invest in such 'hegemonic' endeavours are subordinated as part and parcel of achieving a hegemonic masculinity – and how the school in formal and informal ways supports this process (e.g. playground policies, classroom management). Indeed, I have been particularly interested in exploring the ways in which fighting and football practices, as pedagogies of violent and sporting masculinities, are normalised through a gendered discourse of 'boys will be boys' and a developmental discourse of 'play' (what I have referred to as the 'gaming of violence').[4]

I have also been keen to point out the anxieties and pressures reported by boys (within the privacy of their own friendship groups) as they attempted, yet regularly failed, to project convincing performances of an increasingly adult-centric hegemonic masculinity. Many of the boys seemed to be experiencing similar themes of 'excess' in the projection of particular hegemonic masculinities that many of the girls were negotiating in the sexing-up of their girlie-femininities in the previous chapter. Boys' heterogendered discourse of 'hard but not too hard' paralleled girls' heterosexualised discourse of 'tarty but not too tarty'. While many girlie-girls and wannabe hegemonic boys (at Tipton) were preoccupied with body image and body size, the appropriation of 'older' gender/sexual identities differed significantly between boys and girls. Boys, for example, could either try on and play around with embodying 'older' ('cooler') heterosexualised masculinities or, perhaps more importantly, pass on doing so. Most girls, on the other hand, were expected if not encouraged to labour in the production of their heterosexualised femininities as part of an increasingly normalised teening of girlhood.

Chapter 5

Girls, girlfriends and (hetero)sexualities

Pleasure, power and danger

Introduction

This chapter continues the leitmotif that 'sexuality is what little girls are made of' (or perhaps draw upon to make themselves and make each other) by exploring girls' preoccupations with heterosexual relations of desire and intimacy. I have already explored how the majority of girls were fashioning their femininities within a heterosexual framework of 'impressing the boys' where to be romantically desirable was almost a validation of themselves, as 'normal' regular girls. This chapter extends the discussion of the construction and regulation of (hetero)sexualised femininities as girls negotiate an increasingly salient boyfriend/girlfriend culture and recount their erotic attachments to media stars (see Hatcher 1995; Kehily *et al.* 2002; Ali 2003) and other imagined heteronormative futures with key boys (their age) within and beyond the school gates. What results is an intricate and complex cast of heterosexualised performances and intimacies in which girls are the producers, directors and casting agents of a heternormative script that is difficult to both interpret and re-write. Indeed, girls' take-up of multiple and competing sexual subject positions empower and disempower in a range of contradictory ways.

Introducing girls' hetero-relationship cultures

There are a small number of research studies that have begun to debunk the myth that heterosexual relations symbolise entry into 'adolescence' or that there are 'clear stages' when girls and boys 'go out' (Griffiths 1995). Epstein (1997) and Connolly (1998), among others, have highlighted the salience of the heterosexual positions 'girlfriend' and 'boyfriend' and the practices of dating, dumping and two-timing amongst four- and five-year-olds. Others have indicated the intensity and increasing pressure of heterosexual relations towards the later primary school years (Thorne and Luria 1986; Thorne 1993; Redman 1996; Ali 2003). Whilst most of these authors (myself included) conceptualise such heterosexualising practices and cultures as preparatory, as a form of induction 'into the meanings of heteroseuality in anticipation of their practice'

(Kehily *et al.* 2002), this is not to deny or dilute children's early sexual experiences and relations. Rather, it is to situate them within the temporal present (i.e. the here and now) and within the gendered generational life course (as pre-teenage 'girlfriends' within a primary school setting).

Throughout my fieldwork at both Tipton and Hirstwood, I was struck by girls' collective preoccupation with all things romantic and (hetero)sexual. For the girls who desired the dominant 'girlie' femininities outlined in the previous chapter, group interviews became hothouses for ongoing evaluations of a range of heterosexualised performances – from the latest 'break-up' to who they wanted to 'pull' at the school disco. Over the year I was witnessing a daily heterosexualised social and cultural network that was all pervasive. It permeated almost every facet of school life. Beyond the girls' own emotionally charged discussions of who 'liked', 'loved' or 'fancied' who, girls' heterosexual practices included: kissing and holding hands; the setting, fixing or breaking up of relationships (usually by 'messengers' delivering secret love letters or dumping letters); sexualised playground games (such as 'blind-date'); empirically testing a range of consumer products (including a computerised 'Match-Making Diary' and a mini 'Snog Log Book' from a popular girl's magazine). Some girls reported setting up their own 'Agony-Aunt Problem Solving Magazine' for 'matters of the heart' and a 'Telephone Love-Line' where friends could ring in and pour out their romantic troubles or dilemmas. Collectively these heterosexualised practices were a central and increasingly compulsory component of the ways in which girls were 'doing girl'. Even those that resisted or rejected the sexualisation of contemporary girl culture were ultimately positioned in relation to it. One example of this was the ways in which girls were identifying each other as either 'girlfriends' or 'single'. This sexualised positioning was in stark contrast to the ways in which boys were positioned (see Chapter 6).

What does it mean to be 'going out'?

Despite the active connotation of the phrase 'going out', rarely did 'couples' physically go anywhere together on a 'date' (see Skelton 2001: Ch 7). Most 'relationships' were school bound, insofar as the school was the main social arena for the heterosexualised practices outlined above. 'Going out' was a particular discourse which signified and made available the subject positions, 'boyfriend' and 'girlfriend'. For most boys and girls it also signified monogamy and, for a few, provided a legitimate discursive space for physical sexual activity, often no more than kissing and holding hands. Some of the more 'popular' Year 6 girls and boys, who were regular participants in their local boyfriend/girlfriend network, achieved a sense of notoriety, if not 'celebrity couple' status amongst their peers (and lower down the school). 'Going out' for these girls and boys was a highly visible practice and 'couples' could easily be identified within different school contexts. For example, during assemblies girls and boys in the upper juniors very rarely chose to sit next to each other. If, however, they were 'going out', it was not uncommon to see 'couples' sitting next to each other, or behind each other, secretly holding hands. Similarly, it was unusual to see girls and boys 'hang out' together on the playground unless that interaction was in some way heterosexualised (see below).

Ironically, the 'out' of going out was almost redundant, as it transpired that status and popularity gained from being a 'boyfriend' or 'girlfriend' seemed only possible if girls and boys were 'going out' in school. For example, girls who claimed to have boyfriends outside school grounds were not accorded the desired status of those who had boyfriends in school (unless they had a history of 'being a girlfriend'). To some extent, 'going out' signified a kind of hetero-sexual 'coming out' within the school arena – a 'coming out' that was pivotal to a successful accomplishment of a heterosexualised 'girlie' femininity (as dis-cussed in Chapter 3). Girls' aspirations and pressures to be a 'girlfriend' was such that many admitted 'going out' with or 'fancying' a boy whom they disliked or who was abusive to them. The power relations and heterosexual hierarchies involved in girls' interpellation into the local and wider social and cultural world of heterosexual relations and desires is an enduring theme and is taken up in a variety of ways in this chapter.

'Messengers': maintaining the boyfriend/girlfriend culture

Epstein *et al.* (2001b) observed how the practices of 'going out' and the subject positions 'girlfriend' and 'boyfriend' varied markedly between schools, some resembling 'more adolescent style practices much more closely than the other' (2001b: 14). I also observed some differentiation within the local boyfriend/girlfriend culture at Tipton and Hirstwood. Pupils took up 'older' heterosexu-alised identities and practices at Tipton, whilst more children (girls *and* boys) at Hirstwood drew upon discourses of childhood (sexual) innocence and sexual practices as 'grown up' or as a means of delaying or denigrating 'over-sexualised' behaviours (the significance and interrelationship of sexuality and classed iden-tifications are discussed later in this chapter). A cross-cutting theme, however, was the celebrity status that some couples acquired, usually those boys and girls who were most popular with their peers.[1] Across both Tipton and Hirstwood, only a small number of girls (approximately seven) were regular participants on the local boyfriend/girlfriend scene. By no means, however, were other girls redundant or inactive in what seemed rather an exclusive boyfriend and girl-friend club. Rather, the heterosexualised practices involved in 'going out', 'dumping' and 'fancying' were maintained by a raft of what Adler and Adler (1998) have termed 'intermediaries' and what the girls in my study referred to as 'messengers'.

Being a 'messenger' was an exclusively female role. It involved mediating and relaying love letters, dumping letters, verbal proposals such as 'will you kiss X' or 'go out with Y'. Messengers were crucial to the maintenance of the relationship cultures in both schools, particularly as girls and boys rarely 'asked each other out' or 'dumped each other' face to face. So integrated was the role of the messenger within the usually short life span of a relationship (the shortest I recorded was 20 minutes) that the traditional dyadic 'couple' often represented more of a love triangle. At times, as Sally's story below illustrates, 'messengers' were often more keen on the business of matchmaking than the two protagonists involved:

SCHOOL: HIRSTWOOD

ER: So tell me how you met him then ... how did you get him to go out with you, what happened …

Debbie: Danni fancied him

Sally: Yeah she kept looking at him and I go, 'you fancy him don't you' and she says, 'noo' and I go, 'you do', and she goes, 'noooo' and I go, 'yes you do, don't lie' and she goes, 'yeah, I think he's sweet' and I say, 'do you want me to go and talk to him and see if he likes you?' and she goes, 'yeah', so I went over to him and go, 'do you like Danni?' and he goes, 'who's Danni?' and I pointed to her and I go, 'you like her don't you?' and he goes, 'she's all right' and I go, 'you do don't you' and he goes, 'yeah' and I go, 'right' and I ran back to her and said, 'David likes ya' and then I went back to him and go, 'do you like her a lot?' and he goes, 'I don't know really' and I go, 'you do don't you' and he goes 'I dunno' and I go, 'you do, take it from me, you do' so I ran back and said, 'he likes you a lot' and then next week, Annabel kept going, 'will you go out with Danni will you go out with Danni will you, will you' (spoken hurriedly and excitedly).

ER: To David?

Sally: Yeah, and she didn't even want to go out with him at the time.

ER: Did you mind or not?

Danni: I dunno, it's annoying yeah but ...

ER: Now you're glad that it happened?

Danni: Yeah (sounds unsure).

Sally's efforts to 'fix up' her best friend Danni with the boy she thought was 'sweet' (like an agent might secure a prized business deal) was not representative of most 'messengers'. More often than not they were 'wannabe girlies' and used their mediating role as a way of aligning themselves with high-status female peers and their friendship groups:

SCHOOL: TIPTON

Alison: I don't mind being a messenger .../

ER: What does being a messenger mean?

Julia: Well right when Claire and Martin, Martin asked Claire out and when sort of about ... Claire was sort of going, 'go and tell Martin I'm thinking about going out with him' and I go back to Martin and tell him that, and he'd go, 'well is that a yes or a no?' and we will sort of be going like that all around the classroom and/

ER: So does being a messenger mainly involve being a go-between, between girls and boys?

Jo and Julia: Yeah.

Alison: Once Aaron and Martin had asked Claire out and Claire had to choose one of them, we were there between half past three and about four o clock waiting for her to choose who she was going out with/

ER: And this was outside of school?

Alison: Yeah ... it took her that long.

ER: So how do you feel, are you ever in a position where you can send a messenger out for yourself?

All: No no/ no.

ER: So why do you do it?

Jo: Coz they are/ your friends.

Alison: Because you don't want to like lose your friends.

Julia: And erm I reckon they ask you to take messages because they are too embarrassed to do it themselves.

The girls' fear of 'losing their friends' if they did not participate as agents and mediators of heterosexualised practices offers an interesting parallel to the number of studies which describe how girls' adolescent friendships can be jeopardised when they *do* begin to 'go out' (Lees 1993; Griffiths 1995; Hey 1997). Perhaps the ways in which relationship cultures were (bar one or two exceptions) a collective project negotiated and practised within girls' own peer groups in which boyfriends and girlfriends very rarely spent time with each other as 'couples', consolidated rather than fragmented friendships. As Epstein *et al.* (2001b) noted in their study of relationship cultures in Year 5, girls' friendships not only seemed to act as a site for learning about romantic and sexual relationships but were ultimately formed and bounded by the different ways in which girls were taking up and 'doing' sexuality and gender:

> The children deployed heterosexualised talk and practice in ways that they hoped would make them desirable as friends to significant others. In the process, these friendship practices solidified and enacted particular modes of heterosexualised gender.
>
> (2001:14)

Thus rather than romantic norms violating friendships norms (see Walton *et al.* 2002), meaning and values attached to dominant discourses of romance (i.e.

having a boyfriend) not only created friendship boundaries but hierarchies of (hetero)sexual 'insiders' and 'outsiders'. Located at the periphery of the popular 'girlie' and 'top-girl' friendship cliques, neither Alison, Julia nor Jo were in a position to enlist 'messengers' themselves (see section below). Being able to call upon a messenger was, it seemed, not so much about being 'too embarrassed to do it [ask out or talk to boys] themselves' but one of the ways in which power relations and heterosexual hierarchies were produced and reproduced.

The Power (?) of Love: (peer) pressures of compulsory heterosexuality

Strikingly, every girl in the research positioned themselves within heterosexual relations of desire in some way. In direct contrast to most of the boys' group interviews, rarely did the girls' interviews conclude without some discussion of current, past or future heterosexual relationships and erotic attachments. Most common were discussions revolving around girls as wannabe 'girlfriends' of boys in their class. Other heterosexual positionings included fantasy romances with celebrities, such as professional footballers and pop stars. In a few cases, girls who were not interested in boys their own age would look to older teenage boys or adult men as their object of desire. Marie, for example, 'fancied' Dean, her 28-year-old neighbour (he had 'a nice bum'). Even girls who regarded their peers' current preoccupation with boys and romance as trivial and unfulfilling (e.g. middle-class high-achieving girls at Hirstwood) firmly positioned themselves within heterosexualised futures as older 'girlfriends', or as 'married' or 'divorced'. However, while some girls became excited at the thought of being and becoming a 'girlfriend', this was not always the case, as Georgina describes below:

SCHOOL: TIPTON

ER:	What about you Georgina
Georgina:	Wh/at?
Rachel:	You've never had a boyfriend.
Georgina:	I don't have a boyfriend.
ER:	Do you think much about boys?
Georgina:	I don't particularly want to go/ out with any of them.
Rachel:	She does (to Jenna).
[...]	
Rachel:	We're too young for boyfriends at this moment.
ER:	Do you think so?
Jenna:	I don't (laughs).
Georgina and Rachel:	Yeah.
Georgina:	When I go to the comp. I'll probably feel more sensitive and give in a lot more.

Georgina would often tell me that she thought she was too young for 'boyfriends' and shuddered at the thought of sexual activity such as 'kissing'. Nevertheless, she was envisaging and passively resigning herself to an inevitable heterosexualised future, when she says 'when I go to the comp, I'll probably ... give in'. Moreover, within the privacy and security of her own (marginalised) peer group, much like Kehily *et al.*'s (2002) 'diary group girls' she would often carve out a fantasy space in which Stuart from the boy band 'Boyzone' was her boyfriend.

Located in a dominant friendship group, however, where fantasy boyfriends didn't 'count' as 'proper boyfriends' the pressure to story oneself as heterosexually desirable seemed overwhelming for some girls. In the following example, Carrie (considered to be one of the least romantically desirable girls in her class) delved back to her infant days, desperate, it seemed, to let me and other girls know that she 'had a boyfriend' once upon a time:

SCHOOL: HIRSTWOOD

Carrie: I had a boyfriend in play-school once. It was really strange coz I just did whatever he wanted and followed him everywhere apart from into the boys toilets of course and em one day when I was playing with him and I was just doing whatever he did ... and then I needed the loo but I couldn't be bothered to go, coz I wanted to be with him ... so I wet myself (Carrie and all the other girls burst into fits of laughter)

Carrie here reflects upon how her need to 'be' with a boy, even at pre-school age, resulted in forgoing a necessary bodily function! While this is and was an amusing tale it does recapitulate the pressures for girls to project and position themselves within a fairly unremitting heterosexual matrix. Indeed, Carrie's story was a prologue to a catalogue of similar sacrifices on the route to project a 'proper' heterosexualised femininity. Tina, for example (see below), admitted to 'going out' with a boy she did not fancy as it enabled her to participate in the heterosexualised talk so prevalent amongst the 'girlie-girl' peer group:

SCHOOL: HIRSTWOOD

Tina: I met this boy erm, we go down to our caravan every year and there was this boy, he was next door, in a caravan. He is a year younger than me but I'm going out with him ... but I don't really fancy him, but he writes though.

'Coming out' as a 'girlfriend', as heterosexually desirable and desiring, was so important to some girls (usually 'wannabe' girlies and those on the periphery of dominant friendship groups) that they would 'go out' with boys who were verbally abusive to them. Or, in their words, 'treated us like dirt' by routinely 'dumping' them and going out with their friends:

SCHOOL: HIRSTWOOD

Claire: Right I was going out with Tom and then Tom dumped me for Annabel and then/

Annabel: He's just dumped me for Danni and he sent that to me (she brings a letter out of her pocket).

ER: Can I read it out?

Annabel: Yeah.

ER: 'Dear Annabel, I know you are a really nice girl, and you are but I like Kate and Danni as well. You'll probably hate me and that I'm a two timing whatever, but I'm going to go out with Danni. I hope we can still be friends although you probably won't, but I'll still be your friend if you want me and please don't take it out on Danni and Kate. Lots of love from Tom. P.S. I hope we can stay friends'.

[...]

Trudy: It's not fair that he keeps dumping everyone coz he's dumped Claire and now he's dumped Annabel/

Claire: Yeah I know I was crying for four days.

Annabel: He dumped me and we'd only be going out for four days and then he just dumps me and then in four days he'll probably just dump Danni for Kate and it'll just go round and round.

Claire: Yeah.

Annabel: It's not fair.

Trudy: He's just /treating us like dirt.

Annabel: Yeah he's treating us like dirt, everybody/

ER: Sorry what was that Claire?

Claire: I don't fancy him as much as before

ER: But you still do a little bit?

Claire: Yeah.

ER: So why do you still fancy him if he keeps dumping you?

Claire: I dunno, it's like I get a chance in the future (laughs)/

SCHOOL: TIPTON

Harriet: The thing with Todd though is that when he dumped Sophie, Sophie hadn't done anything and he goes, like, he dumped Sophie for Fiona and then he goes like 'oh there's a nasty smell around here' and Sophie didn't even do anything just coz he decided to dump Sophie then he starts being really nasty to her.

Amanda: She can't stop fancying him, even when/he does something really horrible to her she can't stop it

Sophie:	Yeah I know
ER:	Why ?
Sophie:	I don't know really
Harriet:	I said that she is just going to have to get rid of him for good and she just like says, 'oh yeah' and then she doesn't/she just goes back out with him, she loves him too much
Sophie:	I know, but I can't help it/

There was much drama and excitement to be had from regular break-ups and consolement parties, where girl-friends collectively rallied round the 'dumpees', (usually in the privacy of the girls' toilets). Being 'dumped', however, was also a painful process. Most break-ups seemed to be experienced by girls as an emotional rollercoaster regulating and generating feelings of insecurity and unhappiness as girls were frequently passed over for their friends. Indeed, the girls who constructed their femininity predominantly through discourses of love and romance (e.g. Harriet's comment: 'she loves him too much') were often the very girls who reported most stress and upset from being 'dumped'. This finding is not surprising. To be cast as 'girlfriends' within dominant romantic storylines (Davies 1989a) is essential to the scripting and performance of a hyper-heterofemininity. Whether it be through enforced matchmaking, inventing fictive boyfriends, or knowingly subjecting themselves to abusive or unsatisfying 'heterosexual relationships', the need to competently perform as heterosexually desirable and to access/perform an active heterosexuality was a seductive and persuasive pressure that many girls felt unable to resist. However, girls were not the only ones to be dumped (see Chapter 6), and power relations could be overturned when girls took it upon themselves to terminate relationships.

Some 'popular' (girlie) Year 6 girls accrued notoriety and power by 'being a girlfriend', not only by attaching themselves to the most 'popular' and 'desirable' boys (usually footballers, bad boys or traditional 'romantics', see Chapter 6) but specifically in the ways they conducted their relationships with boys. Nowhere more transparent was this feeling of control and power than in the practices of terminating relationships, as Sally testifies in the last line of the extract below:

SCHOOL: HIRSTWOOD

ER:	Do the boys get really upset if you dump them?
Tina:	No they just act all tough but I think they're really hurting deep down inside.
ER:	What do you mean by acting tough?
Carrie:	They say 'Oh who cares I was going to dump her anyway'.
Sally:	Yeah that's what, that's exactly what Philip said.
ER:	Do you have more power if you dump them?
Sally:	Yeah you feel like ha-ha-ha.

Being able to start and finish relationships publicly positioned girls and boys as competent heterosexual actors. 'Dumping' was a time when partners asserted their dominance. There was always a struggle and sometimes a race to be the first to deliver the 'you're dumped' message. The confusion, annoyance and ultimate powerlessness reported by boys is discussed in Chapter 7. For the purposes of this section, I want to draw attention to the ways in which some girls were using the boyfriend/girlfriend circuit in playful, pleasurable and essentially powerful ways, viewing relationships as 'not serious' by frequently rotating their boyfriends. For some girls, heterosexual relations were the only relations where they could exercise some power over the boys. It was the one arena within the social context of their schooling lives where they could undermine 'traditional' sexual relations (e.g. female passivity) and assert their dominance without rendering themselves 'unfeminine' (see Chapters 3 and 7). Using boys, rotating boyfriends and dumping relationships was not just about exploring 'older' relationship cultures and emerging sexualities but a way of being powerful in contexts, such as the sports field or the classroom, where they are generally subordinated and powerless.

'Boys aren't just for boyfriends': negotiating and resisting 'hetero-friendships'

Harriet: Like Adrian, we get on with. We don't fancy him of course. He doesn't fancy us. But we get on with him like a friend, coz boys aren't just for boyfriends and girls aren't just for girlfriends … you can have close friends that are boys.

Given that sitting next to, or borrowing a pencil from, the opposite sex can result in sexualised innuendo and teasing (Davies 1993), it was hardly surprising that girls tended to view their interactions with boys in terms of heterosexual relations (e.g. as intimate or distant 'sexual' Others).[2] Although some girls, like Harriet, suggest that it is possible to 'have close friends that are boys', developing and maintaining non-sexualised, platonic friendships with boys was fraught with tension and contradiction:

Harriet: The other people on the table, all I do is talk to them, I don't want to be boyfriends or girlfriends or anything.

Mandy/Sophie: Yeah.

Harriet: Like Pete, her boyfriend (Mandy), I just to talk to him, it's not … he's just like a friend, not boyfriend or girlfriend … coz you need some boys to talk to sometimes not just all girls all the time but you don't want to get in a … like a relationship with them … *but you still do* (shrugs her shoulders).

Mandy/Sophie: Yeah, yeah.

Even when a 'heterosexual relationship' is not sought after or desired ('I don't want to be boyfriends or girlfriends or anything'), the girls above admit that it almost inevitably happens ('you still do'). When cross-gender friendships were heterosexualised many of the girls would refer to the ways in which initial emotional intimacies and friendships with boys dissolve (i.e. 'you talk less' and ultimately 'lose your friendship'). The difficulty of maintaining close friendships once relationships are heterosexualised and the confusion surrounding the desire to form or not to form heterosexual relationships are the topic of discussion for Amanda and Harriet (below) as they contemplate 'going out' with one of their 'friends' Pete:

SCHOOL: TIPTON

Harriet: I'm not sure if I'd really go out with Pete coz it's like I just want to be friends with him, but

Amanda: I want to be good friends

Harriet: Yeah.

Amanda: Like I, I'd want to go out with him, but I like being friends with him/ if you know what I mean.

Harriet: Yeah coz if you go out, then like we said, like, you haven't got that.

Wanting to be 'good friends' (Amanda) rather than 'just friends' (Harriet) seemed to tip the balance for Amanda. Two weeks after the interview she successfully hooked Pete as her boyfriend. Their status as 'couple', however, was relatively short-lived. As predicted, their once-close friendship rapidly dissolved and 'they weren't really talking anymore' (Harriet):

ER: So you didn't get on as well when you were going out with him?

Amanda: No.

ER: Why do you think that is, because it seems to happen quite a lot?

Harriet: I dunno.

Amanda: You don't know what to say.

Harriet: And then they end up dumping each other because they aren't talking to each other and then they get bored/ and then they get more friends and then they say 'can we just be friends' and then they say 'yeah' and then they start fancying each other, then they ask them out again, then they dump them ohhhh (despairingly).

The cycle that Harriet outlines above in which heterosexualised intimate friendships are formed, disbanded and re-formed was a common occurrence at both Hirstwood and Tipton (see Chapter 6). Given the pressure to heterosexualise cross-gender interactions and the heteronormativity clouding and constraining the formation of boys' and girls' friendships with each other (within the public arena of the school, at least) they might be better conceptualised as 'hetero-friendships'.

Perhaps we should not be too surprised at the heterosexualisation of children's friendships given the ways in which adults tease even very young toddlers as 'having a little boyfriend or girlfriend' when children strike up boy–girl friendships or when teachers unwittingly manipulate the 'taboo' of physical and emotional proximity between girls and boys as strategies for classroom management (Clarricoates 1980; Best 1983; Paley 1984; Thorne 1993). As we saw in Chapter 4 the threat, 'if you don't quieten down I'll sit you boy girl, boy girl' was very effective at Tipton and resulted in screams and gasps by both girls and boys.

Platonic friendships with boys were still sought after by girls, although primarily by the girls who enjoyed what they considered to be 'boys' pursuits' (those girls who positioned themselves as 'one of the boys' or sought to spend time 'with the boys', see Chapter 3). Harriet's group in particular struggled to strike up and maintain boy–girl friendships. They enjoyed interacting with and having boys-as-friends with comments such as, 'it's nice being friends like, saying things to boys as well as to girls' and 'I like being good friends with boys'. When I asked them *why* they like being friends with boys, they talked generally about boys having a 'different opinion on things'. Kirsty, for example, clearly differentiated her friendship with boys and girls along traditional gendered lines in which humour is constructed as masculine and in opposition to femininity: 'I talk to girls more private-wise and with boys, I like just have a laugh'. Interestingly, when Harriet reflects upon her relationship with boys, she not only differentiates between boys, but through the rigidity of gender categories and their expectations, she finds she has positioned herself as a boy:

ER:	So which boys do you like as friends?
Harriet:	Well there's Darren, Pete, Timothy …
Sophie:	Robert?
Harriet:	Er, William.
Sophie:	Robby?
ER:	What makes them different?
Harriet:	Well some boys are like … say like Aaron he's like 'oh I hate you' and stuff, but these boys they like try and be kind to you and like … they like treat you like a boy and stuff, well not a boy, but they treat you like friends like we are. It's sometimes better to have a boy's opinion than a girl's if you want to find out something or/
Sophie:	Yeah.

To some extent, Harriet's account illuminates the lack of discursive space to describe a friendly cross-gender interaction insofar as she struggles to express her relationship with boys that are 'kind' to her without positioning herself as a boy. By momentarily positioning herself as a boy she can eliminate any heteronormative discourse that may inscribe her interactions as hetero/sexual. Caught in a discursive gender-trap, Harriet exposes the ways in which the heterosexual matrix underscores most boys' and girls' gender identities and social interactions.

We only get on with boys who aren't dorks ...

When the girls did talk about enjoying boys' company or forming close friend-ships with boys, they had particular 'boys' and particular (hegemonic) masculinities in mind. Discussing the ways in which boys and girls 'line-up' to go into school assembly, Harriet not only confirms the ways in which mixed-gender physical proximity is heterosexualised, but that there are 'boys' that you avoid and never want to stand or sit next to and 'friends boys' who they don't 'mind sitting next to':

SCHOOL: TIPTON

Harriet:	We only get on with boys who aren't dorks.
ER:	How would you describe a dork Harriet?
All:	Stuart or Damien.
[...]	
ER:	Do you like having friends who are boys as well as girls?
Sophie:	Yes.
ER:	You all acted very strange when Mrs Fryer sat you next to the boys this morning.
All:	(Laughing) Yeah/No.
Hayley:	I didn't mind/
Harriet:	I had a dork sitting next to me.
Sophie:	So did I (grimaces).
Hayley:	I don't mind Timothy.
[...]	
(Discussing gender and lining up)	
Harriet:	Yeah coz there's like boys, then there's a girlfriend and a boyfriend, then there's all girls /
ER:	Do you organise that on purpose?
All:	Yeah.
Mandy:	We want to sit next to our boyfriends and our girlfriends.
ER:	You want to do you?
Mandy:	Yeah we want to/
Amanda:	We ask them or they go can I sit there or something.
ER:	OK, so if they're not your girlfriend or boyfriend do you then want to sit next to a girl rather than a boy?
All:	Yeah/
Mandy:	Except except/
Sophie:	You never want to sit next to a boy.
ER:	But then you said on your table that you were all good friends/
Harriet:	Yeah I know but/
Amanda:	We don't mind sitting next to friends boys/
Mandy:	I sat next to Darren Hill and (???)/
Harriet:	Darren's OK to sit next to and like Pete and Timothy and stuff/

Harriet's earlier claim that girls and boys should be able to be friends is consolidated further in this extract in which she states that only boys who are properly masculine can qualify for the position of 'friend'. Moreover, the boys referred to (Darren, Timothy and Pete) are not only high flyers on the football pitch but regular players on the local boyfriend/girlfriend circuit. Just as the (much critiqued) 'girlie-girls' were only interested in boys as boyfriends, so the pro-feminist 'top-girls' were only interested in friendships with boys who weren't 'geeks', 'dorks', 'girl-ish' or 'gay', thus further reinforcing the heterogendering of boy–girl friendships in which 'suspect' masculinities are undesirable both as potential boyfriends and boys-as-friends. So pervasive were 'heterofriendships' that girls who did not participate in the boyfriend/girlfriend culture were not only excluded from any form of 'platonic' cross-gender interaction but were more frequently targets of heterosexualised teasing. Many of these girls (discussed in more detail below) expressed their frustration, not only at not being able to secure 'a boyfriend' but also of not being able to develop friendships with the boys outside of the boyfriend/girlfriend circuit. However, as the next section illustrates, just as particular boys were sought after as 'friends', not just 'any' boyfriend would do. Heterosexual hierarchies permeated the boyfriend/girlfriend culture in ways that both maintained and undermined hegemonic masculinities and 'girlie' femininities.

'The right kind of boyfriend': heterosexual hierarchies and heterosexual failures

'Having a boyfriend' did not automatically signify 'romantic desirability' and the hyper-femininity that many wannabe 'girlies' strived for. 'Going out' with the 'right' kind of boy was essential to access the status and power accrued by their more popular peers. Fantasy boyfriends, crushes on older neighbours, erotic attachments to media stars, younger boys (as opposed to same age peers), boys from other schools and significantly, boys who were regarded as undesirable by 'popular' boys and girls (usually those boys who did not conform to dominant masculine norms) failed to generate (hetero)sexual capital. Heterosexual hierarchies between 'popular' girls and boys (i.e. 'celebrity couples') and subordinated girls and boys (see Chapter 7) operated to produce 'illegitimate' or 'failed' heterosexualities. Wannabe 'girlies', and those girls and boys who transgressed gender norms often became frequent targets for sexual ridicule by children at the top of the heterosexual hierarchy. For example, some (usually) 'popular' girls would cruelly try to matchmake romantically undesirable girls as potential girlfriends of 'popular' boys, either, it seemed, as a way of mocking and undermining boys' heterosexual masculinity or simply to 'get one over the boys' (see also Duncan 1999). Consequently, such practices also had the effect of re/producing the girls' status as romantically subordinate.

Other ways in which heterosexual hierarchies were maintained was by matching boys and girls regularly positioned as gender misfits (see Chapter 7) as potential romantic partners. One episode involved two girls teasing Stuart (regularly labelled 'geek' and 'gay') that his perfect partner would be Julia (regularly labelled 'weird' and 'like a boy'). The implication was that Julia as 'failed girl' would be the perfect match for Stuart as 'failed male'. There were also cases of dominant girls sexually intimidating subordinate boys or 'failed males'. Tina and Sally in the extract below seem to delight in sexually teasing Charles, an unpopular (and thus romantically undesirable) boy insofar as their heterosexual advances were unwanted, unwelcome and mocking in their tone:

SCHOOL: HIRSTWOOD

Tina:	Do you remember that time when we kept going round to Charles Hampson … the fat one …
Tina:	He's got ginger hair.
Sally:	He's so horrible.
ER:	Why, because of the way he looks?
Sally:	No, he's just so annoying.
Tina:	Yeah he goes right, if you go erm … he just walks around like this (she displays a 'camp' walk).
Sally:	And he's really a drag and stuff, he's just such a (lowers voice) nobby person (the others laugh).
Tina and Carrie:	Yeah.
[...]	
Sally:	They're scared of us … and you go 'Oh Charlie, Oh Charlie (singing style)
ER:	Are you teasing him?
Sally and Tina:	Yeah.
Sally:	And he goes '*Oh no*' and I go, 'Tina your lover is here to see you' and he runs off and then she goes, 'oh you're really ugly'.
[...]	
Sally:	He's so sad.
ER:	Don't you think this might upset him?
Tina and Sally:	No no.

This was not an isolated incident. There were many occasions when girls of a high heterosexual ranking would use their sexual status to sexually tease and denigrate other less desirable and often effeminate boys (see also Draper 1993; Lees 1993 and 1994; Duncan 1999). Duncan (1999) for example cites the popular practice of 'de-bagging' where a group of teenage girls would pull a boy's trousers and underpants down. Draper (1993) describes a similar incident of girls sexually harassing a boy with learning difficulties. Each conceptualise the incident as an example of female sexual power. The extract above does go some way to challenge old stereotypes of girls as passive sexual beings and perhaps signals an emerging active female (sexual) gaze. Indeed, there were a few girls who radically transgressed 'acceptable' codes of practice in the ways in which they related to their boyfriends. However, these girls are the subject of Chapter 7. The purpose of this section was to highlight the ways in which heterosexual hierarchies operate to police normative heterofemininities (and heteromasculinities). It was also to further address the complex power relations embedded within the boyfriend/girlfriend culture in ways which reinforce and undermine the making of hegemonic heterogender identities and relations.

Pleasures and dangers of 'doing' sexuality within and beyond the school gates

So far, this chapter has discussed how discourses of romance via a range of different subject positions and practices ('girlfriend', 'messenger', 'fancying', 'going out', 'dumping' and 'being dumped', etc.) shape and police girls' emerging femininities and mediate girls' friendships with each other and their friendships and relations with boys in contrasting and complex ways. As stated at the outset of this chapter, sexual activity (such as kissing, touching and holding hands) was not an essential ingredient to children's romantic-erotic attachments and for many girls and boys, 'holding hands' and 'kissing' (usually snatched pecks on the lips) was the extent of their sexual activity (within the school grounds). Although children's sexual activity was not a central focus of the research, conversations relating to the 'doing' of sexuality as an embodied and erotic practice were introduced and observed, most notably by those boys and girls who were established members of the school-based boyfriend/girlfriend network. The following interview extracts reveal how girls (and boys) appropriated different public and private spaces for the performance of different versions of sexuality: from the 'officially sanctioned' heterosexualised school disco to their own 'couples corner', where established boyfriends and girlfriends (e.g. 'celebrity couples') graduated:

SCHOOL: TIPTON

The school disco
ER: What happens at these (school) discos then?
All: We dance/we dance.
Kirsty: And last year I was going out with James and we all asked for a smoochy dance and we ended up smooching like that, all the boys and girlfriends get together and go (Kirsty stands in front of Mandy, takes her arms and wraps them around her shoulders and they sway from side to side)
ER: What about the ones who haven't got a boyfriend or girlfriend?
Kirsty: They just stand around.
All: They just watch.

'Couples corner'

ER:	OK ... so when you have a boyfriend where do you go, on the field?
Kirsty:	Yeah, under the willow (tree), or right at the back of the field.
ER:	You get some privacy there do you?
Kirsty:	Yeah a bit. This one dinner lady Mrs Beadon, she goes 'you're not supposed to cuddle and kiss and hold hands' (in a squeaky voice)
ER:	Really, so you can't get up to much in school?
Kirsty:	Yeah/
Mandy:	Yeah but we do anyway (they laugh).
Kirsty:	We hide.
ER:	Where?
Kirsty:	'Couples' corner' ... it's over there (Kirsty shows me, pointing out the window)
Kirsty and Mandy:	Yeah.
Mandy:	It just moved over to the willow tree.

★★★

> Looking towards the end of the field by the willow tree, I see Kirsty, Neil, Mandy and Pete. They are both lying down on their sides, coupled up, facing each other. Neil has moved to sit on top of Kirsty. His legs straddling her hips. He then lies down on top of her and they start kissing. The two women on dinner duty are chatting together approximately 100 metres away. They do not notice Kirsty and Neil. Kirsty then pushes Neil off her and pushes Mandy off Pete. They all then push and trip each other up and then settle back down in their pairs. Neil gets up and does a cartwheel and then swings his hips in a thrusting movement towards Kirsty. They all start laughing.
>
> (Tipton: fieldnotes)

Collectively these extracts demonstrate the ways in which girls' and boys' relationship cultures are mediated and regulated by the school in different ways: from the sanctioned 'smooching' at school discos (which could almost be described as a pedagogy of traditional heterosexual relations for those participating and watching) to staff interventions policing 'inappropriate' sexual activity on the sports-field. They also highlight children's own strategies to circumvent adult surveillance and engage in sexual activities they 'aren't supposed to' thus perhaps inscribing girls (Mandy and Kirsty) with a sense of power and agency in their subversion of childhood, gender and sexual taboos.

In the extract below, trying on and flirting with 'older' sexualities and sexual knowledges take centre stage within a seemingly unsupervised birthday party. Here school-based 'couples' are provided with an opportunity to play sexual games such as 'spin the bottle' and 'truth or dare' in the privacy of a predominantly child-centered space:

Kirsty:	We play truth or dare, spin the bottle …
ER:	Who with?
Kirsty:	Our boyfriends.
Amanda:	Yeah.
ER:	What sort of things do you ask them?
Kirsty:	Er anything, like 'have you had it off with anyone'?
Mandy:	Yeah (giggles).
ER:	So who went to your party?
Kirsty:	Mandy, Jenny, Fiona, Victoria, Martin, Pete, Todd, Darren.
ER:	And you play these games like spin the bottle?
Kirsty:	Yeah and we played it in the dark and Victoria and Darren ended up snoggin' in the dark.
Amanda:	Throw yourself around and do whatever you like in the dark and just throw yourself around /
Kirsty:	And Todd lifted up my skirt (giggles).

Following this exchange, the girls go on to talk about the fun they had probing each others' sexual histories and sexual limits on what they would or wouldn't 'do' and giggled some more about who they ended up 'snogging' that evening. However, when the same children engage in similar sexual games/activities in the privacy of their 'dorms' on the school-trip, their sexual freedoms 'to do whatever they like' are soon curtailed. The discourse of desire shifts from one of fun and pleasure to one of pathology and shame as children's (private) sexualities are scrutinized within the public ('adult') domain:

> As we all walk back to the Youth hostel I bump into Mrs Fryer in the corridor. She tells me that she has just found Darren and Christine, Kirsty and Todd semi-naked, in bed together (Darren and Christine in one bed, Todd and Kirsty in another). She realised they were missing, but thought Mr Thomson was supervising them. Instead he was watching the world cup football in the TV room. She thinks Kirsty has been 'encouraging the boys' running round with just her towel on. She calls her, albeit light-heartedly, a 'tart'.
>
> (Tipton: fieldnotes)

★★★

(Later, in the evening of the same day)
The children gather in the recreational room before going to bed. The boys are told to leave the room as Mrs Fryer wants to talk to the girls on their own. She tells them how some girls have been behaving in a way

which is 'not appropriate'. She says they 'must not run around the building' unless they are 'fully dressed' and '*must not, at any time, go into the boys' bedrooms*'. It is their job, she continues, to keep the boys out of their bedrooms (for some reason the boys appear to be incapable of doing this themselves!). She talks about how they must 'preserve' their 'reputation – keep it safe'. She then says she will say 'no more about it' and they leave the room and go to bed. On the way out, she tells me that she has already 'had words with' Kirsty and Christine privately regarding their 'behaviour' and the dangers of becoming sexually involved with boys 'at their age' (although all they were doing was 'kissing' Kirsty tells me later). She thinks Mr Thompson will be speaking to Darren and Todd (he doesn't). The boys, as a group, have not been spoken to about these issues.

(Tipton: fieldnotes)

There are a number of *highly gendered* and contradictory discourses operating here regarding the ways in which primary school girls' and boys' sexualities are regulated and policed. I emphasise highly gendered to draw attention to the ways in which the boys seemed to be denied any sexual agency and responsibility. Rather, they are constructed almost as passive 'victims' to their sexual curiosity/'urges' through the widely used global discourse of an 'uncontrollable male sex drive' (see Hollway 1984). Kirsty, in contrast, is simultaneously warned against the 'inappropriateness' and 'danger' of becoming sexually involved with boys *and* disciplined as to the infectious use of her body in enticing and encouraging male sexual advances. Paradoxically, the 'protectionist' discourse denies her sexual agency/desire while the 'polluting' discourse reinstates it: not only by positioning her body as sexually responsible for boys' sexual urges but also for the safety of her own and all girls' sexual reputations. In many ways, this episode literally captures the ways in which girls who blur the boundaries between adult-woman/girl-child and sexual-innocence/sexual-experience become 'sexualised as part of the process of the desexualisation of the school …(and) made to carry the denied (even repressed) sexuality which is everywhere present/absent in the school' (Epstein and Johnson 1998: 119). Moreover, it is no coincidence that as a low-achieving, 'working-class' girl from a one-parent family, it is Kirsty, rather than Christine ('middle-class') who is labelled a 'tart' and constructed as the carrier and signifier of female sexuality and the dangers of (hetero)sexual excess (see Hey 1997).

Discussion of the dangers and pleasures of girls' (hetero)sexualised relations have so far centered around their same-age peers and broadly within the context of the school (home and away). The following two extracts offer some insight into the ways in which girls negotiate the potential and actual dangers of projecting (hetero)sexualised bodies beyond the school gates, when the usual markers of sexual innocence (i.e. school uniform) are absent and social and gendered generational boundaries of 'childhood' and 'adolescence' are blurred. The first fieldnote re-visits the school trip and Mandy and Kirsty's encounter with a couple of older boys they meet at the park. The second extract picks up and develops themes raised in the first extract around 'older' male sexualities and girls' negotiation of un/wanted sexual advances, sexual intimidation and wider narratives of sexual risks and dangers in public places (see also Valentine 1997):

> We are at the park half a mile away from the youth hostel. Most of the boys are playing football with a team from another school (also staying at the youth hostel). Approximately 20 metres away are Kirsty and Mandy, dressed in denim mini skirts, short cropped tops, pink jelly-bean shoes and fully made-up (eye-shadow and lipstick). They are leaning against a fence that is separating the playing areas from the wider field and have been approached by and are chatting with two seemingly older boys (they both have deep voices). While Mandy's prepubescent body represents her young age, Kirsty's pubescent body betrays her (looking as she does, about 13/14). I overhear one of the boys say, 'do you know what a blow-job is?' to which Kirsty and Mandy giggle and Kirsty says, 'yes', and mutters something about orgasms. The boys then seem to be trying to arrange to meet them later and the taller of the two tries to persuade Kirsty to drop her boyfriend (Todd) and 'go out' with him. Throughout this episode the girls look over at me and smile. Sometimes, it looks as though they want rescuing. Mrs Fryer then sees me watching them and walks over and joins in their conversation – they no longer talk about blow-jobs, orgasms and boyfriends.
>
> (Tipton field trip: fieldnotes)

SCHOOL: HIRSTWOOD

Trudy:	Once when me and Debbie went to the park right and these boys were on these swings, I think we were about nine and I had these short jeans on and this boy (she starts laughing) and this boy goes, 'I want your body' and once/
ER:	How did you feel, did you feel scared then?
Debbie and Trudy:	Yeah, yeah.
Trudy:	Once er, me and Debbie and Kelly were on the 'landing' (grassy hill in local park) and oh you tell her/
Debbie:	Right OK, then, me and Michele and Trudy were on the landing at the park and these boys were walking past and suddenly stopped and pulled their pants down (they laugh)
ER:	How did you feel?
Debbie:	Horrible/
Hannah:	Well erm this boyfriend er we met him at Godfrey Lane park and he started, on the way back coz we wanted to get away from him because we didn't really know him. He kept pinching my bum (the others laugh) and I was trying to run away and he kept pinching my bum.

ER:	What did you do?
Hannah:	I just pretended I weren't bothered/
Trudy:	I would've slapped him round the face (she says in fits of laughter).
ER:	You would have slapped him would you?
Trudy:	Yeah.
ER:	More seriously, if he went too far would you run off or hit him or/
Hannah:	I'd kick him there (shows me that she'd go for his genitals)
ER:	Would you?
Hannah:	Yeah definitely ... and then while he's like that (down on the floor) I'd punch him round the face and throw him in the road coz I I dunno, then/
Trudy:	Older boys they like, they can like ... go for you more
ER:	What do you mean? ... you mean physically?
Hannah:	Yeah, coz they're older
Debbie:	Coz, taller people, they, and then older boys, thirteen or fourteen, they think that you're a lot older /
ER:	Because you can look older than you are can't you?
Debbie and Trudy:	Yeah.
Trudy:	And then also we were walking down at the back of the park and this boy said 'hello' and we didn't even know him, what did he say again?
Debbie:	'Hi girls', or something.
ER:	Did you feel intimidated?
Hannah:	Well you hear this stuff ... if like Trudy/
Trudy:	It's nice getting all the attention but/
Hannah:	If I was at a park and this boy pulled down his pants, I dunno, coz you hear these stories of getting raped and stuff and I'd be really scared 'oh what's going to happen' and you hear these stories about people dying, well not dying but ... (school bell rings and the interview is cut short).

Hannah's 'older' boyfriend's persistence to 'pinch her bum' and the sexualised comments ('I want your body') and performances (boys who 'pulled their pants down') confirm Kelly's (1989: 51) observation that from a very young age, girls are learning that 'male sexuality is predatory and abusive'. Certainly their imagined fears of 'getting raped' and their experiences of unwanted sexualised attention because 'boys think you're a lot older' cannot fail to evoke a protectionist response. However, while it is important to register how 'horrible' some of these encounters made the girls feel, it is just as important not to overlook or downplay the ways in which they managed these risks and dangers either by 'pretending they weren't bothered', 'running away' or imagining how they might defend themselves in potentially sexually abusive situations ('I'd kick him *there*', 'I'd punch him round the face').

The first extract also illustrates the slippage and blurring between sexual pleasure and danger (very rarely discussed as a positive element in girls' sexualities) and further complicates a simple reading of 'risky' sexual relations as Kirsty and Mandy are 'chatted up' by two local boys on the school trip. One interpretation as to why Kirsty and Mandy are keeping close to the perimeter fence (that seems to symbolically differentiate 'school children' from 'non-school children) is because they are experiencing sexual encounters beyond their control and are aligning themselves with the school and the safety and protection provided by the teachers in 'loco parentis'. Additionally, they might also simultaneously be enjoying the sexual attention (see Trudy's earlier comment) and perhaps displaying and consuming sexual knowledge that they may not engage in with their peers at school. However, the ways in which girls experienced and negotiated sexual pleasures and dangers is never a straightforward picture of school = safety and outside = danger. Girls were regular targets of various forms of sexual harassment within the school. The next section explores the often neglected stories of young girls' experiences of physical sexual harassment from their male peers. Using sexual swear words and other forms of indirect sexual harassment is discussed in Chapters 6 and 7.

'We're used to it': girls' experiences of physical sexual harassment

Several primary school studies of children's gender relations have commented upon the grey area and fine line regarding the ways in which some heterosexual games and sexualised interactions (e.g. kiss chase) can be experienced as both harassing and pleasurable (Best 1983; Thorne 1993; Redman 1996; Connolly 1998; Skelton 2001). Because of this ambiguity, experiences that are conceptualised as harassment in the accounts that follow are defined in terms of the harm and pain of the recipient (rather than solely relying on what particular types of behaviour might constitute harassment). For example, 'bra-pulling' has several conflicting meanings. It could be experienced by girls positively (e.g. a welcome sign of a boy's romantic interest) or negatively (e.g. a humiliating recognition of their sexual maturation). Consequently, if it was experienced as fun and amusing I *would not* categorise it as harassment. If, however, it was experienced as unwanted, unwelcome and made the girl involved feel uncomfortable, it *would* be categorised as harassment.[3]

While the most common form of sexual harassment was verbal sexual abuse (see also Chapters 6 and 7), some girls were experiencing what they considered as unwanted sexualised forms of physical harassment from their male classmates. Just as girls' harassing behaviour towards low status boys seemed to be about exercising sexual agency and power, the physical sexual harassment engaged in by boys towards girls also seemed to be another means of being powerful in social circumstances which often rendered them powerless or out of control (see Mac an Ghaill 1994). Such practices were often engaged in by boys who were located lower down the heterosexual and masculine hierarchies. The following extract is an example of one of the most extreme cases of physical sexual violence/harassment reported by girls towards the end of the study. The boys' response to the incident is described in Chapter 6.

SCHOOL: HIRSTWOOD

ER:	Do boys pick on you like they do their friends?
All:	No.
[...]	
Trudy:	They punch you in the boobs.
Annabel:	Yeah they punch you in the boobs sometimes and pull your bra and that really kills.
Trudy:	Yeah, they go like that (shows me)
ER:	Who does that?
All:	Stu.
Annabel:	And Ryan and that.
ER:	So what do you do to that/
Annabel:	Nothing, we just walk away going like this (hugging chest), 'don't touch me'.
ER:	Do you think that's some form of harassment?
All:	Yeah.
Annabel:	Yeah, but/we don't tell.
ER:	You don't tell anyone?
Annabel and Carla:	No.
ER:	Why not?
Kate:	Because you ... /they might think it's a big deal.
Trudy:	Because w/e're used to it.
Annabel:	No, we *do* think it's a big deal, but if we told someone/ like Miss Wilson, she'd just say 'oh don't be so silly'
Trudy:	The/y'd laugh.
[...]	
Carla:	And I'd be too embarrassed.
Annabel and Kate:	Yeah.
Trudy:	Yeah and we don't like causing an argument, we don't ... I don't like causing an argument.
[...]	
ER:	Don't you punch him back? (when he hits you)
Trudy:	No, coz you can't really.
Annabel:	You don't ...
Carla:	They hurt you.
ER:	Sometimes/
Trudy:	Girls really don't fight boys.

While echoing the widely established relations of sexual violence within the secondary school (Davies 1984; Jones 1985; Mahony 1985; Halson 1989; Herbert 1989; Lees 1993; Duncan 1999; Leonard *et al.* 2002; Sunnari *et al.* 2002), my research, alongside Margaret Clark's (1990) in Australia and Nan Stein's (1996) in the US, reveals that such experiences are by no means peculiar or restricted to teenage girls and secondary schools. Clark (1990), for example, describes similar reports of primary school boys punching girls in the breasts and Stein (1996: 149) describes 'Friday flip-up days' where 'boys in the first through to third grades flipped up the dresses of their female classmates'. My research confirmed the findings of other studies which suggest that often such incidents are typically dismissed as mutual, voluntary or playful playground behaviour. And like so many reports of sexual harassment, girls tend to use discourses that serve to invalidate and undermine their experiences as a form of harassment (Kelly and Radford 1996).

None of the girls reported these incidents to the teaching staff at either Tipton or Hirstwood. In fact the girls above only disclosed the incident to me in my final week at the school. When I asked them why they didn't tell anyone, their responses seem to reflect and echo wider cultural issues around girls' and women's socialised passivity, desire for conformity and subordination to men and authority more widely. They explained to me how 'telling' was not an option for them because of fears of: confrontation and conflict ('causing an argument'); being subject to ridicule ('they'd just laugh'), raising and discussing personal topics ('embarrassment') and not being taken seriously by their class teacher ('she'd say oh don't be silly'). Each girl's experience not only remained untold, but, unable to retaliate, given the pervasive discourse that 'girls don't fight boys', they also went unchallenged. Unfortunately, this had the knock-on effect of reproducing the boys' behaviour as 'normal' and 'natural' (Blackmore 1995).

Concluding notes

This chapter has explored the ways in which all of the girls in this research study were actively negotiating an increasingly compulsory, yet multiple and hierarchical heterosexual matrix. This matrix, fuelled by a discourse of romance and home to the local boyfriend/girlfriend culture, permeated and regulated girls' social relations/hips with each other, their relations/hips with other boys and their imagined sexual futures. Given the pressure to project increasingly sexualised femininities (see Chapter 3), it was perhaps not surprising to find that the organisation and maintenance of the boyfriend/girlfriend culture was a predominantly all-female enterprise (see also Skelton 2001: 149; Hatcher 1995; Thorne 1993). I was particularly struck by the ways in which girls' relationship cultures operated as a collective project with an inclusive yet hierarchical range of heterosexual subject positions. Girls' peer group cultures not only seemed to be a key site for much of their sexual learning (Epstein *et al.* 2002) but operated to create and police a range of heterosexual hierarchies. Indeed, a central part of

the chapter was dedicated to exploring the pleasures, pressures and personal sacrifices of aspiring and belonging to a variable yet salient boyfriend/girlfriend
culture, in which being a 'girlfriend' could bolster or undermine the successful
accomplishment of a heterosexualised 'girlie' femininity, depending upon where
a girl was situated within the peer group's heterosexual hierarchy.

The chapter also introduced the concept 'hetero-friendship' to make visible
the heterosexualisation of boy–girl friendships. Some girls were using the
boyfriend/girlfriend culture (positioning boys as either potential boyfriends or
sexual outcasts) to cultivate and project heterosexualised 'girlie' femininities.
Other girls (the 'top-girls' at Tipton, see Chapter 3), however, were not only
struggling to maintain friendships with boys who had become their
'boyfriends', but resisting the ways in which any close mixed-gender friendship
is almost automatically (hetero)sexualised (within the school grounds at least,
see Chapter 7). Indeed, I suggest that the adult-centric tendency to conceptualise the relentless cycle of multiple 'dumping' as children trying/practising
'older' sexualities or as an indicator of immature relationship cultures is perhaps
to overlook two related issues. First, it overlooks the ways in which some children use heterosexual subject positions to strike up legitimate boy–girl
friendships. Second, it underestimates the difficulty to think 'otherwise' – that
is, outside of the hegemonic heterosexual matrix (Butler 1990).

The last section of the chapter explored the pleasures and dangers of girls
appropriating a range of social spaces to explore, experience and negotiate
more overt sexual practices and activities. An emerging theme here was the
ways in which girls, in multiple and contradictory ways, blur the sexual boundaries between public/private, (sexual)innocence/(sexual)experience,
child/woman and safety/risk within and beyond the school gates as they
engage with what some might conceptualise as 'older' or 'inappropriate' (e.g.
DfEE 2000a) sexual discourses and practices. Girls like Hannah, Trudy,
Annabel, Kirsty and Mandy were all learning how their bodies, as erotic and
sexual, could be both exciting and threatening: a source of power, pleasure and
potential danger (Vance 1992). Given the increasing recognition of girls' sexual
knowledge and awareness (Epstein et al. 2003; Kehily et al. 2002; Pallotta-
Chiarolli 1997) their experiences can no longer be wished away as 'isolated
incidents' (Smith and Sharp 1994). Such a recognition is absolutely crucial if
we are to encourage girls to speak out about and develop practices of resistance
to some of the more dangerous aspects of sexual relations (e.g. sexual harassment). The ways in which sexuality education (Redman 1994) and the DfEE
(2000a) SRE guidance can be harnessed to address some of these issues are
briefly discussed in the concluding chapter.

Chapter 6

Boys, boyfriends and (hetero)sexualities

Fears and frustrations

Introduction

Chapter 5 explored the salience of an active boyfriend–girlfriend culture at both Tipton and Hirstwood (although stronger at Tipton) and a number of heterosexualised practices and discourses (such as 'going out', 'two-timing', 'fancying' and 'dumping'). As other studies have noted, girls were central to and ultimately the key protagonists for the production and maintenance of each school's boyfriend–girlfriend culture via an intricate network of matchmakers and messengers. For most girls, being a girlfriend (albeit the 'right' kind of girl-friend) and participating within the boyfriend–girlfriend culture, whether as a messenger or a girlfriend-to-be, was one of the key ways to access a high status femininity. It was also the means by which girls could publicly register their desirability and attractiveness and signal their commitment and transition to older (hetero)sexualised femininities and romantic futures.

With local and global representations of young (hetero)sexualized femininities all around them (from 'girl' magazines to TV soaps and advertising), investing in an 'accelerated femininity' was an available, if not expected, trajectory for girls to aspire to. Being a boyfriend, on the other hand, was a much more precarious role for young boys to jump into and take up. Indeed, the sexualisation of femininity and the feminisation of erotic innocence more widely has resulted perhaps in an underdeveloped theorisation and neglect of boys' everyday sexual cultures and relations beyond their representations of 'dirty talk' or 'sex play' usually framed within discourses of normative and maturing masculinities (Fine 1987).

The purpose of this chapter is to critically explore the ways in which pre-teen boys differently engage with a range of heterosexualities and show how integral yet complex and contradictory heterosexual performances are to the production of young boys' masculinities. I explore how boys negotiate their local boyfriend–girlfriend culture, how they respond to a heterosexualised female gaze, and how they look upon and experience the role of boyfriend. In particu-lar, the chapter illustrates how most Year 6 boys in this study experienced the boyfriend–girlfriend culture as an emotional cocktail of fear (of the 'feminine') and frustration (inability to access 'traditional' patriarchal power positions). It suggests how many boys seem to rescue and resecure sexual power through (hetero)sexualised storytelling and symbolic sex-play, anti-girl and anti-gay talk and the sexualised harassment and objectification of female classmates. In contrast to girls' always-already sexualised femininities, it also details how many boys can more easily opt out of their local heterosexualised world of boyfriends and girlfriends by drawing upon developmental discourses of child/boyhood innocence and sexual immaturity (this option seemed only available to the 'academic' middle-class girls at Hirstwood). The rest of the chapter focuses on three individual case studies in which a minority of boys achieve 'celebrity couple' like status and invest in a privileged hyper-heterosexual masculinity as 'professional boyfriends'. Here, I develop some of the themes above to illustrate the very different ways in which the subject position 'boyfriend' and discourses of 'heterosexuality' are re/produced in gendered and age-specific ways.

Girls, girlfriends and the problematics of boy–girl intimacy

Participating in the boyfriend–girlfriend culture was only one of the routes to affirm and project a hegemonic masculinity. Furthermore, levels of participation in terms of the number of boys engaged in 'fancying', 'asking girls out' and 'going out' differed markedly between the two schools. Over the year, 7 out of the 13 boys in Mrs Fryer's class, compared to the 3 out of the 13 boys in Miss Wilson's class, reported 'going out' or 'having a girlfriend'. At Tipton, heterosexualised practices, and 'being a boyfriend' in particular, were more visible, more public and more frequent and seemed to be one of the defining features of a hegemonic masculinity in contrast to the Hirstwood boys. Most boys at Hirstwood shunned the role of boyfriend and engaged more in sexual storytelling and imagined (hetero)sexualised futures. As the following extract reveals, however, there was still a sense that having a girlfriend and being a boyfriend was no simple or straightforward signifier of a boy's heterosexuality or hegemonic masculinity.

The following group interview extract goes some way to show how 'coming out' romantically, even in schools with a strong boyfriend–girlfriend culture, was a complex and contradictory process fraught with tension, anxiety and confusion. It highlights the pressures, pleasures and fears of the heterosexual matrix at work via a ritualised language of 'fancying' 'love' and 'embarrassment':

SCHOOL: TIPTON

ER: OK, you can talk about what you like ... .
Martin: Erm erm erm erm cool ... erm Jenna fancies Michael, Michael fancies Jenna
Michael: No I don't.
Martin: Only joking.

ER:	How do you /feel about Jenna fancying you Michael?
Martin:	I was only joking.
Michael:	Not very good.
ER:	Why not?
Martin:	Sh/e's a fat cow.
Colin:	She put, she put on his dictionary, erm, 'good luck, I love you'.
ER:	Really? … (he nods). Have you spoken to her at all?
Michael:	(shakes his head to signify 'no')
Martin:	He's shy …. he's getting embarrassed.
Colin:	I'll speak for him, 'no'.
Martin:	She's a cow.

Competing discourses surrounding the sexually innocent girl-child and the sexual adolescent (Chapters 3 and 4) created contradictions and conflicts for many girls in ways that were not reported or observed in boys' sexual cultures. The difficulty the majority of boys faced was an awareness that constructing their masculinities usually involved publicly disassociating themselves from anything 'feminine', which included physical proximity or emotional closeness with girls. However, being a 'boyfriend' and being 'romantically desirable' (which could involve engaging in both physical and emotional closeness) could also bolster their masculinity.

Proximity to girls could thus give rise to the teasing behaviours described above (because of the association of fear of the feminine) and/or an expression and confirmation of a boy's heterosexual masculinity. Teasing and ridicule most often happened to boys who either rarely deployed or were trying on hetero-sexual/romantic discourses for the first time or when there was a lack of boys in the group who were 'going out' or who previously had a 'girlfriend' (Hirstwood boys in particular). Furthermore, attempts to resecure 'masculinity' often led boys to draw on alternative hegemonic discourses such as misogynist comments which usually involved the objectification of girls ('she's a cow'). The fine line between romance and sexual harassment (see also Skelton 2001) is discussed in more detail later in the chapter.

Despite the connection, heterosexual performances, or 'having a girlfriend', did not automatically signify hegemonic masculinity. It was usually only the boys who were good at sport (usually football), and who were deemed 'hard', 'tough', 'cool' or 'good-looking' by their peers, who were reported to be the most romantically desirable. While more gentle and non-sporting boys invested and participated in the heterosexual network of boyfriends and girlfriends, they were more often positioned as 'heterosexual failures' and teased for pursuing or being pursued by 'non-desirable' girls. For the majority of girls in this study, the most sought after boys constituted the 'A' team (football). Unwittingly, then, the school's own pedagogical strategies to rank sporting competence created heterosexual hierarchies, and the cycle of heterosexuality, sport and hegemonic masculinity was reinforced.

'It's always the girls that use you'

Most of the boys who only fleetingly took on the role of 'boyfriend' and the heterosexualised practices and talk of 'fancying' and 'going out' rarely felt at ease or reported any sustained pleasure. Many boys, like Colin and Martin below, described their experiences in a less than positive light particularly in terms of the associative pressures accompanying their new role:

SCHOOL: TIPTON

ER:	What do you think has been the hardest thing to cope with being a Year 6?
Colin:	Girls.
ER:	Martin?
Martin:	SATS.
Colin:	Girlfriends.
Martin:	Yeah, coz if you have a girlfriend you have everyone saying 'oh can you come and kiss me/, can you come and kiss meee' (singsong)
Colin:	Yeah it's all that/ and the next day.
Martin:	Will you kiss me, will you kiss me, will you kiss me?
ER:	And you don't want to?
Colin:	*No* and Harriet/ is like
Martin:	Jane and Hayley, they'll be going, if you don't kiss me you're dumped.
Colin:	Yeah and stuff like that.
ER:	Who says this?
Martin:	All the girls.

While some boys were teased for not having a girlfriend, those who did were often overwhelmed by girls' expectations of boys to express their commitment in a physical way ('will you kiss me', 'if you don't kiss me, you're dumped'). Martin's concern over kissing further emphasises the ambiguity surrounding the desire for, yet resistance to, sexual maturity and 'older child identities' (see Redman 1996). Alternatively, other boys (below) experienced what they considered to be more than their fair share of 'dumping'. As outlined in the previous chapter, it seemed that a great deal of power could be exercised and experienced by being able to 'dump' relationships and girls were more ready to change their partners and did so more frequently than boys:

SCHOOL: TIPTON

Pete:	I used to be going out with Fiona but I didn't like having a relationship with her because she always used to dump me.
Darren:	Yeah that's what Victoria used to do – what she used to do when I was in a stress was she used to get in a bigger stress and then dump

me ... and then about five minutes later she always comes back to me and thinks it's all right again, 'do you still love me' (mimicking Victoria's voice), and she expects everything to be all right again.

ER: And what does that make you feel like?

Darren: They just use you ... it's not fair.

[...]

Colin: On the practice walk, Hayley asked him out.

ER: Did she?

Darren: Yeah but now she wants to go out with Adrian.

ER: So what happened to the other girls, did they dump you/ or did you

Darren: They dumped me, they always dump me, it's not fair.

Colin: They always dump me.

ER: So why, why do you think it happens Darren?

Darren: I dunno, Victoria dumped me because she wanted to go out with someone else, so I can sort of understand that, but but, Mandy dumped me because she said I was boring, I know it's so stupid.

Colin: Same as me.

ER: Why what happened/ to you Colin?

Colin: I got dumped.

★★★

ER: What about you Aaron?

Aaron: I did have Claire, but she's a cow.

ER: Why is she a cow?

Aaron: Because she always uses me, the last time she used me/

Liam: Go on, and lets get the popcorn.

ER: What happened last time?

Aaron: Well when I was going out with her I, I, she dumped me right, and I go, 'why did you dump me?' and she didn't say anything and about an hour later she goes, 'I was using you anyway'.

When I asked what were the most difficult times during their final year at primary school, Colin, Darren and later Martin agreed that it was 'girlfriends'. The feelings of powerlessness embedded in Darren and Colin's frustration at being 'always dumped' and 'used', and the pressures of engaging in 'older' sexual activities (Martin) suggest that neither one of these boys experienced the dominant subject position and power relations associated with the more traditional heterosexual discourses in which boys and men are 'on top' (see Holland *et al.* 1998). At best, most boys experienced heterosexual relationships as fragile, ambiguous and with a mixture of unease and tension. Given these experiences, it seems difficult to understand why many boys continued to pursue girls for 'girlfriends' or subject themselves to the precarious role of 'boyfriend'. Possible explanations could include: the increased pressure to 'be a boyfriend' at Tipton;

the status attached to 'older (sexually mature) identities' (at Tipton); and the wider media/cultural discourses that bind heterosexuality with hegemonic masculinity (from TV to magazines) – all of which leave boys little discursive space for any systematic resistance without throwing their 'masculinity' into doubt. However, as I stated earlier, being a boyfriend and engaging in a more sexualised masculinity wasn't the expected or main route to being a boy.

I play football instead: compulsory heterosexuality?

Liam: Aaron fancies Kirsty, Aaron fancies Kirsty.
Aaron: I don't. I play footy.

As other studies examining young boys' masculinities have noted, the central route through which boys define their masculinity is through sport. Regardless of the presence or absence of a dominant boyfriend–girlfriend culture, it was possible for many boys to resist the pressure to actively engage in the boyfriend–girlfriend culture by involving themselves in sporting activities. Demonstrating skill and competence in the field of sport was almost equivalent to demonstrating skill and competence in the field of love and romance. For example, Ryan's positioning, as successful 'sportsman', immediately follows his negative response to having a girlfriend:

SCHOOL: HIRSTWOOD

ER: So what about you three, any girlfriends, David? (shakes his head), Ryan? (shakes his head), Jake? (shakes his head) …
Ryan: I got up to novice two in [go]carting.

In the following two examples, the two subject positions of 'boyfriend' and 'footballer' are almost interchangeable.

SCHOOL: TIPTON

Darren: I still like a girl I used to go out in the comp with called Amanda.
ER: I remember … what about you Timothy?
Timothy: I haven't got a girlfriend.
ER: Would you like one?
Timothy: No, not really.
Pete: No, he's more into football.
ER: You're more into football are you?
Timothy: (Nods)

★★★

ER: What about you Adrian, are you into girls as girlfriends/
Adrian: No, not yet (wolf whistles and laughter from his friends) … I'm into
         sports, canoeing and stuff.

Adrian's expression, 'no, not yet' was indeed another legitimate discourse drawn
upon by boys who actively resisted 'being a boyfriend' and engaging in the various practices of 'fancying' and 'going out' as the following section reports.

'I'm waiting until the comp': delayed (hetero)sexualities and re(a)lationships

Many boys (particularly those at Hirstwood where few boys regularly participated in the boyfriend–girlfriend culture as practising boyfriends) drew
upon a discourse of delayed sexuality either by expressing a desire for a
'proper' relationship following primary school, which would involve intimate
sexual activity, or, by stressing that they were 'too young' or 'not ready' to
have a girlfriend:

SCHOOL: HIRSTWOOD

David: We don't really care about the girls in our school.
Ryan: Yeah.
ER: At other schools?
David: In Year 7, but they're too old for us.
[…]
ER: Why's that?
Sean: Coz we don't want to/
Jake: I'm waiting until the comp/
ER: You're waiting until the comp are you?
Ryan: Yeah, and I'm waiting till my brother brings one home then I'll know
         what to do

★★★

(responding to a discussion on the lack of sexual activity amongst boyfriends
and girlfriends in their class)
Ryan: They don't do anything, they just hold hands.
David: Yeah, real boyfriends and girlfriends kiss properly and stuff and go
         around each other's houses.

SCHOOL: TIPTON

Darren: Yeah, but I've got my eye set on this other Amanda in the comp?
ER: Have you?

Darren: Yeah (laughs) coz I like/
Colin: She's older than him.
Pete: Yeah, but not by much/
Darren: I like older women (raises eyebrows).

Many boys drew upon developmental discourses of childhood innocence (i.e. sexual immaturity) and exposed and positioned their peers' school-based relationships as phoney (not 'real'). Ryan, David, Jake and Sean, for example, provide a legitimate rejection of participation in the heterosexualised culture of their peers, whilst simultaneously confirming their imagined, and perhaps superior ('proper'), albeit delayed, heterosexualised trajectories, as older comprehensive boys. It also allowed them to position boys who 'just sit and talk' with their girlfriends as subordinate and (hetero)sexually inferior. However, it was not an easy position to maintain. Their 'heterosexuality' could be called into question if they failed to successfully demonstrate hegemonic forms of masculinity in other ways (usually through 'fighting' or 'football'). As the next section illustrates, the need for boys to outwardly perform their heterosexualised masculinity to others could not solely be achieved by demonstrating their sporting skills. In the pursuit of a hegemonic heterosexual masculinity, which seemed to be increasingly undermined by the refusal of girls to occupy passive sexual subject positions in 'real' boyfriend/girlfriend relationships (see also Chapter 5), heterosexual identifications were sought out in ways that were not directly undermined or challenged.

'God, I wish I could have sex': heterosexual fantasies, 'sex talk' and misogyny

Most boys, including those who did not regularly 'go out' or who were not interested in establishing heterosexual relationships, would define and construct their 'heterosexuality' through public displays of a range of heterosexual fantasies and desires. They located themselves firmly as (hetero)sexual subjects both within and outside classroom spaces (including the group interviews) in a variety of ways from public and private declarations of desire for greater sexual knowledge to the sexual objectification of girls and women:

Public desire for sexual knowledge

SCHOOL: TIPTON

(discussing their Year 6 sex education lesson)
Pete: We want to know more about the girls.
ER: OK, so what did you want to know more about the girls?
                 ... (few seconds silence and embarrassed looks)

Pete:	We are interested … because when you get older you've got to sometime er er … coz when I'm older I won't be able to 'do it' will I, I won't be able to/
Colin:	Yeah sometime or other you'll have to do something beginning with 's' and ending in 'x'/
ER:	Sex.
Colin and Darren:	Yeah.
Timothy:	You wouldn't know how to would you/
[...]	
Pete:	What's the point of having sex education if you, if it's not really showing it and it's just showing your genitals and all that stuff
[...]	
Timothy:	Today when that bloke was shaving naked they had him on for about three minutes and had the girl on/
Darren:	For three seconds bathing this other girl.
Pete:	All it shows was their boobies
ER:	So you wanted to see more?
Darren:	More breast stroke (they all laugh).

Sexualising classroom talk

Mrs Fryer tries to quieten the class down. She asks them to put their lips together. Adrian shouts out 'oo err, I'm not kissing everyone in this class'. Many of the boys and girls start laughing. Mrs Fryer looks at me, smiles, rolls her eyes and gives Adrian a long look (of disapproval?).

(Tipton: fieldnotes)

Sexual objectification of girls and women

David and Sean prepare the tables for group artwork by covering them in old newspapers. As they spread the newspapers around David comes across a picture of three topless women posed in an intimate embrace. 'Cor – look at this – I wouldn't mind a bit of that' and he shows up the picture to Sean and a number of boys crowd round. The boys start giggling and Mrs Fryer walks over, saying 'what's the fuss, they're just naked, haven't you seen naked ladies before?' She takes the paper from them and goes back to her marking.

(Tipton: fieldnotes)

Sexualising 'song' lyrics

The bell rings, signalling the end of break-time. Adrian walks across the playground singing out loud his version of Michael Jackson's 'Earth song'

which has a number of lines beginning 'what about...'. He changes the end
of the line with sexual acts: 'what about erections?', 'what about sex?',
'what about masturbation?'

(Tipton: fieldnotes)

Sexualisation of genitalia

SCHOOL: TIPTON

Timothy: Stuart gets erections.
Colin: Yeah (they all laugh) he was talking when the (sex education) video
         was on and goes 'I've got a stiffy' (more laughter)

Sexual story telling

Jake is laughing and joking with his friends. He tells them with a serious,
but cocky face, 'I had Pamela Anderson in my bedroom last night'. He then
explains how he has a picture of Pamela Anderson directly above his bed.
They all fall about laughing again.

(Hirstwood: fieldnotes)

Jake is telling Ryan a story concerning Nick Park's characters, 'Wallace and
Gromit'. I overhear the sentence, 'yeah, and Wallace is fucking a sheep covered in Mustard and he's going 'uh uh uh uh' (Jake mimes 'fucking' a
sheep). They both burst into laughter.

(Hirstwood: fieldnotes)

Positioning themselves as dominant sexual subjects was achieved in a number
of ways. David's public declaration of his sexual desire for supermodels (in this
case, 'topless' models) and Darren's sexualisation of the girl in the sex education
video through his call for more 'breast stroke' illustrate how some boys drew
upon traditional heterosexual discourses in which 'women are represented as
passive objects of male sexual urges, needs and desires' (Mac an Ghaill 1994:
92). Other (hetero)sexualised performances were maintained through more
light-hearted engagements, such as altering song lyrics to sexualise their content, and interweaving sex and violence with humour. Jake, for example,
generates a lot of laughs from his immediate peer group by sexualising Wallace
and the Sheep (drawn from the cartoon 'Wallace and Gromit) whereas Adrian,
the class 'joker', introduces sexual innuendo into everyday classroom relations.
As the title for this section and the first extract highlights, some boys' thirst for
hetero/sexual knowledge far exceeded 'official' sex education programmes.
Like Mac an Ghaill's (1994) findings amongst older teenage boys, the boys'
'sex-talk' seemed to validate their heteromasculinity in quite public ways to
both their male friends and their peers and teachers as a whole.

While all the extracts to some extent reveal boys' experimentation with sex and sexuality and the fun, power and excitement at transcending 'official' school sexual discourses, they also point to the ways in which humour is central to boys' sex-talk and a vital component in their rescue attempts at producing more dominant (hetero)masculinities and (hetero)sexualities (see Kehily and Nayak 1997). In contrast, Pete's fear of being caught out, not knowing what to do (when the time comes) in future sexual relationships, does suggest that some boys could express their private sexual feelings and insecurities without first lacing them with humour (see also Frosh *et al.* 2002; Ashley and Lee 2003). Pete's story is discussed in more detail below.

Boys and (hetero)sexual harassment

'He called her a fucking bitch': verbal (hetero)sexual harassment

Heterosexual harassment from boys to girls commonly took the form of denigrating girls (and women) through sexually abusive and aggressive language. Despite its widespread practice, in most cases, girls did not report sexualised verbal attacks to staff. Verbal insults predominantly centered around a girl's sexual status and included terms such as 'bitch', 'slag', 'tart' and 'slut'. Other studies have highlighted the ways in which boys unsettle girls through sexually abusive language. Clark (1990: 40) cites examples of girls aged 11 and 12 being called 'big tits' and 'period bag', all of which resonate strongly with the well-documented pervasiveness of heterosexual harassment experienced by girls and young women in the secondary school (Cowie and Lees 1981; Mahony 1985; Lees 1986, 1993; Wolpe 1988; Hey 1997; Duncan 1999; Sunnari *et al.* 2002). While some of the misogyny was delivered and justified through humour (Kehily and Nayak 1997), this was not always the case, as the following two extracts illustrate:

SCHOOL: TIPTON

> Julia starts singing a song when pupils have been told to 'be quiet'. Darren spins on his chair and leans forward in front of Julia. He then mouths the word 'fuck' at her – I have no idea why. He looks annoyed at something. I can't see Julia's response.

SCHOOL: HIRSTWOOD

> The class have been told they can go outside – it is now break-time. Neil gets up and as he is walking out, he stops at Carrie's table. Carrie is still sitting down. Neil bends over in front of her so that his face is parallel with hers and wags his tongue up and down directly in front of her face and then walks off. Carrie looks confused and unsettled for a moment and then continues to chat with her friends.

SCHOOL: TIPTON

ER: So what about you Darren?

Pete: Well he's been out with Mandy, I mean, not Mandy, I mean er er Victoria about three times in the past three months init? or something like that and once he went out with her for about a month didn't ya?

Darren: Mmm (eyes down, looks into his lap).

ER: What happened, why aren't you seeing her anymore?

Pete: Because she, because he called her a fucking bitch.

The first two extracts illustrate how some boys would use sexual swear words and symbolic sexual gestures to unsettle and overtly intimidate girls. The third extract seems to be part of a wider narrative about boys' need to re-instate their heterosexual dominance often undermined and denied through 'real' boyfriend and girlfriend relationships, in which many of the boys as noted earlier claimed they were 'used', manipulated and ruthlessly dumped by girls. On two occasions, a group of boys also took to positioning their class teacher as sexually subordinate (see Walkerdine 1981) by calling her a 'slag' and a 'bitch' (in an interview): first, when football was banned on the playground and second, when they felt they were receiving unnecessary disciplinary treatment in the classroom. These forms of sexualised harassment/offensive sexualised behaviours were often engaged in by boys who were located lower down the heterosexual hierarchies (Darren, for example, was continuously 'dumped' in a string of relationships and was particularly abusive to ex-girlfriends and his class teacher).

'He's a woman beater he is': boys' accounts of physical sexual harassment

Verbal sexual abuse towards girls was sometimes frowned upon by other boys as something they shouldn't really have said or done, but was not regarded as particularly deviant. To most boys, sexually abusive language would not constitute 'harassment' and was not conceptualised as overtly harmful. While physical sexual harassment could be regarded as aberrant behaviour (by the majority of boys), only acts which boys could align with representations of sexual violence from the adult world seemed to 'count' as 'harassment'. More ambiguous and perhaps more 'child-like' acts (which were nevertheless harmful and unwanted by the girls themselves) such as bra-pulling or lifting up a girl's skirt were not frowned upon within boys' peer groups in the same way.

Chapter 5 detailed ongoing physical sexual harassment carried out by two boys towards a group of girls towards the end of their final year of primary school. Like many girls, they did not report the incident to any of the teaching staff and tended to use discourses that served to invalidate and undermine their experiences as a form of harassment (see Kelly and Radford 1996). One of the strongest reasons not to physically retaliate was that 'girls don't fight boys'.

However, as the following extract and analysis illustrates, the discourse that 'boys don't hit girls' was just as strongly felt amongst boys and led the peer group of one of the 'perpetrators' (Stu), to publicly vilify his behaviour and led Stu himself to deny his actions when confronted by myself and his male peers in a later interview:

SCHOOL: HIRSTWOOD

(initial question was prompted by Sam's comment that Stu 'beats girls up')

ER:	So Stu, you don't hit the girls at all?
Stu:	No.
ER:	So are they just making / it all up?
Sam:	I do.
ER:	I know you do.
Sam:	Coz they're always going like this (hair ruffling)
ER:	So you hit them back?
Sam:	Yeah.
ER:	They were telling me that sometimes you thump them in the chest (I obtained the girls' consent to confront the boys)
Sam:	Yeah, yeah he does (laughing).
Stu:	No.
James:	He's, he's a women beater he is.
Sam:	Man slaughter.
Jake:	He's like someone out of *Cracker*.[1]
James:	Stu can't beat up boys so he beats up girls.
Stu:	Oh yeah, I could beat you up (Sam laughs).
James:	Come on then.
ER:	So is it true?
Stu:	No.
Sam:	He's gone /all red.
Stu:	It isn't true.
Sam:	It is.

Stu was situated on the margins of the dominant 'footballer' peer group at Hirstwood and was continuously teased by the other boys for his sporting skill. He often participated in fighting games, such as the mock 'boxing match' described in Chapter 4 in which he was often the loser. One interpretation of why he 'punched girls in the chest' could be part of his struggle to access and project a 'tough' and 'sporting' masculinity. However, hitting girls immediately undermines any attempt to project a tough masculinity because 'real men' don't hit women, as his peers quickly point out in their ridiculing of Stu as a 'women beater'. Perhaps the overwhelming need for Stu to disassociate himself from and subordinate the 'feminine', in the form of physical (and sexual) domination, transgressed the social acceptability of his behaviour. However we try to make sense of Stu's behaviour towards Annabel and Carla, his own response and the response of his peers does highlight what constitutes a socially acceptable 'masculinity' as well as the contradiction and struggle in trying to perform a coherent hegemonic masculine identity, and all that that entails – particularly when girls are physically bigger and sometimes stronger than boys at this age. However, the humour through which Stu's friends interpreted and commented upon his behaviour nevertheless powerfully undermined the harm caused and felt by the girls themselves (see Chapter 5).

Collectively, these extracts illustrate the overt and covert ways in which boys differently 'perform' and confirm their heterosexuality. They also suggest how such performances, particularly the sexual objectification of women and the sexualised harassment (verbal and physical) of their female classmates, all go some way to re-instate boys' heterosexual dominance, often undermined and denied through conventional and 'real' boyfriend/girlfriend relationships, as Mac an Ghaill explains:

> Externally and internally males attempt to re-produce themselves as powerful within social circumstances which remain out of their control.
>
> (1996: 200).

With many boys coupling heterosexual activity with maturity and 'older boys', these sexualised performances could also be interpreted as a direct challenge to the perceived 'asexuality' of the primary school environment and discourses of 'childhood innocence'. They could also be one of the ways in which boys 'collectively explore(d) the newly available forms of authority and autonomy conferred by their position at the 'top of the school' (Redman 1996: 178). Indeed, their entry into and engagement with heterosexualised discourses and practices may well be further reinforced by their chronological positioning within the school, although this was not something that the boys' themselves raised in any direct way.

'They say I'm gay – they say I'm like a girl': anti-gay talk and 'homophobic ' narratives[2]

Many secondary-school-based studies have illustrated how 'homophobic' discourses and anti-gay/lesbian talk and behaviours saturate boys' peer-group cultures, social relations and masculinity-making activities (Mac an Ghaill 1994; Nayak and Kehily 1997; Duncan 1999; Sunnari et al. 2002). Each of these studies has indicated the ways in which anti-gay sentiment, such as calling a boy or his behaviour 'gay' operates to produce and police hegemonic masculinities. More recently, primary-school-based research is beginning to uncover how younger children are also drawing upon the term 'gay' in a number of different ways (Gilbert and Gilbert 1998; Letts and Sears 1999; Swain 2003). Some studies, such as Jon Swain's (2003: 319) ethnography of school-boy masculinities, discovered boys' widespread use of the term 'gay' as a general form of inter-personal abuse which could encompass 'anything from being not very good to absolute rubbish'. Even 'trainers' could be perceived as 'gay' if they were not sporting a designer label. In this study anti-gay and homophobic talk was much less prevalent and was taken-up in different ways by boys at Tipton and Hirstwood. Unlike the boys at Westmoor Abbey in Swain's ethnography, the term 'gay' was not used as a general term of abuse but directed at particular boys. This could include one-off comments directed at boys who got (physically) 'too close' to other boys and more persistent targeting of boys who were considered to be aligning themselves too closely with girls and femininity and/or boys who failed or chose not to access hegemonic masculinities (e.g. football and fighting). In my study it was Damien and Stuart at Tipton, whose masculinity and (hetero)sexuality was routinely called into questioned (by girls, boys and teachers alike) for not meeting the requirements of a recognisable (i.e. socially validated) heteromasculinity. As many other studies which have explored the ways in which sexuality and gender intersect and interact within boys' peer group cultures demonstrate, any boy who dares to deviate from a normative or hegemonic masculinity is potentially subject to both gendered and sexualised attacks. Indeed, the terms 'gay' and 'girl' or 'poof' and 'sissy' are often interchangeable (as the title quote makes visible), which is illustrative of the ways in which homophobia and misogyny operate to police the Other (Kimmel 1987; Epstein 1997).

Some authors (for example, Redman 1996) have suggested that 'homosexual anxieties' are not employed as a means of defining and constituting 'normal' heterosexualities until boys are at least 12 to 13 years of age. Other studies have suggested that anti-gay talk should be conceptualised as expressions of doing and defining 'gender' rather than 'sexuality' (Parker 1996a). I would argue from this study, however, that towards the end of children's primary school years, some boys outwardly demonstrate a fear and loathing of homosexualities and are acutely aware of how anti-gay talk/behaviours (labelling and teasing other boys as 'gay') can police and produce 'acceptable' heterosexual masculinities and create and maintain both gender and sexual peer group hierarchies (see also Swain 2003: 321).

In contrast to the boys at Tipton, I did not observe the boys at Hirstwood publicly positioning other 'non-hegemonic' boys through anti-gay language (although they would regularly call them 'girls'). Homophobic narratives, however, did present themselves in conversations around adult Others (such as media celebrities or next door neighbours). The first extract provides a rare discussion of how adult gay sexualities (in this case gay transgender sexualities) and in particular 'doing gay' are constructed as abnormal and perceived with a mixture of fear and disgust. From 'doing gay' to 'sounding gay', the second extract illustrates how boys attribute particular signifiers (e.g. voice) that constitute a 'gay' identity and how they can be drawn upon in the process of Othering. The third extract continues the theme of men who 'sound gay' and crescendos to a climax of applause at a violent attack on a known gay celebrity:

SCHOOL: HIRSTWOOD

Ryan: There was a programme on the other day (it is AIDS week) I turned
           it off after a while, it was disgusting/
ER: Why?
Ryan: Because it showed these er two men who dressed up as women and
           they were er they were having sex and it was really horrible.
ER: And you didn't like it, so you turned it off?
Ryan: Yeah.
ER: OK ... have you thought about why didn't you like it?
Ryan: Well, like, if you see a woman and a man 'doing it', I don't really care
           and er /
David: Coz everyone does it, every night.
Ryan: You see, you see people 'doing it' that way then you don't really mind
           coz that's what most people do. And then you see like two men doing
           it and you know that's horrible, disgusting.

★★★

ER: When you say 'gay' Jake what do you mean by that?
Jake: You know, like/ really sad.
Sean: A bender (Sean, Ryan and Jake laugh)/
Ryan: And you can sound gay can't you/
David: Simon (boy in another class)/ he sounds gay.
Ryan: And our next door neighbour/

★★★

Jake: You know that *Supermarket Sweep* (game show)?
ER: Yeah.
Jake: Well, there was this man on there/
David: And he (host of show) goes (to another man), 'you're really
                  pretty aren't you?'
Jake: Yeah, and he won it right, about 2000 pounds and he goes up
                  to him and he can't stop kissing him (laughing) he kisses him
                  about 2000 times/
Ryan: Yeah that's like Michael Barrymore/
Jake: Yeah and/he smacked Michael Barrymore in the other day/
Sean and Ryan: Yeah (they all cheer and clap)/
David: Who did?
ER: Why is that good?
Sean: Coz he's gay.

In contrast to the boys at Tipton who directed anti-gay abuse at each other, the
boys at Hirstwood tended to project anti-gay and homophobic sentiment onto

'older' bodies and subjects outside the school. This focus on older or adult Others when discussing homosexuality mirrored the ways in which their heterosexual-talk was often framed in relation to older (and their own delayed) active heterosexualities.

Shouting out and positioning other boys or adult Others as 'gay' all seemed to be ways of asserting a more coherent heterosexual self – in other words, a 'heteromasculinity'. Such processes of differentiation (from 'homosexualities') and subordination (of alternative masculinities and femininities) have also been theorised as boys' negotiating external (social/cultural) and internal (psychic) processes (Mac an Ghaill 1994; Kehily and Nayak 1997; Redman 1997):

> Heterosexual male students were involved in a double relationship of traducing the Other, including women and gays (external relations), at the same time as expelling femininity and homosexuality from within themselves (internal relations).
>
> (Mac an Ghaill 1994: 90)

In Mac an Ghaill's research with teenage boys, those who held and projected strong homophobic attitudes and behaviours were predominantly the low-achieving working-class 'macho lads'. Anti-gay and homophobic talk with primary school-aged boys in this study seemed to be expressed more often by boys who were not regular players on the boyfriend/girlfriend circuit or who were positioned lower down the heterosexual hierarchy in terms of romantic desirability regardless of their social-class positioning.[3] Indeed, the powerlessness experienced by many boys participating in the boyfriend/girlfriend cultures (i.e. being 'dumped' or being 'used'), the precarious position of 'boyfriend' and indeed the ambiguity of initiating physical or emotional intimacies with girls at all, produced some very confusing messages and some rather contradictory heterosexual identities. Jon Swain (2003: 320) also highlights the ways in which boys struggle with the contradictions of naming and defining a 'gay' or 'hetero' sexuality in a discussion of how gender-bending is conflated with (hetero)sexual transgression as three boys discuss how it is possible for one of their male classmates (Travis) to 'hang around' with girls, kiss them and 'act gay'!

'I love girls, it's my living': professional boyfriends and primary school 'studs'

So far, this chapter has briefly outlined how the majority of boys defined and constructed hegemonic heterosexual masculinities through fleetingly entering and engaging in a combination of heterosexualised fantasies, misogynistic, homophobic and heterosexist performances, and the local boyfriend/girlfriend culture. This section examines how three boys, Todd, Pete (both from Tipton) and Tom (Hirstwood) defined their masculinities almost entirely through their hyper-heterosexual status as 'professional boyfriends'. Derived from Pete's answer ('it's my living') to my question about the number of girls who 'fancied' him, I use the term 'professional boyfriend' because it captures the time, commitment and effort involved in the three boys' cultivation of their role as 'boyfriend'. It also signifies their 'difference' from other boys insofar as their heterosexual couplings and romances were a constant reference point for other girls and boys in the class (see also Epstein and Johnson 1998 and Epstein *et al.* 2001a). I have also drawn upon Haywood's (1996) term 'hyper-heterosexuality' to emphasise how they all publicly established themselves as the 'studs' of the school, insofar as they were attributed by girls and other boys to be the most romantically desirable, the most physically attractive and the most 'popular'.

The three boys have many traits in common. They each firmly established themselves as 'heterosexual' through long-term relationships: Todd for three years, Pete for six months and Tom for four months. They then began to engage in a long list of ephemeral, and in the case of Todd, overlapping ('two-timing') relationships. However, as the following three stories illustrate, they drew upon the discourses of 'heterosexuality' and invested in and capitalised on their dominant status and position of privilege as the 'stud' of their class in very different ways.

Todd ('mean and keen')

Harriet: Todd always needs a girlfriend so he can be cool. Even if he doesn't love her he goes, well no he doesn't go out with everyone, but whoever's good-looking. He doesn't care about their sense of humour, he just goes for the looks. He just goes out with people just for the sake of it, so he can be cool.

Todd matches the description of Haywood's (1996) original 'hyper-heterosexuals' who were 'working class', low academic achievers and whose resistance to school seemed to be achieved through a constant public projection of their heterosexuality. Over the years, however, Todd engaged with different versions of heterosexuality, moving from a romance-based heterosexuality (discussed below) to a more misogynistic 'mean and keen' heterosexuality. Until Year 6, Todd had firmly established a romantic heterosexual identity in a three-year relationship with his classmate Sophie. They would often sit together in class and spend time together at playtimes, usually holding hands or 'snogging in the corner', as one girl put it. Over time, they came to represent the 'official' couple of the school, each firmly established as the most romantically desirable and popular pupil. However, the increasingly visible, worryingly monogamous (when other children of the same age were conducting numerous and overlapping 'relationships') and often physical nature of their relationship led their class teacher to place them in different Year 6 classrooms (at the end of Year 5). This strategy was a direct attempt to 'stop us getting too serious' (Sophie) and prevent them from 'conducting a relationship beyond their years' (Class Teacher, Mrs Fryer).

Consequently, their 'relationship' soon dissolved and throughout Year 6 Todd engaged in a number of short-lived 'two-timing' relationships. Cultivating a reputation as 'stud' of the school by capitalising on his earlier 'romance-based' heterosexuality Todd began carving out a different heterosexual identity by drawing upon the traditional 'treat them mean keep them keen' discourse. Epstein *et al.* (2001a) in their own study of children's relationship cultures also note 'the way in which the girls valued boys who 'treated them mean' using their power to reinscribe themselves and the boys in very traditional gendered relations' (Epstein *et al.* 2001a: 165). Indeed, Mrs Fryer's decision to physically separate Todd and Sophie seemed more about regulating, controlling and ulti- mately disbanding their monogamy (which was perceived as unhealthy), than their emerging (hetero)sexualities. Thus, the heteronormativity operating in the junior years in this school appeared to be about disrupting monogamous 'relationships' (including spending time in mixed-sex pairings) with a view that in doing so it offset more 'serious' sexual acts. However, the outcome of the break-up saw Todd as 'stud' of the year, rejecting 'romance' and 'emotional inti- macy' and investing in 'older' forms of heterosexuality which tended to prioritise physical intimacy.

However, there being no 'professional girlfriend' subject position, Sophie, unwavering in her attachment to Todd, continued to 'pine' (her words) for him, despite the barrage of verbal insults he threw her way. Although I have used some of this extract earlier to demonstrate heterosexualisation of girls' attrac- tiveness, I am using it here to focus upon Harriet's analysis of Todd's relations/hips with girls as girlfriends:

SCHOOL: TIPTON

ER:	Does Todd ever say anything about the way you look?
Harriet:	Yeah he does, he calls her/
Sophie:	Yeah, he says that I'm ugly when I'm not going out with him ... he thought I had nice legs when I was going out with him
Harriet:	And now he says that she's really ugly and everything ... the thing with Todd is he likes having girlfriends, but he dislikes girls.
[...]	
Harriet:	Just coz he dumped Sophie, he starts being really nasty to her
Amanda:	She can't stop fancying him, even when he does something really horrible to her she can't stop it/
Sophie:	Yeah I know.
Harriet:	She loves him too much.

As Harriet eloquently illustrates, Todd 'likes having girlfriends, but dislikes girls' – that is, he enjoys and invests heavily in girls as (hetero)sexual objects/posses- sions insofar as they mark and parade his heterosexual masculinity, yet rejects girls insofar as they represent a contaminating 'femininity'. Todd rarely positively interacted with girls who were not his girlfriends, or potential girlfriends. It was 'relationships' not 'friendships' that Todd was interested in and he went to great lengths to cultivate the sort of image that he considered 'cool' and attractive to the opposite sex. Differentiating himself from what he considered his 'immature' peers, he invested in an older identity and participated heavily in what I have termed the 'grooming' discourse and a 'heterotextuality' of the body. This involved public and ritualised performances such as frequent gelling and styling of the hair (in front of windows and mirrors), wearing aftershave and discussing their different fragrances. He even took to wearing a tie to school (which was not part of the formal school uniform) thus aligning himself more with older secondary school boys and the (male) head teacher. Interestingly and disturbingly, however, while many girls openly thought that he was 'too cool', went 'over the top' and disliked him and his patriarchal and misogynist attitude, he was hardly ever without a girlfriend![4]

Todd mobilised a particular form of heterosexuality on a number of levels. The constant grooming and public boasting of his physical (hetero)sexual interactions with girls were all ways in which he heterotextualises his body and concomitantly his (hetero)gender and (hetero)sexual identity. Like many boys, his misogyny and re-working of the 'treat them mean, keep them keen' discourse seems to be much more about the pressure to negotiate, perform and consolidate an 'older' (and often contradictory) heterosexual masculinity than it is about enjoying heterosexual relations with girls as friends or as girlfriends. Indeed, Todd's story provides an important contrast to Pete and Tom's investment in heterosexual discourses and practices as 'professional boyfriends'.

Pete ('love and romance')

Pete: I've been out with about five people so far, but I've always dumped them because I didn't like them. But now I've found Mandy, she's someone I really like and I want us to stay together ... (whispers) I am so in love.

At the beginning of the first term in Year 6 Pete was already admired for his sporting skills, particularly football. Unlike many of the boys, he rarely engaged in 'fighting' practices and openly enjoyed talking and spending time with girls both inside and outside the classroom. As if to compensate for this, however, he went to great lengths to firmly locate himself as a 'boy', as 'masculine'. For example, if he was not playing football at playtime, and sat and chatted with the girls instead, he would always carry his football magazine under his arm. Pete was also the boy who publicly declared his 'masculine' status with the comment: 'I don't like roses I like mud', in response to one of the ancillary support teachers bringing some flowers into class (see Chapter 4). Pete's hegemonic masculinity, however, was initially achieved via his status as 'footballer'. Indeed his rising status as football 'star' seemed directly to correlate with his status as 'professional boyfriend' and after the first half term Pete engaged in a six-month relationship with Mandy.

In contrast to Todd's misogynistic 'mean and keen' hyper-heterosexuality, Pete draws upon traditional romantic and heteronormative discourses of love, loyalty and imagined futures of marriage and babies – thus confirming Epstein *et al.*'s (2001b) suggestion that children's engagement with sexuality in the primary school 'is often subsumed within a kind of heterosexual familialism':

SCHOOL: TIPTON

ER: When you say someone is your girlfriend, what do you mean?
Darren: You love them/
Pete: Yeah you love them, you love them ... like you know when you get
            married to people when you're older, it's just like a little bit off that ...
            a little bit off marriage.

In ways almost identical to Todd and Sophie in Years 3 to 5, Pete and Mandy became the 'celebrity couple' for their current Year 6 classes. They also became very close friends, which makes more complex Thorne's (1993) finding that boys and girls are rarely 'friends' when they become heterosexually involved. Pete used to tell me how Mandy helped him talk about the 'troubles he was having at home' when his parents divorced and when his step-father was applying for custody of his daughter. Pete's popularity amongst the girls seemed to be driven by his sensitivity and ability to talk and listen to *all* girls, irrespective of whether or not they were potential 'girlfriends'.

Even when Pete and Mandy's relationship ended, Pete continued to invest in the romance-based hyper-heterosexuality and maintained close friendships with many of his female classmates. Now 'single' and 'available', however, Pete was the boy that 'everyone fancied'. At one stage he had four girls who, through various 'messengers', put themselves forward as 'Pete's girlfriend to be'. He took over a week to make up his mind on who to choose! During the latter half of Year 6, he embarked on a series of monogamous 'relationships' (often lasting no more than a couple of weeks) and was described by some girls as the 'swapping boy':

SCHOOL: TIPTON

ER: You go through quite a lot of girlfriends Pete don't you?
Pete: I know.
ER: How's that?
Pete: I can't help it.
[...]
ER: You've changed a lot /haven't you since you were first a Year 6?
Adrian: Everyone fancies him, so that must be the reason.
Timothy: Everyone on our table, apart from Kirsty, me and Martin fancy him.

[...]

ER:	Why do you think that is?
Pete:	I dunno, I can't help it, I can't help it
ER:	Do you like it?
Pete:	Yeah, I like girls, it's my living. I don't need to worry about how I look/coz girls just to come to me
Timothy:	Yeah (reluctantly).
Adrian:	Yeah (sighs).

Basking in his new found hyper-heterosexual status as 'professional boyfriend', which Pete developmentally describes as 'the stage', he also heavily invested (with Todd from the parallel Year 6 class) in a number of grooming discourses and practices. He went to great lengths to position himself as desirable (which included sporting the latest fashion, hair-cut and wearing Lynx aftershave, see Chapter 4). As the extract below highlights, he (and some of his friends) were anxious to consume all the knowledge they could around sexual practices and contraception. Pete even discussed with his sister how he should negotiate 'the stage' and spent time sifting through her *Sugar* and *Just Seventeen* magazines to achieve the 'right look' and 'learn more about girls':

SCHOOL: TIPTON

Pete:	I read, like I read horror books at night and magazine, like *Shoot*, like, and I go over to the shop and get some like *Match* and sometimes my sister buys erm like/
Darren:	Erm like music magazines/
Pete:	*Sugar* and all that/
Darren:	And like *Just Seventeen*
Pete:	Coz my sister knows that I'm going through the stage coz my sister's two years older than me and she knows that er she's been through the stage before and she knows that I'm growing up and I want to know about it/
Darren:	And like *Just Seventeen*.
Pete:	She goes to the shop and just buys me a magazine like with all the stuff in and like sex pages and everything.
ER:	So your sister/
Pete:	Helps me get through it.
[...]	
Pete:	Yeah it (sex education video) hasn't got enough detail, it hasn't got enough details.
ER:	So you want more detail?
Pete and Colin:	Yeah.
Pete:	We want to know we want to have a man and a lady real having it off/

Colin:	They didn't show you how to put the condoms on and all that
[...]	
ER:	OK so from the videos you've seen, how relevant are they to you now as eleven year olds. Sexually what sort of stage are you at with your girlfriends?
Pete:	Snogging/
Darren:	Cuddling, hugging.
Pete:	That's all it is at the moment but how can we get like nineteen, I mean that's only seven to eight years and by the time that comes and we haven't got enough details in these sex education videos we wont know how to do it/
ER:	But you do get sex education in the comprehensive as well.
Pete:	Yeah, but I want to know how to do it now because I want all the details today.

Pete differs significantly from Todd. He rarely engaged in misogynistic or homophobic discourses and performances. However, his status as 'professional boyfriend' did, by default, subordinate other masculinities and femininities, as girls were unable to occupy this dominant heterosexual subject position and non-hegemonic boys were often ridiculed if they spent time or played with girls. So established was his hegemonic heterosexual masculinity that Pete could transgress and play around with gendered boundaries. He often declared how it might be fun to be a girl and sometimes positioned himself as 'gay' (albeit through humour) – something that I had not observed with any of the other boys in the study without incurring some form of penalty. His ability to communicate his feelings and private insecurities within the group interviews was also unique. His freedom of expression also seemed to encourage other boys to express themselves more openly and led to some very productive interviews in which a number of boys openly expressed their private insecurities and anxieties about 'being a boy' and the pressures of compulsory heterosexuality. For example, Pete and his friends could talk openly about enjoying being a 'boyfriend', the pleasures of kissing and the possibility of future romances. At other times they could express their concern over not knowing enough about 'sex' or contraception or worrying about 'being dumped' and feeling powerless.

Tom ('just good friends')

Rachel: The only decent boy is Tom – he's so nice, he has all the girls after him.

Throughout Year 6, Tom was well known as the boy whom 'all the girls fancied'. From a professional middle-class family, Tom's heterosexual status as 'professional boyfriend' and 'stud' goes some way to indicate that it is not a position exclusively occupied by working-class boys. However, there were clear differences and these are outlined below. Like Pete, Tom's romantic desirability seemed to stem from his sensitivity and easy manner with *all* girls:

SCHOOL: HIRSTWOOD

ER:	So why do you still fancy him if he keeps dumping you?
Claire:	I dunno, it's like I get a chance in the future (laughs)/
Annabel:	He's a boy that you can talk to but/
Trudy:	Yeah like all the other boys you can't say like a word without them calling you names and stuff, but Tom you can talk to.
ER:	What can't you talk to other boys about?
Trudy:	Erm/
Annabel:	Everything.
ER:	Can you talk to your girlfriends about the same sorts of things you can talk to Tom about?
Annabel:	Er yeah/
Claire:	Yeah, mostly/
Annabel:	He's just like a girl really (they laugh)
ER:	So how does he get on with other boys?
Carla:	Not very well.
Annabel:	Coz he fell out with all his boy friends and started hanging around with all the girls and then the boys got really sick of him and they started to hate him and none of the boys play with him.
ER:	Why do the boys hate him?
Annabel:	Because he hangs around with the girls and he doesn't care about erm about playing with the boys anymore/

Unlike Pete, he did not participate in any of the 'grooming' practices or engage in any sexual activities, such as kissing. His intimacy with girls extended only to 'holding' hands. However, by utilising the heterosexualised boyfriend/girlfriend discourses, Tom managed successfully to achieve and develop close friendships with girls without undermining his cultivation of a hegemonic masculinity. When Tom became a close friend with a girl, he or they would ask the other 'out', thereby heterosexualising their relationship and avoiding ridicule. Fine (1987: 106) also notes that only 'high status' boys could develop involved and committed heterosexual relationships and could 'let girls replace other boys as the focus of their attention' without 'being ridiculed by their peers'.

However, because the boyfriend/girlfriend culture was less prevalent at Hirstwood, other boys would become agitated that Tom and his close friend Michael no longer played football with them:

SCHOOL: HIRSTWOOD

David:	They just hang around with girls all the time, they never play football, they're really disappointed when ??? 'oh I'll play now', when they've just been talking to the girls.
Ryan:	We keep on asking 'do you want to play, do you want to play' and it's 'no I'm talking to the girls'. So you fix the teams and then like half an hour later he comes up and says 'oh can I play now' and then when we say 'no' and he gets in a real mood.
[...]	
ER:	So, once you have got a girlfriend then, is it quite difficult to have a girlfriend and play football?
David:	They just have to see them every single playtime.
Ryan:	Yeah.
ER:	So you think they spend too much time together?
David:	Well, they're not exactly going to last all the time, it's only going to be stupid, they're never going to do anything.

Other pressures included girls' and boys' expectations for Tom to express his commitment in a physical way:

SCHOOL: HIRSTWOOD

David:	We go (to Tom), 'are you actually going to get off with each other'?
ER:	So they don't kiss each other?
Ryan:	I asked Tom the other day, and he's been going out with Melissa for two weeks, two months sorry and he just sits with her and *talks* to her!
[...]	
ER:	So they're really just friends then, but because they spend so much time together, they are boyfriend and girlfriend?
Ryan and David:	Yeah.

Ryan's refusal to let the 'boyfriends' join in, when it suited them, could also be interpreted as a form of gate keeping in an attempt to limit Tom's (and Michael's) access to both heterosexual and sporting masculinities. Moreover, given the weaker boyfriend/girlfriend culture at Hirstwood, their position as 'professional boyfriends' was not as easy to occupy in Hirstwood as it was at Tipton.

Tom's platonic-based heterosexuality only seemed possible because of his spatial location within the primary school insofar as it symbolises an institutionalised childhood innocence and asexuality. Pete's developmental positioning as 'pre-teen' also enabled him to draw upon discourses of childhood sexual innocence and thus legitimately refrain from sexual activity, such as kissing, without too much speculation. However, Ryan's comments in the last few weeks of the study echo some of the sexual pressures associated with heterosexual relationships directed and experienced by boys in the secondary school and broader sociological studies of heterosexualities (Wood 1984; Holland *et al.* 1993; Mac an Ghaill 1994, 1996). Ryan's amazement at Tom's platonic relationships with Melissa ('they just sit and talk') also highlights the increasing difficulty for Year 6 boys to talk and be friends with girls without a hetero/sexual agenda. Collectively, these case studies illustrate the multiple ways in which the subject position, 'boyfriend' and the discourses of love, romance and sexuality were negotiated in ways that challenged or reinforced their ascribed gendered generational position as 'boy-child', their sexual generational position as 'innocent-child' and their hierarchical pedagogical position within the school as Year 6 boy-pupil at the 'top of the school'.

Concluding notes

In an article exploring the regulation of childhood at the end of the millennium, Valerie Walkerdine (1999) focuses on the subjects and subjectivities of 'violent boys' and 'precocious girls' in terms of how they represent the Other to normal childhood. I argued in Chapter 2 how media and public concerns over the increasing eroticisation and sexualisation of girls and femininity and the masculinisation of violence has resulted in the neglect and under-theorisation of the (hetero)sexualisation of masculinity in young boys' gender cultures. The purpose of this chapter has been to make explicit and break the silence around boys' sexual cultures and expose how the organisational heteronormativity of the primary school regulates and polices the ways in which boys invest and engage with hegemonic heterosexual masculinities. Through a critical presentation of empirical observations and boys' own accounts of rather complex and contingent heterosexual identifications, Butler's 'heterosexual matrix' can be seen to operate in different ways for boys (than girls), although being a 'proper' boy still involves projecting some kind of recognisable heterosexuality.

For the majority of boys, overt heterosexual practices, such as being 'fancied' or being 'a boyfriend' did not automatically signify hegemonic masculinity (particularly at Hirstwood, where the boyfriend/girlfriend culture was weak). For most boys, emotional and physical intimacy with girls (in school) could paradoxically be masculinity confirming (via a discourse of sexual prowess) and masculinity denying (via a discourse of gender contamination). With heterosexual masculinities occupying such a fragile and contradictory status, many boys seemed to go on and define their heterosexuality through heterosexual fantasies and imagined (hetero)sexual futures and the policing and shaming of Other gender and sexual identities and practices. Some of the latter performances include: misogynistic and sexual objectification of girls and women, homophobic/anti-gay performances towards particular boys (Tipton) or embedded in boys' talk (Hirstwood), and direct and indirect forms of sexualised harassment towards girls and women more widely.

In contrast to the girls' compulsory interpellation into the heterosexualised world of romance and relationship cultures, many boys could legitimately delay their participation by drawing upon discourses in which 'proper' sexualities are for 'older' boys. I also explored how alternative 'masculine' subject positions (e.g. footballer) were not only interconnected, but often interchangeable with the 'sexual' subject position of 'boyfriend'. Indeed, the last third of the chapter explored three boys' rather unique engagement with their hyper-heterosexual positioning as 'professional boyfriends' to illustrate the different ways in which 'heterosexuality' can be taken-up at this age for boys and to emphasise the plurality of heterosexual masculinities produced within, and specific to, the primary school.

Pete and Todd's interest in 'older' sexual activities signify how a rejection of childhood innocence and investment in the symbolic, discursive and embodied production of (hetero)sexual practices and knowledges can be mobilised to bolster and confer status and power within an often fragile world of boyfriends, girlfriends, dating and dumping. Alternatively, Tom's story illustrates how the very same discourses of childhood innocence can be drawn upon as a way of legitimately avoiding (hetero)sexual practices and maintaining (albeit temporarily) a physical and emotional intimacy with girls. Where Todd created and defined his heterosexuality through patriarchal and highly oppressive heterosexist, misogynist discourses, Pete and Tom produced a hyper-heterosexual masculinity that not only enabled them to develop close friendships with both dominant (popular and desirable) and marginalised (unpopular and undesirable) groups of girls but avoided the practices through which many boys constructed their hegemonic masculine identities (e.g. anti-gay behaviours and misogyny).

It must not be forgotten, however, that although the majority of boys experienced a range of pressures and fears as they entered the hegemonic world of heterosexuality, the power relations involved in their practices overtly (and indirectly) denigrate and subordinate femininities and marginalised masculinities, even in the cases of Tom and Pete. For although each boy opened the discursive space for less oppressive gendered performances and interactions, the subject position of professional boyfriend, was, in both schools, only available to boys, there being no 'professional girlfriends'. Girls were still subject to the tyranny of the sexual 'double standard' and boys who transgressed or deviated from the heteronormative gendered script were open targets for gender-based or sexualised bullying (Chapter 7). Nevertheless, the stories of the three 'primary school studs' and the different ways in which they engaged in their hyper-heterosexuality ('keen and mean', 'love and romance', 'just good friends) does provide a more nuanced analysis of the ways in which masculinity, (hetero)sexuality and childhood intersect and are negotiated and experienced by pre-adolescent boys as they make sense of their emerging gender and sexual identities and relation(s)/hips.

Chapter 7

'We're not like most girls and boys'

Being the gendered and sexualised Other

Introduction

> The outsiders who are not-our-group and thus who in part define our group must be attended to.
>
> (Davies and Hunt 1994: 398)

Previous chapters have highlighted how rare it was for children in the study to sustain any comfortable security with their gendered and sexual identities, produced as they were in a constant flux of power and powerlessness. As we have seen, many children articulated personal struggles and pressures in trying to get their gender/sexuality 'right' and most had, at one time or another, been subject to some form of gender-based or sexualised teasing (or Othering) for stepping outside of or failing to project appropriate 'masculinities' or 'femininities'. However, this chapter is not about those wannabe hegemonic boys or wannabe girlie-girls who were routinely subjugated for struggling to pull off convincing gendered/sexual performances. Rather, it is about those children who experienced the same intense feelings of marginalisation but continued to actively resist normative gender and sexual discourses and ways of being.

This chapter builds upon and develops the literature of those gendered and sexual Others such as Best's (1983) 'losers', Thorne's (1993) 'sissies', Eder's (1995) 'isolates' and Davies and Hunt's (1994) 'outsiders'. The central aim of the chapter is to re-conceptualise the process of Othering and explore more fully the interrelationship between hegemonic and non-hegemonic gender identities through the concepts *doing Other*, *Othering* and *being Other*. In particular it explores how marginalisation does not signify powerlessness in any simple sense (see Gordon 1996; Hey 1997). Focusing on how it feels and what it means to do gender/sexuality in non-hegemonic ways, I map out some of the different ways in which girls and boys trouble 'traditional' (hetero)genders and (hetero)sexualities, from girls as powerful and predatory sexual Others to the use of humour in boys' queering of heteromasculinities. The chapter also outlines the strategies of survival and the maintenance of Other gendered/sexual subjectivities through a range of sophisticated discursive and collective resistances and how these differ for girls and boys from different social backgrounds, academic abilities and between the schools themselves. The chapter concludes by further reiterating how school-bound and thus context specific many of the accounts of doing gender and sexuality are by reporting children's very different experiences of their relationships with each other beyond the school gates.

Gender and sexual fugitives: Othering, doing Other and being Other

According to the Oxford English Dictionary, a 'fugitive' is 'a person who has escaped from captivity or is in hiding' (2002: 331). The emancipation of escape from rigid gender binaries coupled with the need for a private refuge or hide-away (whether it be spatial, social or psychological) was an enduring theme for boys and girls who defied gender and sexual norms. I have been using the term Other throughout this book to conceptualise those transgressive identities that cross or blur hegemonic sex/gender boundaries or what Butler (1990) refers to as 'unintelligible genders' (see Chapter 1). However, what gets defined as the gendered or sexualised Other can vary markedly between schools as well as over time. Othering practices in relation to gender and other 'differences that make a difference' are both temporally and contextually contingent. In this study, the gendered Othering pivoted around the multiple and shifting interactions of social class, age, academic ability and sexuality (see Connolly 1998, 2003; Ali 2002; Bhana 2002 in relation to ethnicity).

As the four previous empirical chapters have illustrated, all of the children in the study were actively engaged in articulating and embodying their sense of boy-ness or girl-ness in relation to and opposition against an Other in quite complex ways. Some were, in part, constructed in relation to other dominant heterofemininities and heteromasculinities (e.g. some girls defined their femininity as 'non-girlie' and some boys defined their masculinity through the culturally exalted status of sport rather than the heterosexualised subject position of 'boyfriend'). While all girls and boys could be subject to a range of Othering practices (even from their 'friends'), children who asserted their 'difference' and rejected and resisted gender norms were routinely targeted and articulated stronger feelings of marginalisation than others. Dominant subject positions and in particular those struggling to access dominant gendered identities (the wannabes) were constructed through the policing and shaming of Other 'non-hegemonic' identities (discussed below) to produce what other studies have referred to as dichotomous in-groups and out-groups (e.g. Adler and Adler 1998). However, before I go on to explore what it means and how it feels to take up non-hegemonic masculinities and femininities which blurred (hetero)gender and (hetero)sexual norms, I want to further problematise the notion that children who transgress gender/sexual norms follow a trajectory of marginalisation and subordination.

Just as boys and girls who invested in dominant and normative masculinities and femininities only temporarily (if ever) felt their high-ranking cultural status, so those children who engaged in non-hegemonic practices were not always subordinately positioned. As we have seen in previous chapters, there were girls and boys who could transgress gender boundaries and take up 'non-hegemonic' discourses so long as they successfully accessed other 'hegemonic' discourses and practices – in particular, heterosexualised discourses. For example, Pete (Chapter 6) could opt out of many of the masculinity-making activities such as football and fighting games. He could also 'hang around' and strike up friendships with girls (that he was not interested in pursuing as 'girlfriends) and publicly articulate his anxieties about 'growing up', secure and revered in his romantic status as 'stud' of the school. It is then possible for some children to try on Other non-hegemonic identities without being subjected to the derogatory labelling that usually accompanies such performances.

To understand the complex relationship of what Thorne (1993) has termed gendered 'border crossings', I have drawn upon Davies and Harre's (1991) dual notion of 'reflexive' and 'interactive' positioning. *Reflexive positioning* refers to children as active agents who position themselves. *Interactive positioning* refers to how children are positioned by others through social interaction as gendered (and classed, racialised, sexualised and aged) beings. As Pete's identity-work has illustrated, locating one-self as Other (reflexive positioning) does not necessarily mean that he is positioned subordinately as Other by his peers (interactive positioning). As I will go on to illustrate in the next section, the children who were routinely marginalised were those actively investing in non-hegemonic ways of doing gender/sexuality and were recognised and subordinately positioned by others as such. They were thus interactively and reflexively positioned as Others. Indeed, there were some complex relationships between what I have conceptualised as Othering, doing Other and being Other in relation to children's constructions of their gendered identities (outlined below):

Othering: the daily performances engaged in by all children to delineate their particular gender/sexual identity (in relation to what they are not) and the means by which some genders are constructed as 'normal' and others as 'abnormal'.

Doing Other: the ways in which some (usually dominant) girls and boys could try on and temporarily engage with Other 'non-hegemonic' femininities, masculinities and sexualities.

Being Other: the ways in which girls and boys consistently located themselves and were located by others as 'different' from hegemonic and other dominant forms of masculinity, femininity and sexuality.

The girls and boys at the centre of this chapter are those who inhabited the subject position 'being Other'. Through daily interactive and reflexive positionings they became recognisable as gendered 'outsiders', as Jenna remarks when she said in one of my first interviews with her: 'we're not like most girls and boys'. Almost unbeknown to Jenna, there are plenty of children who do not feel like 'most' girls and boys and who resist gender and sexual norms (see Davies 1993; Thorne 1993; Connolly 1998; Francis 1998).

Is anyone like 'most girls and boys'?

Over one-third of boys and one-quarter of girls were positioned and positioned themselves as Other to the hegemonic heterogendered scripts that subsequently enabled other children to establish their own identities as 'dominant' and 'normal'. They all reported being routinely teased, excluded and humiliated for choosing not to invest in and project (and thus directly challenge and resist) dominant and hegemonic forms of 'age-appropriate' (hetero)masculinity and (hetero)femininity. However, where boys' gendered transgressions provoked feminised (e.g. 'sissy' and 'girl') and (homo)sexualised (e.g. 'gay', 'bender') name-calling, girls' gendered border crossings were never homosexualised. They were, however, sometimes masculinised ('she's like a boy') or given a freakish label, such as 'weirdo'. Derogatory homosexual terms such as 'dyke' and 'lesbo' had not entered the verbal repertoire either at Tipton or at Hirstwood (although see Buckingham and Bragg 2003). The ways in which their Otherness was defined, however, varied more for the girls than for the boys.

There were two friendship groups of boys: one at Tipton (four boys) and one at Hirstwood (six boys) who all, as 'non-footballers' (during the first half of the year), rejected the most obvious route to demonstrating their allegiance to a hegemonic masculinity. Moreover, engaging in studious behaviours rather than 'messing about' in class further reinforced their gendered Otherness (particularly at Tipton, where high-achieving boys were notable by their absence). In contrast, the girls' gendered and sexualised Otherness involved rejecting (Hirstwood) or failing to embody (Tipton) the emphasised 'girlie' heterofemininities and appropriate participation in the boyfriend/girlfriend circuit prevalent at both schools (particularly Tipton). There was, however, a marked difference between the two schools. For most of the girls at Tipton it was their rejection of 'good pupil' (e.g. the 'conscientious', 'hard-working' and 'obedient' school-girl) with their 'loud', 'disruptive' and sometimes violent classroom behaviour that set them apart from acceptable school-based femininities (see Skelton and Francis 2003) – behaviours incidentally that bolster boys' masculinity within a discourse of 'messing about' or 'rough and tumble play' (Chapter 4). In contrast, for the four girls at Hirstwood, it was their goody-goody behaviour and academic flair and success, combined with their anti-girlie image, that in the eyes of their predominantly 'girlie' peer group represented a failed and aberrant femininity (see Renold 2001a). Whether they were engaging in conformist (academic) or rebellious (masculinised) femininities, without the projection of a normative heterosexualised or emphasised femininity, girls were positioned outside legitimate 'subjects of girlhood' (see Hey 1997: 84).

Pushing at the boundaries of (hetero)normative gender was a risky business with some high social and emotional costs and consequences. Indeed, all of the children in this chapter were subjected to a range of heterosexist practices (e.g. gender-based and sexualised bullying) which play a significant part in maintaining the presentation of hegemonic heterosexuality within acceptable gendered boundaries (Hinson 1996; Renew 1996).

Queering gender and sexuality

Previous chapters have already illustrated how heterosexism, as a pedagogy of heterosexuality, is 'used against those children and young people who do their gender in ... non-traditional ways' (Hinson 1996: 235) and thus used as a means of creating and maintaining (hetero)sexual hierarchies. Bearing this context in mind, this section will explore further children's capacity to mobilise and trouble the categories of sexuality, gender and age in fluid and contradictory ways. In other words, it will focus upon children's capacity to queer normative genders and sexualities. The first scenario tells the story of Jo (working-class, high-achiever) at Tipton and Kelly (middle-class, high-achiever) at Hirstwood (introduced in Chapter 5) who trouble the traditional submissive and passive role of 'girlfriend' (adopted by some of their peers). The second scenario explores the queering of masculinity by a group of predominantly middle-class boys (of varying academic ability) at Hirstwood and three boys at Tipton (one working-class low-achiever and two middle-class high-achievers). The third story explores the 'fugitive' element of a marginalised masculinity in the ways boys seek out safe and often private hideaways to escape the gender binary and gender stereotypes of macho masculinities.

Girls as powerful sexual Others

Both Jo (Tipton) and Kelly (Hirstwood) located themselves and were located by their peers as gender misfits. Neither embodied the 'girlie' culture in terms of fashion and preoccupation with body size and they were regularly described as 'weird' (Jo) or 'baby-ish' (Kelly), particularly for their continuation to play 'fantasy games' (I would often observe Kelly playing 'ponies' with younger junior girls). While their location as gendered Others rendered them romantically undesirable by those further up the gender/sexual hierarchies, both girls actively pursued marginalised boys (described above) as potential boyfriends in ways that their peers thought betrayed 'acceptable' codes of practice: not only in their methods of courtship, but in the ways in which they related to their boyfriends. Jo engaged the kinds of 'predatory' behaviour described in Chapter 5 by almost stalking her boyfriend, William. She would chase him round the classroom, follow him round the yard at playtime and pester him for kisses. In fact their 'relationship' was particularly turbulent and sometimes physically violent, as the extract below describes:

SCHOOL: TIPTON

(Note: Jo is at least one foot taller than William)

ER:	So Jo how are things with you and William?
Jo:	All right (smiling).
Amanda:	She whacked him the other day and he had a red mark like a hand shape/
Jo:	That's because he comes round my house and he does this thing with a pipe cleaner ... he takes these little bits off and goes like that (strokes her hand across her cheek) and I got these cuts straight down here (laughing)
Jane:	Eeer/
ER:	He did that/ to your face?
Hayley:	You always hit him, all, all the time
Jo:	Yeah (giggles).
ER:	So you slapped him?
Jo:	Yeah I slapped him/
ER:	Coz he made a mark on your face?
Jo:	Yeah, coz/
Hayley:	He had a hand mark on his back/ (almost defending William)
Amanda:	She slaps him all the time/
Jo:	He hits me (defensive tone)
ER:	So if he hits you, you hit him back/ or do you hit him and he hits you back?
Jo:	Yeah, ... no he hits me and I hit him/ back
Amanda:	If he thumps you though you don't think you'd want normally to keep hitting him do you?
Jo:	(Laughs and nods)
ER:	You like that do you?
Jo:	He doesn't but I do/
ER:	You like hitting him?
Jo:	Yeah/

Jo's violent behaviour towards William (which is framed both in terms of defence ('he hits me and I hit him back') and pleasure ('I enjoy hitting him') was not an isolated practice. Kelly used to hit her boyfriend Simon and stamp on his toes. When he terminated their relationship Kelly left him an anonymous letter in his tray saying '*Watch it, I'll get you*' and continued her threats to kick him and scratch him with her 'super sharp nails'. To some extent both these cases illustrate how some girls were transgressing and transforming conventional heterosexual expressions and performances. While Kelly's actions demonstrate a refusal to be subordinately positioned as a weak and passive 'dumpee', Jo's physically turbulent relationship with William echoes much of the boys' play-fighting practices, albeit with a romantic twist. However one interprets these scenarios, both Jo and Kelly's assertive and aggressive 'relationships' certainly make more complex previous accounts (e.g. Davies 1993: 136) of girls' heterosexual engagements as predominantly fragile and vulnerable. They also highlight how some girls draw upon their physical capital at this age to undermine hegemonic heterogender identities and relations and seek out ways in which they can momentarily position themselves as a powerful sexual Other. Jo and Kelly's stories also reinforce the idea that pushing at the boundaries of femininity and (hetero)sexuality does not signify powerlessness in any simple sense.

Humour and boys' queering of (hetero)masculinity

The next two extracts offer one of the few examples of how boys use humour: not as a reinforcer of masculinised practices and subjectivities (see Chapter 6), but as a way of parodying and subverting conventional gender and sexual dichotomies. The first extract highlights Stuart's attempt to win back his volatile and fragile friendship with Damien through their shared interest in (homo)sexual story-telling. The second extract offers a window onto boys' early sexual games and fantasies.

SCHOOL: TIPTON

ER:	Are you two still friendly with Stuart now? (they had 'fallen out' a number of times that week)
Damien:	We're about the same.
ER:	Before/
Damien:	He's OK.
Stuart:	Am I OK when I make you laugh Damien? ... Like what's that door (Damien laughs) it's yellow, it's made of metal, and it's gonna jump on top of you (he screams and I ask him to try and 'keep it down a bit') ... it's got glass on it and there's a padlock on it and there's a silver knob on it and it's gonna jump on top of you and the knobs gonna wiggle (Damien is in fits of laughter along with Murray and William)
Murray:	Here we go again (rolls his eyes).
Damien:	He told that one on the Lake District about the green door.
Stuart:	It's green, it's hard, it's wiggling and it's going to jump on top of you (high pitched screaming and laughter)

★★★

Toby and Steven tell me that some of their favourite games when they were in Year 4 (age 9) were fantasy games and they still play them today. I ask them what did they used to play when they were younger. Steven replies: 'Well we used to play one game where we were in my bedroom and we made a van out of stuff. We used to pretend that we broke into the school using the van and drove into the playground to kidnap the girls we used to fancy at the time ... after we got them into the van we pretended to have it off with them on the bed'. Steven then continues to describe that they used to act 'having it off' with each other. One of them would pretend to be the girl and one the kidnapper. At this point, Simon interjects with 'so did I' and informs the group that he and his best friend used to play the same game at home. They all fall about laughing (at the coincidence? Or over the game?).

(Hirstwood: fieldnotes)

Collectively, these extracts draw upon playful sexual imagery of overt and covert phallic ('door knob'), patriarchal (the boys' coercive and dominating actions in the van) and sexually violent (hijacking and 'rape' of the 'young girls' in 'the van') discourses. Stuart, for example, in his humorous description of how the 'door knob' will 'tickle and wiggle' into (?) Damien evokes an imagery of penetrative same-sex behaviour. Steven and Toby, in the second extract, lace ostensible 'heterosexual' activity with a homoerotic twist as they express and perform their private heterosexual fantasies (with each other) in the privacy of their bedrooms (yet telling me and each other in the context of the classroom – see Renold 2002a).

The second extract, in particular, potentially gives rise to a number of queer readings. On one level the boys could be trying on and exploring 'gay' desires/subjectivities but positioning their performance in (socially validated) heterosexual discursive practices. Or, they could simply be practising 'heterosexual' acts with imaginary future girlfriends in mind. Alternatively, these boys could have just been exploring and experimenting with their emerging awareness and experience of sexualities, bodies and gender boundaries – and perhaps the power positions within the 'role' they enacted (coercive male, passive female). While it is perhaps all too easy to superimpose adult sexual representations and categories (e.g. 'gay' or 'homo-erotic') to make (adult) sense of the boys' sexualised storytelling, I do feel that to some extent the boys are involved in both trying on or practising 'older' sexualities and enjoying producing and reflecting upon their own junior sexual cultures and creating their own subversive sexual humour – whatever those 'sexualities' may be/come. They may also be gaining some pleasure in the temporary transformation of their ascribed powerless status as gendered and sexualised Others. Unfortunately, I couldn't explore issues of interpretation and meaning with the boys further at the time because the interview was interrupted by the school bell signalling the end of break and the classroom quickly returned to (and was re/produced as) a heteronormative pedagogic space. It was also too sensitive a subject to raise for discussion at a later date and the boys themselves didn't return to it (see Renold 2002a). What the interview extracts do perhaps lend themselves to is a feminist poststructuralist (and queer) reading of gender and sexual identity construction (see Davies 1997) insofar as the boys quite freely performed and seemed to delight in playing around with multiple and contradictory gender, sexual and generational subject positions.

Boys, intimacy and safe spaces

Finding and inhabiting spaces that disrupt the disciplinary gaze of the school in which gendered norms and behaviours are policed and maintained comes at a cost. For a minority of boys, however, it was obviously desirable and worth pursuing as the following two fieldnote extracts at Tipton illustrate:

> Peter, Damien and Murray have offered to tidy up the classroom and are staying in this playtime. They are not doing much tidying though – they are playing on the computer. I notice that they are behaving very differently now that they are on their own. They are not quiet or subdued, but are openly joking and laughing with each other. I overhear Damien tell the others: ' I like it in here, it's much quieter and you can do what you like'. They are huddled together, leaning over the computer. Damien reaches over and strokes Murray's hair. Murray smiles at Damien and looks back at the computer. They have never interacted this closely before. In fact, I have never observed such tender physical intimacy free from teasing and ridicule.
>
> (Tipton: fieldnotes)

★★★

> Damien, Mark and Murray spend another playtime in 'the environment corner'.[1] They have been telling me that it is a place they can go to where no other children are allowed. Damien tells me that it is a safe place where they can talk about what they want without 'the bullies cornering us'. They have spent most of the spring term here.
>
> (Tipton: fieldnotes)

As gender fugitives, retreating to the secluded and private environment area in the school grounds was a common strategy used by the boys at Tipton. It legitimately enabled the removal of themselves from the physical spaces occupied by hegemonic and wannabe hegemonic boys. Both groups of boys in my study, as outlined earlier, also reappropriated the classroom at break-times, usually under the guise of continuing with their class work or helping the teacher in some way. However, their motivation to occupy these spaces involved more than seeking out a safe retreat or hideaway. The privacy afforded the boys at these times and in these contexts offered them key moments to engage and interact in non-hegemonic ways – particularly in the 'trying on' and embodiment of 'soft' and 'intimate' masculinities, which in any other context (particularly within the high surveillance of the playground, which is the key arena for the posturing of hegemonic masculinities) would not have been possible.

Strategies of survival and the maintenance of Other gendered subjectivities

All of the girls and boys who experienced sustained gendered and sexualised bullying highlighted the futility of the teaching and ancillary staff in either a supportive or preventative role. The most common 'advice' reported by the boys from staff on playground duty was to 'keep away' and 'ignore them'. However, as Simon says, this didn't prevent some of the more targeted bullying because 'you walk away to the other side of the playground and they just follow you'. Unfortunately, previous experience led many of them to abandon the idea of informing a teacher well before they entered Year 6:

SCHOOL: HIRSTWOOD

Neil: (bullied for lack of football skill and interest) I used to 'tell' (the teachers) in Years 4 and 5, but they just used to say 'stop telling tales'.

SCHOOL: TIPTON

Julia: (bullied for being 'fat') I used to tell my mum and she goes in and tells Mrs Church (deputy head teacher) and Mr Edwards (head teacher) but they never did anything, so we've just given up on that.

Many of the girls reported confiding in, and being supported by their 'mums' (and older sisters) in ways that they said made them 'feel better'. Most of the boys, however, either kept the fact that they were bullied to themselves, or found they were supported in ways that only served to reinforce the very macho forms of hardened masculinity that they were trying so hard to resist (e.g. fighting):

SCHOOL: HIRSTWOOD

Graham: My dad told me to stick up for myself, but he doesn't know them like I do (almost in tears).
Simon: If I do tell my mum and dad, what happens is, coz my dad, he teaches me some moves, he teaches me how to block, by putting two arms in front of me.
[...]

Simon: ... and if I do get into a fight and I tell my mum and dad and say 'well I just thumped them and I just ran off', my dad says 'so you won the fight then' and I go 'yeah' (unconvincingly) and my mum and dad go 'good for you' (big sigh)

Later in the interview Graham and Neil highlight a further paradox regarding intervention when they explain that staff on playground duty only 'come over' when they are 'crying' or 'lying on the floor'. However, the very act of crying leaves them open to more verbal abuse ('you wimp'):

SCHOOL: HIRSTWOOD

ER: Could you tell the dinner ladies about this or don't you/
Graham: No I don't.
ER: Why not?
Graham: Coz they won't really bother.
[...]
Neil: You /need to be crying before they take any notice
Graham: They (other boys) call you a wimp then.
Simon: You have to be either crying or lying on the floor with loads of people round you.
ER: For?
Simon: To get any attention.
[...]
Graham: I feel like crying but I I I just called a baby if I do cry

Some girls and boys did achieve some success at physically retaliating. Rick, for example talked at length about his strategy to 'hit them on the back and then run away'. Jo and Marie used their chunky platform shoes and height (as the tallest girls in the school) to stamp hard upon on the toes of one of their frequent tormentors.

Working the discourse: power as/of resistance

The most common and perhaps most successful form of retaliation was discursive. Many girls and boys demonstrated a deep awareness of the power relations at play in the very gendered discourses which marginalised and subordinated them. They were thus able to 'turn the tables' on their attackers in quite sophisticated ways:

SCHOOL: TIPTON

ER: What do they call you?
Rachel: Fatso and fat slob, and fat (she mouths the word 'bitch').

ER:	Fat?

ER: Fat?
Rachel: Fat bitch and stuff like that.
ER: Who does?
Rachel: Adrian/ and Liam
Georgina: Adrian, I find /really easy to get along with.
Rachel: Liam and Aaron sometimes does that and Martin.
ER: Do they?
Rachel: Yeah.
ER: What do you say back to them?
Rachel: I just say, 'I may be fat but at least I'm not ugly, and I can diet'

Rachel, Julia and Jenna (Tipton) were regularly teased by a number of boys for their body size with comments such as 'fatso', 'fat slob' and 'fat bitch'. Rachel's counter attack to one boy, 'Well I may be fat, but at least I'm not ugly and I can diet' symbolises her refusal to passively endure being subordinately positioned by his comment. It also captures her ability to draw upon a discourse of resistance in a way that enables her to take on a more powerful and agentic position. Her comment implies that yes, she 'may be fat' but that is her choice and she can change her weight and 'diet' if she wants to. By positioning her perpetrator as 'ugly' she fixes his undesirability by implying that he *cannot* change his face in a way that she *can* change her body-size (as boys don't wear make-up and cosmetic surgery has an age of consent). She thus inscribes herself with choice and agency in which *she* now has the power to name and shame.

One could argue that Rachel has been able to mobilise the ways in which discourse as power can operate as a point of resistance (Foucault 1978: 101) and to great effect. I am not suggesting that she wasn't upset by these comments or that she even believed she could change or was happy with the way she looked. What this brief scenario illustrates, however, is how children who endure the kinds of gendered taunts and teasing that Rachel and her friends routinely experienced are not automatically placed in a position of passive powerlessness. Neither are they on a fixed emotional trajectory of oppression and marginalisation. While discourses clustered and congealed to give an appearance of fixity (and thus cultural hegemony) there were many examples and practices in which dominant discourses were undermined and exposed as both fragile and illusory.

Producing counter-gender/sexual politics: subverting and reinforcing hegemonic norms?

During the research process, the group interviews were often hijacked by the more marginalised children as a kind of forum for the enactment of a critical gender and sexual politics in opposition to the hegemonic ways of being a 'boy' and a 'girl' in their respective schools. We have already seen in Chapters 3 and 5 how Julia and her friends often used the interviews to articulate a powerful critique of the heterogender hierarchies which frequently positioned them as gendered and sexual outsiders (Others). The following extract reveals how boys also (at Hirstwood) used the group interview to debate the inequities and injustices of inhabiting the category 'boy' which they felt prevented them from engaging in behaviours, activities and popular culture which were deemed 'feminine' or only suitable for 'girls'.

SCHOOL: HIRSTWOOD

Simon: The school isn't free anymore now that we've got erm those Year Sixes, like Sean.

ER: What do you mean it's not free?

Simon: Well it's just that you can't say what you used to be able to say. Like erm, like go up to someone like Ryan and go 'Oh I like Michael Jackson, how about you?' and he'd go 'Michael Jackson' (laughs sarcastically) I like Guns and Roses better than that duuuurrr' ... and bla bla bla.

ER: So you can't be open about what you like?

Simon: Yeah you can't/ you can't ...

Toby: You can't like any of the soft music coz they, like Michael Jackson/ used to be used to be/

Simon: Coz they think they're big, they think they're big and they can control/ other people.

[...]

Simon: Yeah which makes you try to erm try to not like what you do like.

ER: Does it?

All: Yeah/

Toby: They used to like Michael Jackson and Meatloaf

Simon: Yeah Ryan, erm there was this group and we used to sing one of the Meatloaf songs in the playground and Ryan used to sing it with me and now he just thinks Meatloaf is kind of like a flower, kind of really stupid and dumb and everything.

Neil: Yeah/

[…]

Jay: The girls are always/

Simon: The girls act differently, they kind of make fun of you/

Jay: The girls/

Toby: The girls like the music/ we like

ER: So they like the stuff you like?

Toby: Y/eah.

Simon: Precisely.

Jay: And just because they're girls and we're boys doesn't make us any different. Why can't we support, like erm lets say I like Boyzone or something like that, why can't we like them? ... It's not fair on us/ just because we're not girls, then we can't like it

[...]

Simon: Like me, and Toby, likes Whitney Houston, there's nothing wrong with that, and some of the girls do, but Ryan and that don't pick on the girls.

ER: For liking Whitney Houston?

Simon: Yeah, because there's there's no law in anything that boys can't like Whitney Houston.

With the increasingly visible ways in which girls moved between 'masculine' and 'feminine' subject positions without getting 'picked on', Simon and his friends could only see as far as their *own* struggles and the unequal power relations at play in the marginalisation of their *own* 'non-hegemonic' masculinities. From their perspective, girls not only 'made fun of them' but were able to engage in a culture without penalty in a way they could not. Furthermore, while the boys' gender politics offered up possibilities for them to interrogate the stylised masculinist practices that seemed to construct gendered symbolic laws in which only girls can like 'Whitney Houston' or 'Boyzone', they still needed to project their sense of 'boy-ness'. For most of them, (with the exception of William and Simon) the main ways in which they did this was detaching themselves physically and emotionally from girls and femininity. Girls were not only generally avoided but many of the group interviews took on quite a misogynistic streak.

Over the year, it became apparent that a large part of their gender-identity work as 'boys' was achieved through the denunciation of girls and women (e.g. girls in their class, in parallel classes and their mothers and sisters at home). More so than by other boys in the study, these boys described girls as 'weak' and generally 'inferior' to them, despite and perhaps precisely because their opinions and stories were continuously undermined by their everyday interactions with 'real' girls and powerful femininities. These boys were often picked on, humiliated and pushed around by both the dominant and marginalised girls in the class (see Chapter 5). As we have seen, the boys' interactions and relationships with the girls often placed them in a powerless position. And the more they were positioned as 'feminine', as 'failed males', or 'failed heterosexuals' the more they seemed to traduce the feminine and take back a little bit of power for themselves (see also Renold 2002c).

Where the marginalised boys constructed their sense of boy-ness through either avoiding the company of girls and/or attempting to construct girls and women as subordinate, the marginalised girls tended to deploy any discourse, whether feminist or sexist, to momentarily position others as powerless and re-position themselves as powerful in contexts where they were produced as subordinate or powerless. For example, some of the girls (particularly those like Jo, Jenna and Marie who were significantly taller and stronger than the boys in their class) would retaliate to physical attacks by physical counterattacks, fully aware that 'boys aren't allowed to hit girls'. On one occasion when one of the boys did physically defend himself, Jenna ran crying to one of the staff on playground duty and the boy was seriously reprimanded. At the same time all three girls were fully supportive of the idea that girls should not hit boys and boys should not hit girls, with Jenna stating that 'men should be gentleman' and 'girls should be lady like'. Thus, fighting back with the wider knowledge that boys cannot physically retaliate both disrupted and reinforced the discourse of weak and passive femininities. At the same time, engaging in physically violent behaviour only served to reinforce their gendered Otherness.

It seemed that the very discursive strategies drawn upon by boys and girls to transform their subordinate positioning often worked against them and ironically reinforced the very forms of hegemonic masculinity and femininity that marginalised their own alternative ways of doing boy and doing girl. What these children (especially the boys) had not developed yet was an aware-ness of (or concern for) the struggles and processes of marginalisation felt by the opposite gender – an empathy which could develop into a more sophisti-cated understanding of the ways in which non-hegemonic masculinities and femininities have the potential to intersect as social allies to the forces of hege-monic masculinity. As we have seen, however, they were critically aware of the social and emotional costs experienced by deviating from their own gender norms (as 'girls' or as 'boys') but were only able to sustain their non-hege-monic position through a strong friendship group, or what Lees (1993) has called a 'collective resistance' (see Chapter 4) – resistance which was both gen-dered and classed.

Collective resistance: the significance of gender, class and academic ability

The boys

There were two groups of boys, one at Tipton (William, Damien, Stuart and Murray) and one at Hirstwood (Simon, Neil, Graham, Jay, Rick and Toby) who all, at the beginning of Year 6, actively constructed non-hegemonic masculini-ties. In both schools this involved the rejection of football and fighting games, and generally detaching themselves from the company of girls. The level of shared solidarity and friendship between the two groups, however, differed markedly and there was a clear classed dimension to the core group of boys who were able to sustain a non-hegemonic masculinity.

The boys at Tipton, for example, did not enjoy the shared history of a close and supportive friendship experienced by the boys at Hirstwood. Rather, their 'friendship' involved a range of shifting loyalties and interests throughout Year 6. Such changeable group dynamics often led to mistrust, hostility, teasing and defensive interactions within group interviews and amongst themselves. Their alliance did not promote a safe and secure environment within which they could share and disclose experiences free from ridicule in ways created by the boys at Hirstwood. However, even for the Hirstwood boys, as the dominant classificatory system of football/non-football became more entrenched towards the end of Year 6, many of them were reporting an increased sense of loss and mourning for the 'freedom to play the games we want'.

By the last term, three out of the four boys at Tipton and two out of the seven boys at Hirstwood finally defected to the dominant peer groups and masculinities; some with more success than others. Success, it seemed, was strongly related to their social class positioning, academic ability and academic ethos of the school. All of the boys bar Stuart (see Chapter 4) were of low-average ability and working class. While this left a core group of middle-class high achievers at Hirstwood, with collective and shared solidarities for maintaining an alternative masculinity, Damien, at Tipton, the only boy persisting to be alternatively masculine, was on his own. Indeed, given the greater number of high-achievers and the strong 'academic' ethos at Hirstwood (in comparison to Tipton) it could be argued that the institutional production of discourses which made available 'softer' non-macho masculinities were more readily available. Perhaps if Stuart and William attended Hirstwood, they may have been in a stronger position to resist the pull and pressures of projecting the hegemonic masculinity operating at Tipton.

The girls

Collective resistance was just as important to the two groups of girls. They all actively subverted the conformist 'good student'/'nice-girl' discourses with their rule-breaking and persistent 'loud' behaviours (Tipton). They also regularly critiqued girlie obsessions to emulate the (hetero)sexualised 'thinning' femininities they saw in magazines and, of course, their preoccupation with boyfriends (Tipton and Hirstwood). However, such challenges only seemed possible to sustain (as we saw in the maintenance of the 'top-girl' subject position) though a shared resistance. Nowhere more apparent was this than in the swift shift of allegiance to a more dominant 'girlie' femininity by the 'new-girl' Janine who entered Miss Wilson's class in the final term of Year 6.

Janine's 'loud' and physically 'rough' behaviour was routinely commented upon by both the 'girlie-girls' and 'square-girls' in terms of its unacceptability. While she may have found a like minded peer group among the girls at Tipton, both in terms of her subversion of 'girlie' gender norms and in terms of her background (working class) and ability (low-achiever), she was very quickly ostracised by all her female classmates at Hirstwood:

SCHOOL: HIRSTWOOD

ER: So what else has happened since I've been away?
Anna: Janine.

Kate:	Oh yeah. Janine.
Anna:	I didn't dare talk about it before because she was there/
ER:	O/K.
Kate:	Janine's weird. She's dead rough, she keeps on grabbing people and whacking them/
Debbie:	God yeah/she pulls people's hair.
ER:	Did you tell her or/
Anna:	I didn't really dare I didn't, I didn't know what to say, I feel like just saying *'Janine, you're totally different from me, just get a life'*, but you don't dare/
Kate:	She's absolutely, she's dead rough and everything.
[...]	
Anna:	She's very different/
Kate:	I hope she gets on with someone at Hirstwood because I'm getting sick of her whacking everyone/
Anna:	Yeah/
Kate:	She's turning more, she's turning as if we was the boys/
Anna:	Yeah I know.

Within four weeks Janine had curbed her 'boy-ish', 'dead rough' behaviour, talked incessantly about 'boyfriends' in the group interviews, subscribed to *Sugar* (girl magazine) and engaged in a complete make-over to mirror the popular 'girlie' image. While such a radical and rapid transformation did not fool her peers, she became less ostracised and developed friends with a couple of other wannabe 'girlies'.

Rejecting 'girlie' femininities for the 'square-girls' at Hirstwood also seemed only to be sustained by strong parental support and friendship, especially best friend dyads. Here, differences could be diffused as each friend reflected and to some extent confirmed the other's behaviour as normal, acceptable and legitimate. Valerie Hey explains:

> A girl's best friend is her best friend because (at least theoretically) girls can find the reflection of a self – confirmed as 'normal' since the face that smiles back is our own
>
> (Hey 1997: 137)

There were two girls, Penny and Alicia, who, more than any other girl in the study, openly and persistently rejected the dominant discourses which produced the 'girlie-girl' subject position so prevalent in their class. Despite constant teasing and sniggering from their female peers regarding their 'weird' clothes and 'show-off' academic identities in which they publicly presented themselves as the highly competent pupils they obviously were (e.g. answering and raising questions, finishing work first and asking for more), they were both unwavering in their convictions and academic femininities.

The slight twist in this story is that Penny and Alicia were identical twins and twins who had developed a bond so close that they independently described each other as 'best friends'. Thus, the reflection that Hey writes of, that confirms the other as the 'same' and enables us to construct difference as normality, is not only a metaphorical cultural mirror, but in the case of Penny and Alicia, a literal mirror image of themselves. The need for the other to sustain their particular form of gendered Otherness became most salient in a throwaway comment by Miss Wilson, their teacher. She told me how when one twin was away from school (e.g. due to illness) the sister twin would also stay home. True enough, they only ever appeared at school together or not at all. Collective resistance became a very literal and physical manifestation.

Just as the 'low-achieving' working-class boys towards the end of Year 6 actively took up more dominant masculinities, it was the low-achieving working-class girls at Tipton who began to crave a girlier femininity, enhance their romantic desirability and secure a boyfriend. However, where the boys physically split off and literally hung around the more dominant boys as wannabe hegemonic boys, the desires of the wannabe girlie-girls were assimilated within their existing peer groups. Competing femininities were accommodated in ways that competing masculinities were not. It was almost as if the boys had to be seen to physically switch peer groups and overtly signal the shedding of their non-hegemonic masculinities. With the non-hegemonic boys reappropriating the classroom at break time (Tipton and Hirstwood) or retreating to the secluded and private 'environment' area in the school grounds (Tipton) and thus removing themselves from the physical spaces occupied by wannabe and hegemonic boys, their absence (on the pitch) and presence (in the classroom) was significantly enhanced. Girls, on the other hand, seemed to appropriate a range of spaces and subject positions at playtimes without too much suspicion or penalty. For example, staying in class at break time as a 'class helper' (while not every girl's choice and subject to some ridicule) did not compromise their femininity because compliant and conscientious behaviour is normatively constructed as 'feminine' (Walkerdine 1990). The only girls able to sustain their resistance to the overt (hetero)sexualisation of femininity were the more conformist high-achieving middle-class girls. (Middle) class and (high) academic ability were thus key signifiers for both girls' *and* boys' construction and maintenance of non-hegemonic (hetero)masculinities and (hetero)femininities.

For the girls at Hirstwood, however, their rejection of girlie femininities and overt embracement of academic success not only positioned them as Other by their peers, but their achievements were undermined by their own class teacher who described one of the girls, Alicia, to me as 'bossy', 'over-confident' and 'not as clever as she thinks she is' (see Renold 2001a). In contrast, while the boys' non-hegemonic masculinities made them targets for a range of bullying behaviours, their academic identities as high-achievers were fully nurtured by their class teacher with a range of positive adjectives that not only drew upon notions of 'natural intelligence' (e.g. 'he was born clever, that one') but opened up rather than closed down their potential (e.g. 'he'll go a long way'). Indeed, little appears to have changed in the last 20 years in relation to the gendered constructions of achievement (see Walden and Walkerdine 1985, Browne and France 1985; Clarricoates 1987) as other more recent research has also highlighted (see Skelton and Francis 2003 for an overview). Drawing from the feminist literature on high-achieving young adults in the secondary school and university, one could even pessimistically speculate a trajectory of anxiety for middle-class girls as they wrestle with the pressures of 'expected' academic success and an increasingly looming compulsory heterosexuality (see Walkerdine *et al.* 2001; Lucey and Reay 2002; O'Flynn and Epstein 2004; Renold and Allan 2004). In stark contrast, the currently 'non-hegemonic' masculinity constructed by the high-achieving middle-class boys in the primary school is perhaps one version of an 'older' hegemonic masculinity that may pay dividends later in the secondary school (note Mac an Ghaill's (1994) 'academic achievers' and Redman and Mac an Ghaill's (1997) sixth-form 'muscular intellectuals').

Home and away

An increasing number of sociological and ethnographic accounts are beginning to map out the ways in which children themselves negotiate multiple identities and relations between, within and across different social and cultural contexts such as the home, the school, the park, the neighbourhood and the wider community (see Mayall 1994b; Alanen 2001; Christensen and O'Brien 2003). Recent educational ethnographies exploring issues of gender, race, disability and class have also been exploring how children's school-based identities are shaped and produced within the wider community context in which the school is located (Connolly 1998, 2003, 2004; Ali 2000, 2002; Skelton 2001; Benjamin 2002; Bhana 2002). All of these studies stress the importance of locale and how 'differing forms of masculinity and femininity will emerge as hegemonic in differing schools' (Connolly 2003: 125). With only a few educational ethnographies straying beyond the school gates, we know very little about how young children's gender and sexual identities are negotiated and lived out across different social contexts at the level of complexity of children's school-bound social worlds (although see Ali 2000 and Connolly 2004). Alas, my own study is no exception.

Like many other studies, however, conversations often turned to life and relationships with peers and family outside the school, as some of the chapters have already highlighted. Thorne (1993), in her exploration of boundary-maintenance and border-crossings in relation to the gender divide, noted that mobility between gendered subject positions and interactions within and between girls and boys increased in pupils' own neighbourhoods and in less crowded and public arenas. One of the reasons I have left an extended discussion of the relationships between neighbourhood and school until this chapter is because it was the children at the margins (the gender and sexual fugitives), more than any other children in the study, who time and again raised how very different their relationships with their classmates were in their streets and neighbourhoods.

One of the most enduring themes was the reports of the very different gendered interactions and feelings of injustice at being able to hang out with the more popular peer groups outside of school, but being avoided and excluded by the very same girls and boys once back inside the school. The following two extracts detail Georgina's relationship with her next door neighbour, Mandy (a popular 'girlie-girl') and Alison and Jenna's encounter with Pete (one of the most romantically desirable Year 6 boys, see Chapter 6):

SCHOOL: TIPTON

Georgina:	Me and Mandy get on OK because we live next door to one another and we're always chatting over the fence and that, but when she gets with Kirsty and that lot, when she's got one or two of their friends round they're OK, coz they're in Mandy's back garden and I live next door and they can't tell me to get lost coz I live next door, but when we're in school they can tell me to get lost.

★★★

Alison:	When it was chucking it down last night I went to Pete's and I had a game of football there and erm I ??? kicked the ball and it knocked down a vase
ER:	Oh no … who were you playing with again?
Alison and Jenna:	Pete.
ER:	From this class?
Alison and Jenna:	Yeah.
Alison:	It was really chucking it down, and he walked home with us and he said we could go in and dry ourselves off and have a cup of tea and that, so we did and we stayed there for about an hour.
ER:	Whose we?
Alison:	Kerry/ and I
[...]	
ER:	Did you enjoy it?
Alison:	Yeah, he gave me a ten nil head start so I had thirteen and he got sixteen (goals)
ER:	So if you can play it at home and enjoy it, why can't you play it on the field?
Alison:	It's embarrassing.

| Jenna: | Too many boys. |
| Jenny: | And most of them are violent. |

Whilst I was not surprised by the ways in which Mandy used Georgina as her 'contingency friend' (see Davies 1982) which she resurrected from time to time, I was initially shocked with Pete's invitation of a cup of tea and a game of footy to Alison and Jenna. According to my fieldnotes and observations, they had rarely spoken to each other in school (beyond the occasional class project). Almost in fairy-tale style, as the school clock strikes (marking the end of the school day) Pete, Jenna and Alison 'hang out' and enjoy a 'kick-about' free from sexual innuendo, gaming violence and the policing eyes of their peers (albeit with the knowledge that they return to their separate gender-ridden paths once inside the school gates!). Just as Wulff (1988) noted over 15 years ago in her ethnography of a group of 12–16 year olds in a working-class area of London, girls and boys of different ages and ethnicities would hang about together on street corners, but the moment they entered school grounds the same pupils separated by gender, ethnicity and age. Indeed, a core group of the girlie-girls and footballers at Hirstwood often returned to school after school hours and hung about with their class mates, sitting, chatting and 'mucking about' in ways not observed during school hours. The ways in which gender and sexual relations between and within groups of girls and boys are mediated across different social contexts is surely an area ripe for future ethnographic research.

Concluding notes

This chapter has been concerned with exploring the experiences of those girls and boys in the study who perceived themselves and were perceived by others as gendered and (hetero)sexual outsiders. A conceptual distinction was made between Othering, doing Other and being Other, to differentiate between the ways in which all children construct their gender identities in relation to Other gender identities (e.g. Othering). I also explored how some girls and boys could momentarily try on Other non-hegemonic masculinities and femininities without penalty (doing Other) from those children who consistently located themselves as marginal to dominant peer groups and gender/sexual identities, and were positioned by others as such (being Other). Over a third of children in the study persisted in actively pushing at and transgressing the boundaries of (hetero)normative genders and sexualities in a range of ways that both empowered and disempowered.

Contrary to Butler's thesis, their violation of gender/sexual norms was regularly punished (via a range of gendered and sexualised bullying). As we have seen in previous chapters, children were more than ready to expose the gaps, cracks and transgressions of others in ways that consolidated and reinforced rather than undermined or thwarted gender norms. Nevertheless, they developed a range of strategies to circumvent and maintain living out the category 'girl' and 'boy' in the ways that they wanted – peripheral to mainstream positions. The girls, in particular, were acutely aware of the power relations at play in the gendered discourses that subordinated them and were well practised in discursive retaliations (see also Gulbrandsen 2003: 119). Physical retaliations seemed to have mixed success in destabilising gendered power relations for both girls and boys, and tended to reinforce rather than destabilise or undermine the gendered and heteronormative status quo (with girls' sexual and physical dominance labelling them 'freaks', and boys' often failed attempts to fight back rendering them 'wimps' and in some cases 'gay').

Collective resistance (i.e. sharing and supporting each other's gender-agenda) and seeking out and appropriating safe spaces within school (especially for the boys) seemed to be crucial to cultivate and maintain non-hegemonic masculinities and femininities. Intersections of class and academic ability also seemed to impact upon the maintenance of non-hegemonic gender identities, with most of the working-class girls and boys ditching their 'difference' for more normative ways of being. Perhaps one of the most significant findings of this chapter was the ways in which the boys seemed to be defining and constructing their sense of 'boy-ness' almost entirely through disassociating themselves from and traducing all things feminine and female or 'girlie' (and particularly girls who troubled or transgressed normative gender binaries). This surely has serious implications for any gender equity programme encouraging boys to drop dominant ways of 'doing boy'. It seemed that neither the marginalised girls or boys had much awareness that their retaliations (e.g. girls' use of sexism, or boys' misogyny) effectively reinforced the very forms of hegemonic masculinity/dominant femininity that curtailed their own alternative versions. Perhaps by hearing each other's own stories of marginalisation (within and beyond the school gates) they could, through debate and discussion, begin to understand the knock-on effects of holding onto these feelings and challenge the oppositional gender trap they were caught up in (see Davies 1993). The ways in which the small group interviews were regularly hijacked by the more marginalised girls and boys to reflect upon and share their feelings of marginalisation (and power and pleasure of being 'different') suggest that some children are more than ready to share and perhaps hear each other's stories. Children's capacity to engage in some sophisticated critical gender and sexual politics is taken up in the final, concluding chapter.

Chapter 8

Thinking Otherwise about girls, boys and sexualities

Some concluding thoughts

Introduction

This book has explored children's everyday gender and sexual cultures, identities and relations in their final year of primary school in a semi-rural market town in the East of England. It has shown how children actively locate the school as a key social and cultural arena for creating, appropriating and redefining a range of spaces through which they can share, display, hide and ultimately negotiate their gendered and sexual selves. Focusing on the sexualisation of children's gender identities, one of the overarching 'findings' of the study was identifying heterosexuality as a pervasive and normalising force mediating and regulating children's school-based relations and relationships in ways that constrain and empower how they live out their gendered identities as 'girls' and 'boys'. In this concluding chapter, rather than provide a summary of each individual chapter, I have identified a number of salient points from the empirical chapters that expand upon this central theme. I have selected issues and topics that are relatively underdeveloped in the research literature by way of contributing to and articulating 'new' knowledge about boys, girls, sexuality and primary schooling. They include the following:

- Gender identities and relations are produced within a heteronormative framework of 'compulsory heterosexuality'.
- Children have, and actively negotiate, their own romantic/relationship cultures, produce and regulate their own (hetero)sexual hierarchies and experience their romantic/sexual selves in multiple and contradictory ways.
- Gendered and sexualised bullying and harassment are the means by which children create and consolidate gender and sexual norms.
- Resistance and challenges to normative gender and sexual discourses are most successful as collective enterprises, but tend to simultaneously subvert and fortify hegemonic masculinities and heterosexualities.
- Children are policed and police each other's sexual identities and practices through a range of often contradictory and highly gendered 'age-appropriate' discourses.

- Children's sexual cultures and identities are mediated by and cannot be separated from other social and cultural differences or from space (e.g. school context) and time (in 'childhood').

Collectively, these key 'findings' illustrate the reality and diversity of children's own gender and sexual cultures. The rest of the chapter is dedicated to outlining the limits, possibilities and challenges of current UK governmental sex education guidance. Particular attention is drawn to the contradictory advice offered by the DfEE's Sex and Relationship guidance on designing and delivering 'age-appropriate' sex education programmes that remain sensitive to and can effectively address children's own sexualities (e.g. sexual identity, sexual knowledge and sexual behaviour). Findings from this research suggest that 'starting from where children are at' is essential in meeting and supporting children's needs and experiences (see Ray and Jolly 2002: 5). But, it will involve some brave and radical disruptions in what we think children should or shouldn't know, be or do to fully reflect the pleasures, pressures and pains of children's own gender and sexual cultures.

Key 'findings' in brief

Gender identities and relations are produced within a heteronormative framework of 'compulsory heterosexuality'

All of the empirical chapters have explored the extent to which Butler's hegemonic heterosexual matrix features as a compulsory presence in the social and cultural worlds of girls and boys, as Year 6 pupils. Chapter 3 highlighted the ways in which the heterosexualisation of femininity was a strong and powerful feature of girls' school-based peer group cultures (Walkerdine 1999; Ali 2002; Russell and Tyler 2002) with over two-thirds of the girls in the research investing and policing each other's bodies as heterosexually desirable commodities ('for the boys' discourse). In contrast, the heterosexualisation of masculinity was more present by its absence with hegemonic discourses of masculinity revolving around violence and sport rather than any obvious notion of heterosexuality. However, with success at sports and being tough as key signifiers of romantic desirability, and deviation from or constant failure to achieve hegemonic forms of masculinity resulting in anti-gay and/or anti-girl jibes, boys as well as girls can be subject to and active agents of a heterosexual male gaze. Where boys seemed to have the choice to take up and embody 'older' (more overt) sexualised masculinities, girls, on the other hand, had to actively opt out. The compulsory sexualisation of 'older' femininities was already emerging as a defining feature of contemporary girlhood (Russel and Tyler 2002; Holland 2004), particularly in relation to dominant discourses of romance and romantic relations, as a pedagogy of compulsory heterosexuality.

Children have, and actively negotiate, their own romantic/relationship cultures, produce and regulate their own (hetero)sexual hierarchies and experience their romantic/sexual selves in multiple and contradictory ways

By the time children had entered Year 6, heterosexual games such as 'kiss–chase' (Epstein 1997) or having multiple boyfriends and girlfriends (Connolly 1998) had been superseded by a seemingly conventional and linear dating culture of 'fancying', 'asking out', 'going out' and 'dumping'. I write 'seemingly' because romantic relations at both Tipton and Hirstwood were produced through a number of competing discourses shaping and regulating children's social relations and peer group cultures.

First, *the feminisation of romance* was a pervasive and normalising discourse for girls and boys. Chapter 5 illustrated the centrality of girls to the production and maintenance of each school's boyfriend–girlfriend culture and the expectation and pressure for girls to project heteronormative romantic futures as 'girl-friends' or 'future girlfriends'. Chapter 6 explored boys' fear of romance and romantic relations and the paradox of being emotionally and physically intimate with girls as both masculinity confirming and masculinity denying.

Second, *multiple discourses of romance mediated girls' friendships and consolidated and created hierarchical peer group cultures.* Chapter 4, in particular, explored the ways in which friendships were formed in relation to whether girls perceived themselves to be 'girlie' (where 'romance' was constructed as central and important) or 'non-girlie' (where 'romance' was constructed as 'inevitable', 'immature', 'older', 'constraining' or just something that had to be endured). The ways in which girls (and boys) were active in policing their own and each other's sexual identities and practices through a range of 'age-appropriate' discourses is expanded upon below.

Third, *the subject positions 'girlfriend' and 'boyfriend' (and the practices of 'being dumped' and 'dumping') were seen to both shore up and undermine dominant masculinities and femininities* depending upon where girls or boys were positioned in gender and sexual hierarchies. Thus, being a girlfriend or boyfriend could be experienced as a source of pleasure and power, but also a source of anxiety, powerlessness and pain. Emerging and counter discourses of active and powerful female sexualities competed alongside conventional hegemonic heterosexual discourses and relations (such as the evolving subject position, 'professional boyfriend'). However, boys, as primary school 'studs', were not subject to the sexual double standard and the misogyny often thrown at girls' active participation and management of romantic relations.

Fourth, *discourses drawn upon to delay sexual activity and practice were more easily accessed by boys than girls and contingent upon the strength of the boyfriend–girlfriend culture local to each school.* Drawing upon developmental discourses of child/boyhood innocence, sexual immaturity (and thus 'older' sexualities as 'proper' sexualities) many boys could opt out of the local heterosexualised world of boyfriends and girlfriends. In contrast, by the end of Year 6, the only girls not participating in the boyfriend–girlfriend culture were a core group of 'middle-class' high-achieving girls.

Fifth, *discourses of heterosexuality and romance suffused many mixed-gender interactions, relations and intimacies from the classroom to the playground*. A central finding was how heterosexual discourses simultaneously constrained and enabled the development of boy–girl friendships. We also saw how some girls accessed discourses of romance to transform unequal power relations between themselves and the boys (Chapter 6).

Gendered and sexualised bullying and harassment are the means by which children create and consolidate gender and sexual norms

Over the course of the year, most children (girls and boys) articulated an ongoing struggle in trying to make sense of a range of contradictory discourses of what and how 10- and 11-year-old 'girls' and 'boys' should and should not do or be (e.g. 'hard but not too hard', 'tarty but not too tarty'). Many were acutely aware and offered powerful critiques of the conformative pressures, contradictions and ultimate impossibility of 'achieving gender' and being the 'right' kind of girl or boy. Each of the empirical chapters explored the ways in which normative and hierarchical (hetero)gender identities (i.e. the 'right kind') were maintained via daily evaluations and re-evaluations of their own and each other's gender and sexual performances. For girls, such evaluations tended to revolve around their investment and engagement with, or departure and rejection from, heterosexualised 'girlie' femininities. For boys, their evaluations centred upon their commitment to and competent display of hegemonic forms of masculinity (which at Tipton and Hirstwood could include various combinations of the following: football, fighting, girlfriends, (hetero)sex and anti-gay talk, misogyny).

Although all children experienced some form of gendered and sexualised teasing (see also Francis 1998), it was those girls and boys who actively persisted to subvert and resist dominant and hegemonic identities who were routinely targeted. These children were the main recipients of sustained forms of gendered and sexualised bullying and harassment (see Chapter 7). Indeed, discourses and practices of homophobia, (hetero)sexism and misogyny all operated to consolidate and maintain Butler's hegemonic heterosexual matrix whereby gender (masculinity/femininity) and sexuality (heterosexuality/homosexuality) are both hierarchically and oppositionally organised. A pervasive theme throughout all of the chapters was the ways in which some of the discourses and practices of hegemonic masculinity (e.g. discourses constructing femininity as powerless and polluting, and the practices of heterosexual harassment) were being accessed by an increasing number of girls as a way achieving a more powerful sense of self. The next section explores the possibilities for some quite powerful practices of resistance but in ways that both destabilise and reinforce gender/sexual norms.

Resistance and challenges to normative gender and sexual discourses are most successful as collective enterprises, but tend to simultaneously subvert and fortify hegemonic masculinities and heterosexualities

There were many girls and boys who were challenging discourses that they felt were constraining and pathologising the ways they wanted to do 'girl' or 'boy'. An emerging finding was how normative gender performances could be transgressed or challenged by girls and boys who were established players on the local boyfriend/girlfriend circuit. For example, the Tipton girls' attack on, and successful attempt to overturn, a range of sexist and heterosexist discourses seemed contingent upon their privileged status as 'ex-girlfriends'. Tom's (Hirstwood) ability to hang out with the girls without penalty (i.e. without being labelled a 'sissy', 'a girl') was enabled primarily in his role as 'professional boyfriend'. Thus, although it was possible to challenge a range of normative gender performances (e.g. hanging out with the opposite gender or fighting for equal rights) without being subordinated, such an endeavour was not readily available to those girls and boys positioned lower down the heterosexual hierarchy, although it did not stop children from trying. Over a third of children were actively choosing to blur and queer normative and age-appropriate gender and sexual binaries.

Chapter 7 was concerned with exploring how marginalised girls and boys (i.e. 'gender fugitives') were by far the most acutely aware and critical of the gendered/sexualised power relations subordinating them. They were less aware, however, that their strategies of resistance often tended to reinforce rather than thwart the gendered status quo. 'Collective resistance' (Lees 1993), realised through strong peer group support and thus a shared gender agenda, seemed to be a strong indicator of any sustained critique of gender/sexual hegemonic discourses (the significance of class, age and school ethos are discussed below). While we mustn't lose sight of the desire to disrupt and destabilise seemingly fixed gender/sexual/generational binaries, many of the 'border-crossings', regardless of assigned gender (e.g. 'male', 'female'), particularly towards the end of the school year, were one-way. That is, they were effectively re-configuring traditional discourses of powerful dominating masculinities and powerless dominated femininities (e.g. 'geek' to 'goalie' story). Of particular concern was how subordinate boys (i.e. those resisting and rejecting the dominant masculinity-making activities and practices of their peers) seemed to be constructing their gender identities as 'boys' (and thus reconfiguring their powerlessness) almost entirely through misogynistic discourses (e.g. 'girls are crap').

Children are policed and police each other's sexual identities and practices through a range of often contradictory and highly gendered 'age-appropriate' discourses

In Chapter 2 I introduced the concept 'sexual generationing' to make visible how discourses of 'age', and in particular the temporal duality of 'age-grade' (e.g. tweenager) and 'age-class' (as Year 6 junior school pupils), interact in multiple, yet often regulatory, ways to produce and police girls' and boys' sexual relations, knowledge and behaviour. Each of the empirical chapters explored the ways in which children drew upon and were subject to a range of developmental and age-appropriate discourses. For example, discourses of childhood (sexual) innocence could be used by some children to resist sexual activity (e.g. kissing), were deployed as a form of sexual bullying (e.g. by rendering a child sexually illiterate and ignorant) or were used to undermine children's experiences of sexual harassment (e.g. just mucking about). The notion of 'sexuality as play and preparation' was visible in the 'fun' side of children's sexual exploration and experimentation (e.g. couple's corner and other sexual games). But it also served to silence the more negative aspects of children's sexual(ity) relations (e.g. sexual teasing and physical harassment).

Similarly, discourses of 'sexuality as older' could be drawn upon to denigrate children's emerging sexualities by positioning them outside of 'age-appropriate' discourses, or drawn upon as a source of power and pleasure – all of which was a highly gendered process and contingent upon the local gender/sexual cultures operating within each school. The section above has already highlighted how, in contrast to boys, girls had to actively opt out of projecting overtly (hetero)sexualised femininities (although the misogyny of boys' sex-talk seemed at times to be a compulsory component of hegemonic masculinity). Indeed, girls' embodiment of 'older' sexualities and a more 'accelerated femininity' rendered them particularly vulnerable to a catalogue of derogatory comments, interventions and sanctions by teachers and their peers, not experienced by boys' 'trying on' of older sexualities. It was boys' deviation from 'age-appropriate' masculinities (e.g. playing fantasy games) that evoked gendered and (homo)sexualised insults. However, what constitutes 'age-appropriate' behaviour when it comes to gender and sexuality was continually contested and, as the next section illustrates, contingent upon a range of social, cultural and spatial factors.

Children's sexual cultures and identities are mediated by and cannot be separated from other social and cultural differences or from space (e.g. school context) and time (in 'childhood')

As Debbie Epstein and many other researchers have emphasised, the ways in which children learn and do gender/sexuality and, in particular, the patterns of inequality and power within such performances are inflected with other differences that 'make a difference' (Epstein *et al.* 2003). Although cultural differences, such as minority ethnic identities, and the power relations embedded and embodied in the racialisation of gender and sexuality have not been explored in this study (with all of the children occupying the more privileged powerful side of the binary White/Other), discourses of social class could be seen at work in the production and regulation of children's sexualities in a number of expected and unexpected ways. For example, although the boyfriend–girlfriend culture enjoyed a stronger presence at Tipton, it was the middle-class girls from Hirstwood who invested most in the more sexualised 'girlie' femininities (perhaps as a way of re-positioning themselves from the desexualised, thus de-feminised position occupied by the 'square-girls'). However, it was only at Tipton that I observed teachers directly intervening in girls' performance of sexualised 'girlie' femininities. Indeed, the uneven regulation of sexualised femininities at Tipton seemed to operate to maintain and rearticulate traditional 'working-class' hyper-heterosexualities (Hey 1997; Walkerdine 1997) with its 'boy-studs' and 'girl-tarts'. It was also at Tipton, however, that girls seemed to enjoy access to a more diverse range of femininities, infiltrate masculinist discourses and practices, and engage in more challenges and critiques to a range of sexist and heterosexist practices.

Nevertheless, (middle) class and (high) academic ability seemed to be key signifiers for both girls' and boys' sustained (individual and collective) resistance to heterosexualised femininities and hegemonic forms of masculinity (see Chapter 7), although what was hegemonic in one context may be subordinate and marginalised in another. For example, Tipton's more sexually active boyfriend–girlfriend culture would have possibly rendered Tom's 'just good friend' approach to romance at Hirstwood untenable. Deviation from (hetero)normative 'girlie' femininities also differed significantly for girls at Tipton and Hirstwood. At Tipton, it was loud, disruptive and violent behaviour. At Hirstwood, it was academic flair and success. Moreover, beyond the school gates, many of the hegemonic practices, so normalised and naturalised within the school, were disrupted further: from the seemingly rigid gendered and sexualised peer group hierarchies, to the striking up of mixed-gender friendships free from (hetero)sexual innuendo.

'Appropriate' guidance for 'appropriate' sexualities?: addressing the reality of pupils' sexual cultures

Ten years ago Peter Redman called for a conceptual shift from 'sex education', which focused upon biology and reproduction, to 'sexuality education', which focused upon 'the reality of sexual diversity' within pupils' sexual cultures and schooling processes more widely (Redman 1994: 143). Despite the continued emphasis upon marriage and reproduction which represents heterosexuality as an unquestioned norm, the latest sex and relationship guidance (DfEE 2000a) makes some headway in its message to teachers and governing bodies to be responsive to and support the reality of pupils' own sexual cultures. On 'sexual identity' and 'sexual orientation' the guidance states that:

> It is up to schools to make sure that the needs of all pupils are met in their programmes. Young people, whatever their developing sexuality, need to feel that sex and relationship education is relevant to them and sensitive to their needs.
>
> (p.12, para. 1.30)

The explicit reference to 'young people', however, fails to acknowledge that younger children are also dealing with issues of 'sexual identity'. Indeed, the guidance throughout seems to have a very specific age-appropriate childhood sexuality in mind. In an effort perhaps to maintain and protect the presumed sexual innocence of children, it advises schools on the need to develop 'age-appropriate programmes' (p. 9, para. 1.12) and avoid answering questions that a teacher feels are 'too old for a pupil' and thus constitute 'inappropriate' knowledge (p. 23, para. 4.5). Not only are some sexual knowledges banned from discussion, but all sexual activity, including any 'early sexual experimentation' within the period of childhood is strongly discouraged (see p. 5, paras 5, 7 and 9). On the 'rare occasion' that a primary school child might be 'contemplating sexual activity' (kissing?), 'this should be viewed as a child protection issue' (p. 31, para. 7.8). The continued emphasis on closeting children's sexual knowledge (as 'appropriate' or 'inappropriate') and constructing children as sexually innocent and ignorant highlights and reflects the unease within the DfEE (and 'adult' society more widely) of acknowledging children as sexual beings. Ironically, the only people identified in the guidance as 'finding it difficult to accept (their) children's developing sexuality' are parents and carers of children with special educational needs (p. 12, para. 1.27).

In one of the few ethnographic accounts of a primary school sex education lesson (Year 5) since the introduction of the DfEE's SRE guidance, Debbie Epstein illustrates just how disabling and disempowering working within the constraints of the preferred pedagogic practice can be for teachers and pupils alike. With the class teacher anxious and nervous about 'saying the wrong thing' (Epstein *et al.* 2003: 37) and thus straying from the prescribed guidance, Epstein describes a lesson that adds little to children's existing knowledge and provides 'no opportunity for any kind of real learning to take place', particularly in relation to responding to children's own concerns, knowledge and experiences. For example, children's accounts of 'bad' or 'dangerous' (hetero)sexual encounters, such as sexual harassment, rape and domestic violence were either quickly dismissed by the teacher or framed as experiences that only 'older' teenagers had. Lesbian and gay sexualities raised by the children within the context of 'rude' words or as terms of abuse went unchallenged (deriving partly from the teacher's fears of 'promoting homosexuality', under Section 28). Children's attempts to draw upon their own relationship cultures (e.g. exploring the gendered imbalance of power in heterosexual relationships) were not encouraged or developed. Moreover, the idea that striking up a sexual relationship 'maybe because it's fun' or because 'they both got drunk' or 'the man might like the women's … breasts or buttocks' were either ignored or deemed as 'wrong' answers with their emphasis on sexual attraction, desire and pleasure (variables that have no place in a document that stresses morality and health as its key aims).

Reflecting upon the effects of following constraining, normative and narrow curricula, Debbie Epstein concludes:

> The problem was not that they were incompetent or illiberal or malicious teachers, but that the prescribed approach is pedagogically bankrupt and incapable of offering children the kind of sexuality education from which they might learn and on which they might be able to reflect and build upon their own ways of understanding.
>
> (Epstein *et al.* 2003: 50)

However, what Epstein's analysis does reveal is that the Year 5 children she observed were more than capable of making connections between and drawing upon their own and other (including 'adult') relationship cultures and 'developing' sexual identities and knowledges, from *EastEnders* storylines to their local boyfriend/girlfriend cultures (see also Buckingham and Bragg 2003 and Halstead and Reiss 2003). As this study also illustrates, however, the 'reality' of children's own relationship cultures and sexual knowledge blurs and problematises many of the boundaries set up in the 'official' SRE guidance around what children should or shouldn't know, learn and experience.

Starting points

Kenway *et al.* (1997) stress the importance of using pupil's own experiences as 'starting points' for the development of any sex education or gender equity programme. As we have seen, the DfEE's (2000a) own sex and relationship guidance also emphasises the importance of designing and delivering a sex education programme that can connect with and is thus both relevant and sensitive to children's needs. However, when such 'starting points' are difficult to achieve and define it is often up to the research community to find out and explore 'what's happening' (Mac an Ghaill (1994: 188). By foregrounding children's own accounts of 'doing' gender and sexuality, this research has generated a cluster of 'starting points' and raised a number of issues and experiences often ignored, denied or overlooked by policy and practice.

The Sex Education Forum's fact sheet (Ray and Jolly 2002) on the development of sex and relationship education for primary age children demonstrates that governmental guidance does not in itself prevent teachers or head teachers from working collectively and effectively to address many of the issues outlined in the 'key findings' above. For example, Ofsted has produced a range of learning outcomes derived from both the SRE and Personal, Social and Health Education (PSHE) curriculum which state that by the end of Key Stage 2 (11 years old) pupils should be able to:

- Express opinions, for example about relationships and bullying
- Listen to and support others
- Respect other people's viewpoints and beliefs
- Identify adults they can trust and who they can ask for help
- Recognise their own worth and identify positive things about themselves
- Recognise and challenge stereotypes, for example in relation to gender
- Recognise the pressure of unwanted physical contact and know ways of resisting it

and know and understand:

- The many relationships in which they are all involved in
- How the media impact on forming attitudes
- About keeping themselves safe when involved with risky activities
- That their actions have consequences and be able to anticipate the results of them
- About different forms of bullying people and the feelings of both bullies and victims
- Why being different can provoke bullying and know why this is unacceptable

(Ray and Jolly 2002: 5)

So, for example, if a school wanted to address, and combat, some of the gender-based bullying and anti-gay talk and behaviours experienced by the boys in this study because they dared to deviate from hegemonic forms of masculinity, they would be assisted by a number of policies and guidance. Teachers could draw upon the DfEE's (2000b) anti-bullying pack for schools which offers detailed advice on how to prevent bullying because of perceived or actual sexual orientation alongside the DfEE's SRE (2000a) guidance which explicitly states that 'schools need to be able to deal with homophobic bullying' (para. 1.32). Supported (in theory at least) by Ofsted's learning outcomes above, class teachers could facilitate individual and group projects which invite children to critically reflect upon 'being different', 'challenging gender stereotypes', 'resisting peer pressure' and the 'impact of the media' in the production of hegemonic masculinity. Any one of these activities might generate a discussion about girls' desire for powerful masculinities, boys' struggles to access such perceived 'power' and the role of gender-based bullying in the production and reinforcement of gender and sexual norms. For schools that are committed to encouraging pupils to participate in the design and review of policy initiatives, teachers might also use children's experiences to develop not just their own sex education policy, but also their equal opportunities and bullying policies in ways that reflect how each policy overlaps on particular issues (e.g. gendered/sexualised teasing).[1]

In contrast, however, as Epstein *et al.* (2003) illustrated earlier, the same guidance and learning outcomes can be interpreted in such a way that defines and re-closets some behaviours as 'inappropriate' to discuss and raise with primary school children. Moreover, even if teachers recognised and wanted to address some of the gendered and sexualised teasing within and across boys' and girls' peer group cultures, many lack the training and confidence that such training can often foster (see Ivinson's (2004) discussion of 'tipping points'). Given that providing sex education in UK primary schools is not mandatory but left to the discretion of each individual school (section 352 (1) of the Education Act 1996), some teachers may find both time and resources for training in the area of sex and relationships hard to negotiate (see Warwick *et al.* 2002).

Endnote: learning from children, children learning from each other

It is not the purpose of this chapter to identify or propose what constitutes 'good practice' (see Ray and Jolly 2002; Welsh Assembly Government 2002; Halstead and Reiss 2003; Ivinson 2004). Rather, I want to stress that to support and legislate for not only the more damaging practices of misogyny, heterosexism and homophobia, but also girls' and boys' own 'hidden injuries and paradoxical pleasures of various, somewhat fluid, forms of dominance and subordination' (Kenway *et al.* 1997: 22), educational practitioners and professionals need to disrupt their own normalised assumptions about what constitutes 'age-appropriate', 'gender-appropriate' and 'sexually-appropriate' knowledge and behaviour. They then need to reflect upon the extent to which these assumptions are reinforced in their practice, both within the 'official' and informal school, and in their policy development (see MacNaughton 2000 on how such work can be achieved).

To better understand how girls and boys resist or reinforce heteronormative gender and sexual identities involves both privileging and taking seriously what children have to say about their experiences. It also means recognising how heternormative discourses can constrain their articulation and maintain their silence. Only by developing a sexuality education which speaks to and connects with children's own gender and sexual cultures can educational practitioners and policy makers fully support girls' and boys' individual and collective understanding of 'why they feel the ways they do, what it means for the ways they act and what to do about it' (Kenway *et al.* 1997: 30).

Exploring with and learning from children about the dangers and possibilities of resisting and transforming heteronormative discourses and practices will be no easy task against a socio-political backdrop of governmental and media moral panics around children, sexuality and gender (see Epstein and Johnson 1998; Epstein *et al.* 2003). However, this is a challenge that must be tackled head on if we are to radically transform the experiences of girls and boys who struggle everyday to conform to and perform within contradictory and constraining regulatory heterogendered scripts. While this might seem like an impossible task, if not an impossible fiction, we only have to reflect upon children's own capacity to point out and challenge the unequal power relations that govern and maintain normalised gender and sexual regimes within their own peer relations and identity-work (see also Frosh *et al.* 2002: 262).

Living within an adult-centric world, children are often the experts in understanding and experiencing first hand the distribution, use and abuse of power and privilege. As I hope this research has demonstrated, we (adults) can learn much from girls and boys themselves about the ways in which normative (hetero)sexuality and gender operate to position and re-position children in powerful and powerless ways. By the same token, boys and girls would benefit and indeed have a lot to learn from each other about the costs and consequences of investing in particular femininities, masculinities and sexualities. I want to end this book with a further 'starting point' and a final reminder of children's capacity to think Otherwise and critically interrogate and subvert the power relations at play in a culture that presumes and promotes compulsory and normative heterosexualities. From a discussion (with five girls) of how two eight-year-old boys have been derogatively labelled 'gay' and 'disgusting' by their peers for allegedly being caught 'hugging and kissing', Julia jumps to their defence with the following comment:

Julia: If it was sort of really weird for a girl to go out with a boy, what would you feel like if you wanted to go out with a boy? It wouldn't be very nice would it if everyone was saying to you 'urgh, that's so disgusting'. You should let them do what they want to do.

Appendix

Key to transcripts

…	brief pause
/	when a speaker is interrupted by another speaker
[…]	when material is edited out
(comment)	background information (including body movement, tone of voice, emotion, etc.)
???	inaudible responses
italics	to emphasise a word or phrase
" "	direct quotation within fieldnotes
★★★	to signal that the following transcript is from another interview

Notes

Chapter 1

1 The names of the teachers, children, schools and their locations have been changed to maintain anonymity.

2 I use the term 'sexuality' in its fullest sense, referring to both sexual practices/activities *and* sexual identities and the varied and diverse forms they can take. These include the full spectrum of physical and emotional experiences (e.g. desires, fantasies and pleasures) but most importantly an awareness that sexuality 'is always both material and social, since what is embodied and experienced is made meaningful through language, culture and values' (Holland *et al.* 1998: 23) and will shift and change over time (Foucault 1978).

3 Ironically, as the new social studies of childhood called for recognition of the child as 'being' (i.e. a subject in its own right) rather than 'becoming' (in an effort to move beyond reductive developmental approaches to rigid age and stage models of identity formation), recent social and cultural theory in late modernity has been busy decentring the 'subject' and theorising human identity from a given into an ongoing task (Hall and du Gay 1996; Bauman 2000).

4 Power, in the Foucauldian sense, then, is not conceived of as something that exists 'out there', rather, it is 'constituted in discourses and it is in discourses ... that power lies' (Ramazanoglu 1993: 19).

5 See Renold (2002a) for a discussion of the ethical issues and dilemmas (particularly in relation to renewed consent) when the focus of the research (children's gender relations) develops and changes (to children's gender and sexual relations).

6 Mindful of the debates and recent re-thinking around the fluidity and fragility of defining and categorising 'social class' (Crompton 1998) and sensitive to the ways in which cultural, social, material and discursive resources all play a part in the production of advantage (Skeggs 1997; Reay 1998), the terms 'middle class' and 'working class' are not adopted unproblematically. Rather, they are used primarily as a heuristic device to identify contrasting cultural/socio-economic backgrounds. Although I have primarily made sense of the data 'in terms of distinctive masculinities and femininities across their (children's) class differences' (Holland *et al.* 1998: 18), when 'class' is significant, as other studies have suggested (Pollard 1985, 1987; Clarricoates 1987; Davies 1993; Reay 1998; Skelton 2001; Connolly 2004) it is commented upon and made visible.

7 Children's 'whiteness' was not a visible signifier in their gender/sexual identity-work and relationship cultures and subsequently has not been problematised in the way that Anoop Nayak (1997, 1999) and others have called for.

8 King (1978: 8), for example, questions the possibility of 'understand(ing) the subjective meanings of very small children' and developed sophisticated techniques to avoid eye contact, to the extent that he hid in the Wendy House!

9 Denscombe (1995: 138) cautions that there can be 'problems of domination' in group interviews which can silence 'quiet' children. For example, one boy was particularly vocal in our first interview but almost totally silent when I unknowingly grouped him with an ex-friend/enemy. While, even *within* friendship groups, patterns of domination (talk and interruptions) were not uncommon, I would sometimes intervene and 'bring in' the quiet ones. However, where some would see this as a methodological failing of group interviews in its neglect to access all individual perspectives (e.g Denscombe 1995), I found the the power relations operating within the social climate of the group interview reflected and was thus illuminative of the power relations within the social climate/interaction within the playground and classroom (see Lewis 1992: 416).

10 I adopted a number of strategies aimed at subverting conventional power relations of adult-researcher/child-pupil which involved taking what Mandell (1988: 435) calls 'the least adult' role. While there was no getting away from not being like 'one of them' (see Epstein 1998), I spent as much time as possible 'being with' the children and thus distancing myself from significant adult others (e.g. teachers, classroom assistants, dinner staff, etc.) and focusing upon issues that they raised and deemed significant. As a consequence, the voices and influences of head teachers, governors (and indeed the childrens' own families) are relatively absent in the accounts and chapters that follow.

Chapter 2

1 In many ways and in many Western societies 'adult' has come to signify sex and the realm of sexuality (note the euphemism 'adult' for sexually explicit content in TV, books and films).

2 Both Tipton and Hirstwood had male head teachers.

4 See the Lesbian and Gay Employment Rights' (LAGER) 2004 newsletter for similar examples of the gendered and homophobic harassment and discrimination of gay and lesbian teachers in the UK and the impact of the 2003 European anti-discrimination Employment Directive on sexual orientation.

5 Best's (1983) research was conducted in a central Atlantic state in the United States.

6 Sometimes this involved genital rubbing between opposite gender and same gender couples (termed by the older children as 'fucking').

7 For discussions on the paraphernalia of contemporary boyhood see Chapter 4 (and Redman 1996; Connolly 1998; Swain 2002a).

Chapter 3

1 In her ethnography of 'mixed-race' children and identity, Suki Ali concludes that 'for the children at this age, "race" was less salient in their "reading" of attractiveness and desirability than their perceived ideas about sexual attractiveness' (2000: 237).

2 The term 'girlie' was initially coined by Miss Wilson (Hirstwood) to describe a large group of girls in her class who constructed their femininities through dominant (hetero)sexualised body and fashion discourses.

3 The term 'like' can denote both platonic and romantic intimacy (see Chapter 6).

4 During one interview discussing clothes and appearance, Jo instructs Hayley to tell me 'what your dad says when you get all your gear on'. Hayley replies, matter-of-factly: 'He says I'm a cheap tart'.

5 The re-fashioned femininities of the 'top-girls' strongly mirror the sartorial attire of their male peers and thus, by default, a particular version of masculinity (active, muscular/fit, competitive). Indeed, the girls' desire for unisex fashion neatly coincided with their desire to penetrate and participate in traditionally 'boys only' pursuits.

Chapter 4

1 Drawing upon the language of sexism and equal rights to protect what they considered to be their inalienable right as boys to play football, some boys took to calling (women) staff who enforced the ban, 'bitches'.
2 The decision not to intervene directly to break up the fight, but to intervene indirectly by informing a teacher was my attempt to maintain some kind of non-authoritative position within the school.
3 Although the label 'geek' is often used pejoratively to denote a boy's relationship to technology, at both Tipton and Hirstwood 'geek' was a generic term of abuse directed at boys who were overtly studious or openly pro-school. It was a term more commonly used at Tipton Primary, towards two high-achieving studious boys, Damien and Stuart, who stood out significantly amongst their low-average achieving male peers.
4 The ways in which some activities (e.g. body slams) can be framed as both 'play' and 'violence' present considerable difficulties for any school's anti-bullying policies.

Chapter 5

1 Being 'popular' was usually associated with presenting a coherent dominant femininity/masculinity (see Hatcher 1995; Gilbert and Gilbert 1998).
2 At Tipton, the sexualised teasing on borrowing a pencil was even more pronounced, as Sophie explains: 'Its like, a pencil is a boy's you know what, and a sharpener is a girl's you know what'.
3 While such a definition may be problematic given the multiple and sometimes conflicting interpretations of social interactions and accounts, it was the only working definition that I felt could capture the complexities and ambiguities of sexual harassment and which could differentiate beween children's 'welcome' or 'unwelcome' (boys' and girls') sexualised behaviour. However, it is also necessary to stress that the term 'harassment', while serving a useful analytic function as a concept and language of description, was not a term widely used by the children in the study. Consequently, it is not possible to explore the meaning that 'harassment', as a category of behaviour, has for them (although see Sunnari et al. 2002).

Chapter 6

1 Cracker is the title of a mid 1990s UK television crime drama series in which the central protagonist is a criminal psychologist.
2 I am using the term 'homophobic' to define those behaviours and practices which signify a fear of 'homosexuality' and the term 'anti-gay' to define talk and behaviour that signifies any negative sentiment regarding same-sex identities, practices or relationships. While there is obviously some overlap, differentiating 'homophobia' from 'anti-gay' sentiment offers a way of situating the realm of the unconscious within wider social and cultural relations (see Redman 2000 for a fuller discussion of the usefulness of the term 'homophobia' as an analytic tool).
3 This study did not set out to investigate boys' constructions and perceptions of 'gay' or other minority sexualities. As a consequence it does lack a sustained in-depth exploration of boys' views towards gay sexualities. Because of the sensitivity of discussing non-heterosexualities with primary school children, only the perspectives of boys who instigated discussions on gay sexualities were recorded, alongside observations of the ways in which boys deployed homophobic discourses in the everyday peer group cultures.
4 However, the pressure to maintain his high status position as 'professional' boyfriend (i.e. not single) revealed itself when, during a month in which he was not dating a girl from his own school, he constructed a fictitious girlfriend in another primary school.

Chapter 7

1 The 'environmental area' was a designated and bounded wildlife space that backed on to the concrete playground and grass playing field. It was a space in which children could volunteer to spend their breaktime planting, weeding, feeding the fish/pondlife, etc. It was not, however, popular amongst Year 6 boys (and most girls) who considered it 'work' as opposed to 'play' (or football which was how the majority of boys spent their breaktimes).

Chapter 8

1 The Welsh Assembly Government's (2002) guidance on 'sex and relationships education in schools' explicitly states that 'pupils themselves can also provide a vital contribution to the development of a sex education policy and programme, and their participation will help to create an ethos of involvement and openness'. Using contexts such as a school council or pupil forum (where available) pupils can discuss SRE in order to express their views and needs.

Bibliography

Adler, P.A. and Adler, P. (1998) *Peer Power: Pre-adolescent Peer Culture and Identity*, New Brunswick, NJ: Rutgers University Press.

Alanen, L. (1994) 'Gender and generation: Feminism and the "child question"', in Qvortrup *et al.*, (eds) *Childhood Matters: Social Theory, Practice and Politics*, Aldershot: Avebury Publishing.

Alanen, L. (2001) 'Explorations in generational analysis', in Mayall, B. and Alanen, L. (eds) *Conceptualising Child-Adult Relations*, London: Routledge.

Ali, S. (2000) '"Mixed race" children, identity and schools', unpublished PhD thesis, University of London, Institute of Education.

Ali, S. (2002) 'Friendship and fandom: Ethnicity, power and gendered readings of the popular', *Discourse: Studies in the Cultural Politics of Education*, special issue: Re-theorising Friendship, 23: 153–65.

Ali, S. (2003) 'To be a "girl": Culture and class in schools', *Gender and Education*, **15**(30): 269–83.

Allan, A. (2003) '"Clever girls": how they construct their gender identities', unpublished Masters thesis, Cardiff, University of Wales.

Aries, P. (1973) *Centuries of Childhood*, Harmondsworth: Penguin.

Ashley, M. and Lee, J. (2003) *Women Teaching Boys: Caring and Working in the Primary School,* Stoke-on-Trent: Trentham Books.

Askew, S. and Ross, C. (1988) *Boys Don't Cry: Boys and Sexism in Education*, Buckingham: Open University Press.

Ball, S. (1990) *Politics and Policy Making in Education*, London: Routledge.

Barter, C., Renold, E., Berridge, D. and Cawson, P. (2004) *Peer Violence in Children's Residential Care*, Basingstoke: Palgrave.

Bartky, S.L. (1988) 'Foucault, femininity and the modernization of patriarchal power', in Diamond, I. and Quinby, L. (eds) *Feminism and Foucault*, Boston: Northeastern University Press.

Bauman, Z. (2000) *Liquid Modernity*, Cambridge: Polity.

Bell, V. (1999) (ed.) *Performativity and Belonging*, London: Sage.

Bellous, J. (2002) 'Children, sex and sacredness', *International Journal of Children's Spirituality*, **7**(1): 73–90.

Benjamin, S. (2002) *The micropolitics of inclusive education: an ethnography*. Buckingham: Open University Press.

Benjamin, S. (2003) 'Gender and special educational needs', in Skelton, C. and Francis, B.(eds) *Boys and Girls in the Primary School,* Berkshire: Open University Press.

Best, R. (1983) *We've All Got Scars: What Girls and Boys Learn in Elementary School*, Bloomington: Indiana University Press.

Bhana, D. (2002) 'Making gender in early schooling: A multi-sited ethnographic study of power and discourse: from grade one and two in Durban', unpublished Doctoral dissertation, University of Natal: Durban.

Birkett, D. (2000) 'The end of innocence', *Guardian*, 12th February.

Blackmore, J. (1995) 'Just mucking about?: Students, power and sexual harassment', paper presented at the European Conference for Educational Research, Bath, 11–13 September.

Boldt, G. (1996) 'Sexist and heterosexist responses to gender bending in an elementary classroom', *Curriculum Enquiry*, **26**(2): 113–31.

Boldt, G. (2002) 'Oedipal and other conflicts', *Contemporary Issues in Early Childhood Education,* **3**(3): 365–82.

Bordo, S. (1990) 'Reading the slender body', in Jacobus, M., Keller, E.V. and Shuttleworth, S. (eds) *Body/Politics: Women and the Discourses of Science*, London: Routledge.

Bordo, S. (1993) 'Feminism, Foucault and the politics of the body' in Ramazanoglu, C. (ed.) *Up Against Foucault: Explorations of Some Tensions Between Foucault and Feminism*, London: Routledge.

Bordo, S. (2004) *Unbearable Weight: Feminism, Western Culture and the Body*, Calfornia: University of California Press.

Bradby, B. (1994) 'Freedom, feeling and dancing – Madonna's songs traverse girls' talk', in Mills, S. (ed) *Gendering the Reader*, London, New York: Harvester Wheatsheaf.

Brannen, J. and Nilsen, A. (2002) 'Young people's time perspectives: from youth to adulthood', *Sociology*, **36**(3): 513–37.

Brooks, L. (2003) 'Childish thongs', *Guardian*, 31st March.

Browne, M. and France, P. (1985) 'Only cissies wear dresses: A look at sexist talk in the nursery', in Weiner, G. (ed.) *Just a Bunch of Girls*, Milton Keynes: Open University Press.

Buckingham, D. and Bragg, S. (2003) *Young People, Sex and the Media: The Facts of Life?*, Basingstoke: Palgrave.

Burman, E. (1995) 'What is it? Masculinity and femininity in cultural representations of childhood', in Wilkinson, S. and Kitzinger, C. (eds) *Feminism and Discourse: Psychological Perspectives*, London: Sage Publications.

Butler, J. (1990) *Gender Trouble: Feminism and the Subversion of Identity*, London: Routledge.

Butler, J. (1991) 'Imitation and gender insubordination', in Fuss, D. (ed.) *Inside/out: Lesbian Theories, Gay Theories,* London: Routledge.

Butler, J. (1993) *Bodies That Matter: On the Discursive Limits of Sex*, London: Routledge.

Cain, M. (1993) 'Foucault, feminism and feeling: What Foucault can and cannot contribute to feminist epistemology', in Ramazangolu, C. (ed.) *Up Against Foucault: Explorations of some Tensions between Foucault and Feminism,* London: Routledge.

Canaan, J. (1996) 'One thing leads to another: Drinking, fighting and working-class masculinities', in Mac an Ghaill, M. (ed.) *Understanding Masculinities: Social Relations and Cultural Arenas*, Buckingham: Open University Press.

Carrigan, T. Connell, R.W. and Lee, J. (1987) 'The "sex-role" framework and the sociology of masculinity', in Arnot, M. and Weiner, G. (eds) *Gender and the Politics of Schooling*, London: Hutchinson.

Caspar, V., Cuffaro, H.K., Schultz, S., Silin, J. and Wickens, E. (1996) 'Towards a most thorough understanding of the world: Sexual orientation and early childhood education', *Harvard Educational Review*, **66**: 271–93.

Chernin, K. (1983) *Womansize: The Tyranny of Slenderness*, London: The Women's Press.

Chernin, K. (2004) *The Obsession: Reflections on the Tyranny of Slenderness*, Perennial.

Children's Rights Alliance (CRAE) (2003) Sexual Offences Bill (Committee Stage): CRAE briefing, pp. 1–3 (see www.crae.org.uk).

Christensen, P. and James, A. (2000) *Research With Children: Perspectives and Practices*, London: Falmer.

Christensen, P. and O'Brien, M. (2003) *Children in the City: Home Neighbourhood and Community*, London: RoutledgeFalmer.

Clark, M. (1989) 'Anastasia is a normal developer because she is unique', *Oxford Review of Education,* **15**(3): 243–25.

Clark, M. (1990) *The Great Divide: Gender in the Primary School*, Melbourne: Curriculum Development Centre.

Clarricoates, K. (1980) 'The importance of being Ernest ... Emma ... Tom ... Jane: The perception and categorization of gender conformity and gender deviation in primary schools', in Deem, R. (ed.) *Schooling For Women's Work*, London: Routledge and Kegan Paul.

Clarricoates, K. (1987) 'Child culture at school: A clash between gendered worlds', in Pollard, A. (ed.) *Children and their Primary Schools: A New Perspective*, London: Falmer Press.

Coffey, A., Dicks, B., Mason, B., Renold, E., Soyinka, B. and Williams, M. (2003–04) 'Ethnography for the Digital Age', ESRC-funded research (Ref. H333250056).

Connell, R.W. (1995) *Masculinities: Knowledge, Power and Social Change*, Cambridge: Polity Press.

Connell, R.W. (1996) 'Teaching the boys: New research on masculinity, and gender strategies for schools', *Teachers College Record*, **98**(2): 296–335.

Connolly, P. (1995) 'Boys will be boys? Racism, sexuality and the construction of masculine identities amongst infant boys', in Holland, J. and Blair, M. (eds) *Debates and Issues in Feminist Research and Pedagogy*, Clevedon: Multilingual Matters.

Connolly, P. (1998) *Racism, Gendered Identities and Young Children: Social Relations in a Multi-ethnic, Inner-city Primary School*, London: Routledge.

Connolly, P. (2003) 'Gendered and gendering spaces: Playgrounds in the early years', in Skelton, C. and Francis, B. (eds) *Boys and Girls in the Primary School*, Berkshire: Open University Press.

Connolly, P. (2004) *Boys and Schooling in the Early Years*, London: RoutledgeFalmer.

Corrigan, P. (1979) *Schooling the Smash Street Kids*, London: Penguin.

Corsaro, W.A. (1981) 'Entering the child's world: research strategies for field entry and data collection in a pre-school setting', in Green, J. and Wallet, C. (eds) *Ethnography and Language in Educational Settings*, Norwood, NJ: Ablex Publishing Corporation.

Cowie, C. and Lees, S. (1981) 'Slags or drags', *Feminist Review*, **9**, pp. 17–31.

Crompton, R. (1998) *Class and Stratification: An Introduction to Current Debates*, Cambridge: Polity Press.

Cunningham, H. (1991) *The Children of the Poor: Representations of Childhood Since the Seventeenth Century*, Oxford: Blackwell.

Danish, B. (1999) 'Placing children first: The importance of mutual presence in the elementary classroom', in Letts IV, W.J. and Sears, J.T. (eds) *Queering Elementary Education: Advancing the Dialogue about Sexualities and Schooling*. Lanham, MD: Rowman and Littlefield.

Davies, B. (1982) *Life in the Classroom and Playground: The Accounts of Primary School Children*, London: Routledge and Kegan Paul.

Davies, B. (1989a) *Frogs, Tails and Feminist Tales: Pre-school Children and Gender*, Sydney: Allen and Unwin.

Davies, B. (1989b) 'The discursive production of the male/female dualism in school settings', *Oxford Review of Education*, **15**: 229–41.

Davies, B. (1993a) 'Beyond dualism and towards multiple subjectives', in L.K. Christian-Smith (Ed.) (1993) *Texts of Desire: Essays on Fiction, Femininity and Schooling*, London: The Falmer Press.

Davies, B. (1993b) *Shards of Glass: Children Reading and Writing Beyond Gendered Identities*, New Jersey: Hampton Press Inc.

Davies, B. (1997) 'The subject of post-structuralism: A reply to Alison Jones', *Gender and Education*, **9**(3): 271–83.

Davies, B. and Harre, R. (1991) 'Positioning: The discursive production of selves', *Journal for the Theory of Social Behaviour*, **20**(1): 43–63.

Davies, B. and Hunt, R. (1994) 'Classroom competencies and marginal positionings', *British Journal of Sociology of Education*, **15**(3): 389–409.

Davies, L. (1984) *Pupil Power: Deviance and Gender at School*, London: Falmer Press.

Delamont, S. (1990) *Sex Roles and the School* (2nd edn), London: Meuthen.

Denscombe, M. (1995) 'Explorations in group interviews: An evaluation of a reflexive and partisan approach', *British Education Research Journal*, **21**(2): 131–48.

DfEE (2000a) *Guidance of Sex and Relationship Education*, London: Department for Education and Employment.

DfEE (2000b) *Bullying: Don't Suffer in Silence*, London: Department for Education and Employment.

Dixon, C. (1997) 'Pete's tool: Identity and sex-play in the design and technology classroom', *Gender and Education*, **9**(1): 89–104.

Dollimore, J. (1991) *Sexual Dissidence: Augustine to Wilde, Freud to Foucault*, Oxford: Oxford University Press.

Draper, J. (1993) 'We're back with gobbo: The re-establishment of gender relations following a school merger', in Woods, P. and Hammersley, M. (eds) *Gender and Ethnicity in Schools: Ethnographic Accounts*, London: Routledge.

Dubberly, W.S. (1988) 'Humour as resistance', *International Journal of Qualitative Studies in Education*, **1**(2):109–23.

Duncan, N. (1999) *Sexual Bullying: Gender Conflict and Pupil Culture in Secondary Schools*, London: Routledge.

Duncan, N. (2002) 'Girls, bullying and school transfer', in Sunnari *et al. Gendered and Sexualised Violence in Educational Environments*, Oulu, Finland: Oulu University Press.

Eder, D. (with Evans, C.C. and Parker, S.) (1995) *School Talk: Gender and Adolescent School Culture*, New Brunswick, NJ: Rutgers University Press.

Edley, N. and Wetherall, M. (1996) 'Masculinity, power and identity', in Mac an Ghaill, M. (ed.) *Understanding Masculinities: Social Relations and Cultural Arenas*, Buckingham: Open University Press.

Ellen, B. (2000) 'Too much, too young', *Observer*, 18th June.

Epstein, D. (1993a) 'Too small to notice? Constructions of childhood and discourse of "race" in predominantly white contexts', *Curriculum Studies*, **1**(3): 317–55.

Epstein, D. (1993b) 'Essay review: Practising heterosexuality', *Curriculum Studies*, **1**(2): 275–86.

Epstein, D. (ed.) (1994) *Challenging Lesbian and Gay Inequalities in Education*, Buckingham: Open University Press.

Epstein, D. (1995a) 'Gender and sexuality in the early years', OMEP(UK) Research Update.

Epstein, D. (1995b) '"Girls Don't Do Bricks" Gender and sexuality in the primary classroom', in Siraj-Blatchford J. and Siraj-Blatchford I. (eds), *Educating the Whole Child: cross-curricular skills, themes and dimensions* (pp. 56–9). Buckingham: Open University Press.

Epstein, D. (1997) 'Cultures of schooling/cultures of sexuality', *International Journal of Inclusive Education*, **1**(1): 37–53.

Epstein, D. (1998) '"Are you a girl or are you a teacher?" The "least adult" role in research about gender and sexuality in a primary school', in Walford G. (ed.) *Doing Research About Education*. London: Falmer Press.

Epstein, D. and Johnson, R. (1994) 'On the straight and narrow: The heterosexual presumption, homophobias and schools', in Epstein, D. (ed.) *Challenging Lesbian and Gay Inequalities in Education*, Buckingham: Open University Press.

Epstein, D. and Johnson, R. (1998) *Schooling Sexualities*, Buckingham: Open University Press.

Epstein, D., Kehily, M.J., Mac an Ghaill, M. and Redman, P. (2001a) 'Girls and boys come out to play: Making masculinities and femininities in primary playgrounds', *Men and Masculinities*, special issue: Disciplining and Punishing Masculinities, **4**(2):158–72.

Epstein, D., Mac an Ghaill, M., Redman, P. and Kehily, M.J. (2001b) 'Children's "relationship cultures" in years 5 and 6: A qualitative study', ESRC End of Award Report [R000237438].

Epstein, D., O'Flynn, S. and Telford, D. (2003) *Silenced Sexualities in Schools and Universities*, Stoke on Trent: Trentham Books.

Evans, T. (1987) *A Gender Agenda: A Sociological Study of Teachers, Parents and Pupils in their Primary Schools*, Sydney: Allen and Unwin.

Fine, G. (1987) *With the Boys: Little League Baseball and Preadolescent Behaviour*, Chicago: The University of Chicago Press.

Fine, G. and Sandstrom, K.L. (1988) *Knowing Children: Participant Observation with Minors*, London: Sage Publications.

Fine, M. (1988) 'Sexuality and schooling and adolescent females: The missing discourse of desire', *Havard Educational Review*, **58**(1): 29–53.

Fishman, S. (1982) 'The history of childhood sexuality', *Journal of Contemporary History*, **17**(2): 269–83.

Foucault, M. (1977) *Discipline and Punish* (trans. A. Sheridan), Harmondsworth: Penguin.

Foucault, M. (1978) *The Will to Knowledge: The History of Sexuality* vol. 1 (trans. R. Hurley), Harmondsworth: Penguin.

Francis, B. (1997) 'Discussing discrimination: Children's construction of sexism between pupils in primary school', *British Journal of Sociology of Education*, **8**(4): 519–32.

Francis, B. (1998) *Power Plays: Primary School Children's Constructions of Gender, Power and Adult Work*, Stoke on Trent: Trentham Books.

Francis, B. (2000) *Boys, Girls and Achievement: Addressing the Classroom Issues*. London: RoutledgeFalmer.

Francis, B. and Skelton, C. (2001a) *Investigating Gender: Contemporary Perspectives in Education*, Buckingham: Open University.

Francis, B. and Skelton, C. (2001b) 'Men teachers and the construction of heterosexual masculinity in the classroom', *Sex Education*, **1**(1): 9–21.

Friend, R.A. (1993) 'Choices, not closets: Heterosexism and homophobia in schools', in Weis, L. and Fine, M. (eds) *Beyond Silenced Voices: Class, Race, and Gender in United States Schools*, Albany, New York: State University of New York Press.

Frosh, S., Phoenix, A. and Pattman, R. (2002) *Young Masculinities: Understanding Boys in Contemporary Society*, Basingstoke: Palgrave.

Gagnon, A. and Simon, W. (1973) *Sexual Conduct: the Social Sources of Human Sexuality*, Chicago: Aldine.

George, R. (2004) 'Best friends and worst enemies: an exploration of pre-adolescent girls' friendship within the primary and early years of secondary school'. Unpublished PhD dissertation, Institute of Education, University of London.

Gerard, N. (1999) 'Innocence on the line', *Observer*, 14th November.

Gilbert, P. and Gilbert, R. (1998) *Masculinity Goes To School*, London: Routledge.

Giroux, H. (2000) *Stealing Innocence*, Basingstoke: Palgrave.

Gittens, D. (1998) *The Child in Question*, London: Macmillan.

Gordon, T. (1996) 'Citizenship, difference and marginality in schools: Spatial and embodied aspects of gender construction', in Murphy, P. and Gipps, C. (eds) *Equity in the Classroom*, London: The Falmer Press.

Griffiths, V. (1995) *Adolescent Girls and their Friends: A Feminist Ethnography*, Aldershot: Avebury.

Grogan, S. (1998) *Body Image: Understanding Body Dissatisfaction in Men, Women and Children*, London, New York: Routledge.

Gulbrandsen, M. (2003) 'Peer relations as arenas for gender constructions among teenagers', *Pedagogy, Culture and Society*, **11**(1): 113–33.

Hall, C. and Coles, M. (1997) 'Gendered readings: Helping boys develop as critical readers', *Gender and Education*, **9**(1) pp. 61–8.

Hall, S. and du Gay, P. (eds) (1996) *Questions of Cultural Identity*, London: Sage Publications.

Halson, J. (1989) 'The sexual harassment of young women', in Holly, L. (ed.) *Girls and Sexuality: Teaching and Learning*, Milton Keynes: Open University Press.

Halstead, M.J. and Reiss, M. (2003) *Values in Sex Education: From Principles to Practice*, London: RoutledgeFalmer.

Hargreaves, J. (ed.) (1982) *Sport, Culture and Ideology*, London: Routledge and Kegan Paul.

Harrison, C. and Hood-Williams, J. (2002) *Beyond Sex and Gender*, London: Sage.

Hatcher, R. (1995) 'Boyfriends, girfriends: Gender and "race" in children's cultures', *International Play Journal*, **3**: 187–97.

Hawkes, G. (1996) *A Sociology of Sex and Sexuality*, Buckingham: Open University Press.

Haywood, C. (1996) 'Out of the curriculum: Sex talking, talking sex', *Curriculum Studies*, **4**(2): 229–51.

Haywood, C. and Mac an Ghaill, M. (1995) 'The sexual politics of the curriculum: Contesting values', *International Studies in Sociology of Education*, **5**(2).

Haywood, C. and Mac an Ghaill, M. (1996) 'Schooling masculinities', in M. Mac an Ghaill, (ed.) *Understanding Masculinities: Social Relations and Cultural Arenas*, Buckingham: Open University Press.

Haywood, C. and Mac an Ghaill, M. (2003) *Men and Masculinities*, Buckingham Open University Press.

Hendrick, H. (1998) 'Constructions and reconstructions of British childhood: An interpretative survey', in James, A. and Prout, A. (eds) *Constructing and Reconstructing Childhood: Contemporary Issues in the Sociological Studies of Childhood*, London: Falmer.

Herbert, C. M. H. (1989) *Sexual Harassment in Schools: A Guide for Teachers*, London: Fulton.

Hey, V. (1997) *The Company She Keeps: An Ethnography of Girls' Friendships*, Buckingham: Open University Press.

Hey V. *et al.* (2001) 'Sad, bad or sexy boys?' in W. Martino and B. Beyenn (eds) *What About the Boys?* Buckingham: Open University Press.

Higonnet, A. (1998) *Pictures of Innocence: The History and Crisis of Ideal Childhood*, London: Thames and Hudson.

Hill, M. (1997) 'Research review: Participatory research with children, child and family social work', **2**: 171–83.

Hinson, S. (1996) 'A practice focused approach to addressing heterosexist violence in Australian schools', in: Laskey, L. and Beavis, C. (eds) *Schooling and Sexualities*, Deakin Centre for Education and Change, Deakin University.

Holland, J., Ramazanoglu, C., Sharpe, S. and Thomson, R. (1993) *Wimp or Gladiator: Contradictions in Acquiring Masculine Sexuality*, London: The Tufnell Press.

Holland, J., Ramazanoglu, C., Sharpe, S. and Thomson, R. (1998) *The Male in the Head: Young People, Heterosexuality and Power*, London: The Tufnell Press.

Holland, P. (2003) *We Don't Play with Guns Here: War, Weapon and Superhero Play in the Early Years*, Buckingham: Open University Press.

Holland, P. (2004) *Picturing Childhood: The Myth of the Child in Popular Imagery*, London: I.B. Tauris.

Holly, L. (1985) 'Mary, Jane and Virginia Woolf: Ten year old girls talking', in Weiner, G. (ed.) (1985) *Just a bunch of Girls: Feminist Approaches to Schooling*, Milton Keynes: Open University Press.

Holloway, S. and Valentine, G. (2000) 'Spatiality and the new social studies of childhood', *Sociology*, **34**(4): 763–83.

Hollway, W. (1984) 'Gender difference and the production of subjectivity', in Henriques, J., Hollway, W., Urwin, C., Venn, C. and Walkerdine, V. (eds) *Changing the Subject: Psychology, Social Regulation and Subjectivity*, London: Methuen.

Hostetler, A. and Herdt, G.H. (1998) 'Culture, sexual lifeways and developmental subjectivities: Rethinking sexual taxonomies', *Social Research*, Summer: 1–22.

Hutchby, I. and Moran-Ellis, J. (1998) (eds) *Children and Social Competence: Arenas of Action*, London: The Falmer Press.

Ingraham, C. (1996) 'The heterosexual imaginary: Feminist sociology and theories of gender', in Henessy, R. and Ingraham, C. (eds) *Materialist Feminism*, London: Routledge.

Ivinson, G. (2004) 'Pedagogic discourse and sex education', conference paper presented at *Pleasure and Danger: Sexualities in the 21st Century*. 30th June–2nd July, Cardiff School of Social Sciences, Cardiff University: Cardiff: Wales.

Jackson, S. (1982) *Childhood and Sexuality*, Oxford: Basil Blackwell Ltd.

Jackson, S. (1990) 'Demons and innocents: Western ideas on children's sexuality in historical perspective', in Perry, M. E. (ed.) *Handbook of Sexology Vol. VII: Childhood and Adolescent Sexology*, Amsterdam: Elsevier, pp. 23–49.

Jackson, S. (1996) 'Heterosexuality, power and pleasure', in Jackson, S. and Scott, S. (eds) *Feminism and Sexuality: A Reader*, Edinburgh: Edinburgh University Press.

Jackson, S. and Scott, S. (2004) 'Sexual antinomies in late modernity', *Sexualities*, **7**(2): 233–48.

Jacobus, M., Keller, V. and Shuttleworth, S. (eds) (1990) Introduction, in Jacobus, M. *et al.* (eds) *Body/Politics: Women and the Discourses of Science*, Routledge: London.

James, A and Prout, A. (eds) (1998) *Constructing and Reconstructing Childhood: Contemporary Issues in the Sociological Study of Childhood* (2nd edn), London: The Falmer Press.

James, A., Jenks, C. and Prout, A. (1998) *Theorizing Childhood*, Cambridge: Polity Press.

Janssen, D. (2002) *Growing Up Sexually* Vol. 2: *The Sexual Curriculum*, Interim Report, Amsterdam: The Netherlands.

Jenkins, H. (1998a) 'Introduction: Childhood innocence and other modern myths', in Jenkins, H. (ed.) *The Children's Culture Reader*, New York: New York University Press.

Jenkins, H. (1998b) 'The sensuous child: Benajamin Spock and the sexual revolution', in Jenkins, H. (ed.) *The Children's Clture Reader*, New York: New York University Press.

Jenks, C. (1996) *Childhood*, London: Routledge.

Johnson, R. (1979) '"Really useful knowledge": radical education and working class culture', in Clarke, J., Crichter, C. and Johnson, R. (eds) *Working Class Culture: Studies in History and Theory*, London: Hutchinson.

Johnson, R. (1997) 'Contested borders, contingent lives: An introduction', in Steinberg, D.L., Epstein, D. and Johnson, R. (eds) *Border Patrols: Policing the Boundaries of Heterosexuality*, London: Cassell.

Jones, A. (1993) 'Becoming a "girl": Poststructuralist suggestions for educational research', *Gender and Education*, **5**(2):157–67.

Jones, A. (2003) 'The monster in the room: Safety, pleasure and early childhood education', *Contemporary Issues in Early Childhood*, **4** (3): 235–50.

Jones, A. (2004) 'Social anxiety, sex, surveillance, and the 'safe' teacher', *British Journal of Sociology of Education*, **25** (1): 53–66.

Jones, C. (1985) 'Sexual tyranny: Male violence in a mixed secondary school', in Weiner, G. (ed.) *Just a Bunch of Girls*, Milton Keynes: Open University Press.

Jordan, E. (1995) 'Fighting boys and fantasy play: The construction of masculinity in the early years of school', *Gender and Education*, **5**(2):157–67.

Katz (1996) *The Invention of Heterosexuality*, New York: Plume.

Kehily, M.J. (2002) *Sexuality, Gender and Schooling: Shifting Agendas in Social Learning*, London: Routledge.

Kehily, M.J., Epstein, E., Mac an Ghaill, M. and Redman, P. (2002) 'Private girls, public worlds: Producing femininities in the primary school', *Discourse: Studies in the Cultrual Politics of Education*, special issue: Retheorising Friendship in Educational Settings, **23**(3): 167–77.

Kehily, M.J. and Nayak, A. (1996) 'Playing it straight: Masculinities, homophobias and schooling', *Journal of Gender Studies*, **5**(2):211–29.

Kehily, M.J. and Nayak, A. (1997) 'Lads and laughter: Humour and the production of heterosexual hierarchies', *Gender and Education*, **9**(1): 69–87.

Kelley, P., Buckingham, D. and Davies, H. (1999) 'Talking dirty: Children, sexual knowledge and television', *Childhood*, **6**(2): 221–43.

Kelly, L. (1989) 'Our issues our analysis: Two decades of work on sexual violence', in Mahony, P. and Jones, C. (eds) *Learning our Lines: Sexuality and Social Control in Education*, London: Women's Press.

Kelly, L. (1992) 'Not in front of the children: Responding to right wing agendas on sexuality and education', in Arnot, M. and Barton, L. (eds) *Voicing Concerns: Sociological Perspectives on Contemporary Education Reforms*, Oxfordshire: Triangle Books Ltd.

Kelly, L. and Radford, J. (1996) '"Nothing really happened": The invalidation of women's experiences of sexual violence', in Hester, M., Kelly, L. and Radford, J. (eds) *Women, Violence and Male Power: Feminist Activism, Research and Practice*, Buckingham: Open University Press.

Kelly, L., Wingfield, R. Burton, S. and Regan, L (1995) *Splintered Lives: Sexual Exploitation of Children in the Context of Children's Rights and Child Protection*. London: Barnardos.

Kenway, J. and Fitzclarence, L. (1997) 'Masculinity, violence and schooling: Challenging poisonous pedagogies', *Gender and Education*, **9**(1): 117–33.

Kenway, J. and Willis, S. with Blackmore, J. and Rennie, L. (1997) 'Are boys victims of feminism in schools?: Some answers from Australia', *International Journal of Inclusive Education*, **1**(1): 19–35.

Kessler, S., Ashenden, D., Connel, R.W. and Dowsett, G. (1985) 'Gender relations in secondary schooling', *Sociology of Education*, 58: 34–48.

Kimmel, M.S. (ed.) (1987) *Changing Men: New Directions in Research on Men and Masculinity*, Newbury Park, CA: Sage.

Kincaid, J. (1994) *Child-loving: The Erotic Child and Victorian Culture*, New York: Routledge.

Kincaid, J. (1998) *Erotic Innocence: The Culture of Child Molesting*. London: Duke University Press.

King, J.A. (1997) 'Keeping it quiet: Gay teachers in the primary grades', in Tobin, J.J. (ed.) *Making a Place for Pleasure in Early Childhood Education*, New Haven: Yale University Press.

King, R. (1978) *All Things Bright and Beautiful?: A Sociological Study of Infants' Classrooms*, Chichester: Wiley.

Kitzinger, J. (1990) 'Who are you kidding? Children, power and the struggle against sexual abuse', in James, A. and Prout, A. (eds) *Constructing and Reconstructing Childhood: Contemporary Issues in the Sociological Study of Childhood*, London: The Falmer Press.

Kitzinger, J. (1994) 'Focus groups: Method or madness?', in M. Boulton (ed.) (1994) *Methodological Advances in Social Research in HIV/AIDS*, London: Taylor and Francis.

Klein, A. M. (1993) *Little Big Men: Bodybuilding, Subculture and Gender Construction*, Albany: State University of New York Press.

Lacquer, T. (1990) *Making Sex: Body and Gender from the Greeks to Freud*, London: Harvard Univeristy Press.

Laskey, L. and Beavis, C. (eds) (1996) *Schooling and Sexuality*, Geelong, Victoria: Deaking University Centre for Change.

Lee, N. (2001) *Childhood and Society: Growing Up in an Age of Uncertainty*, Buckingham: Open University Press.

Lees, S. (1986) *Losing Out: Sexuality and Adolescent Girls*, London: Hutchinson.

Lees, S. (1993) *Sugar and Spice: Sexuality and Adolescent Girls*, London: Penguin.

Lees, S. (1994) 'Talking about sex education', *Gender and Education*, **6**(3): 281–92.

Letts IV, W.J. and Sears, J.T. (eds) (1999) *Queering Elementary Education: Advancing the Dialogue about Sexualities and Schooling*, Lanham, MD: Rowman and Littlefield.

Lewis, A. (1992) 'Group child interviews as a research tool', *British Educational Research Journal*, **18**(4): 413–21.

Lloyd, M. (1999) 'Performativity, Parody, Politics', in Bell, V. (ed.) *Performativity and Belonging*, London: Sage.

Lucey, H. and Reay, D. (2002) 'Carrying the beacon of excellence: Social class differentiation and anxiety at a time of transition', *Journal of Education Policy*, **17**(3): 321–36.

Mac an Ghaill, M. (1994) *The Making of Men: Masculinities, Sexualities and Schooling*, Buckingham: Open University Press.

Mac an Ghaill, M. (ed.) (1996) *Understanding Masculinities: Social Relations and Cultural Arenas*, Buckingham: Open University Press.

MacNaughton, G. (2000) *Rethinking Gender in Early Childhood Education*, London: Paul Chapman.

Mahony, P. (1985) *Schools for the Boys*, London: Hutchinson.

Mahony, P. and Jones, C. (eds) (1989) *Learning Our Lines: Sexuality and Social Control in Education*, London: Women's Press.

Mandell, N. (1988) 'The least-adult role in studying children', *Contemporary Journal of Contemporary Ethnography*, **16**(4): 433–67.

Martin, J. (1998) *Women and the Politics of Schooling in Victorian and Edwardian England*, London: Leicester University Press.

Martino, W. and Beyenn, B. (eds) (2001) *What About the Boys?,* Buckingham: Open University Press.

Martino, W. and Pallotta-Chiarolli, M. (2003) *So What's a Boy: Addressing Issues of Masculinity and Schooling,* Buckingham: Open University Press.

Matthews, H. (2002) 'The street as a liminal space: The barbed spaces of childhood', in Christensen, P. and O'Brien,. M. (eds) *Children in the City,* London: RoutledgeFalmer, pp. 110–35.

Mauthner, M. (1996) 'Methodological aspects of collecting data from children: Lessons from three research projects', *Children and Society,* **11**, pp. 16–28.

Mayall, B. (ed.) (1994a) *Children's Childhoods: Observed and Experienced,* London: The Falmer Press.

Mayall, B. (1994b) *Negotiating Health: Children at Home and Primary School,* London: Cassell.

McRobbie, A. (1997) 'More! New sexualities in girls' and women's magazines', in McRobbie, A. (ed.) *Back to Reality? Social Experiences and Cultural Studies,* Manchester: Manchester University Press.

McRobbie, A. and Nava, M. (1984) *Gender and Generation,* London: Macmillan Education.

Mealyea, R. (1989) 'Humour as a coping stategy in the transition from tradesperson to teacher', *British Journal of Sociology of Education,* **10**(3) pp. 275–88.

Messner, M. A. and Sabo, D.F. (1994) *Sex, Violence and Power in Sports: Rethinking Masculinity,* USA: The Crossing Press.

Mills, M. (2001) *Challenging Violence in Schools: An Issue of Masculinities,* Buckingham: Open University Press.

Nayak, A. (1997) 'Tales from the Darkside: negotiating whiteness in school arenas', *International Studies in Sociology of Education,* **7**(1), pp. 57–79

Nayak, A. (1999) '"White English ethnicities": racism, anti-racism and student perspectives', *Race Ethnicity and Education,* 2, pp. 177–202

Nayak, A. and Kehily, M. J. (1997) 'Masculinities and schooling: Why are young men so homophobic?', in Steinberg, D.L., Epstein, D. and Johnson, R. (eds) *Border Patrols: Policing the Boundaries of Heterosexuality,* Cassel: London.

Nilan, P. (1998) Review Symposium: 'The company she keeps: An ethnography of girls' friendship', *British Journal Sociology of Education,* **19**(1) pp. 135–6.

Oakley, A. (1994) 'Women and children first and last: Parallels and differences between children's and women's studies', in Mayall, B. (ed.) *Children's Childhoods: Observed and Experienced,* London: The Falmer Press.

Ochsner, M. B. (2000) 'Gendered make-up', *Contemporary Issues in Early Childhood,* **1**(2): 209–13.

OED (2002) *Oxford English Dictionary,* Oxford: Oxford University Press.

O'Flynn, S. and Epstein, D. (2004) *Schooling the Body: Knowledge, 'Standards', 'Achievements'.* Paper presented at Cardiff School of Social Sciences Seminar Series, 25th March 2004, Cardiff University: Cardiff.

Paley, V. (1984) *Boys and Girls: Superheroes in the Doll Corner,* Chicago: University of Chicago Press.

Parker, A. (1996a) 'Sporting masculinities: Gender relations and the body', in Mac an Ghaill, M. (ed.) *Understanding Masculinities: Social Relations and Cultural Arenas,* Buckingham: Open University Press.

Parker, A. (1996b) 'The construction of masculinity within boys' physical education', *Gender and Education,* **8**(2): 141–57.

Pallotta-Chiarolli, M. (1997) *Girls' Talk: Young Women Speak Their Hearts and Minds*, Sydney: Finch.

Parry, O. (1996) 'In one ear and out the other: Unmasking masculinities in the Carribean classroom', *Sociological Research Online*, **1**(2), www.socresonline.org.uk.

Phillips, A. (2003) 'The child's sex trap', *Guardian*, 9th June.

Piper, C. (2000) 'Historical constructions of childhood innocence: Removing sexuality', in Heinze, E. (ed.) *Of Innocence and Autonomy: Children, Sex and Human Rights*, Dartmouth: Ashgate.

Plummer, K. (1990) 'Understanding childhood sexualities', *Journal of Homosexuality*, **20**(1): 231–49.

Pollard, A. (1985) *The Social World of the Primary School*, London: Holt, Rinehart and Winston.

Pollard, A. (1987) 'Goodies, jokers and gangs', in Pollard, A. (ed.) *Children and Their Primary Schools: A New Perspective*, London: Falmer Press.

Postman, N. (1994) *The Disappearance of Childhood*, New York: Vintage Books.

Qvortrup, J. (1994) 'Childhood matters: An introduction', in Qvortrup, J., Brady, M., Sgritto G. and Winterberger, H. (eds) *Childhood Matters: Social Theory, Practice and Politics*, Aldershot: Avebury Publishing.

Ramazanoglu, C. (ed.) (1993) *Up Against Foucault: Explorations of Some Tensions Between Foucault and Feminism*, London: Routledge.

Ray, C. and Jolly, J. (2002) *Sex and Relationships Education for Primary Age Children*: Sex Education Forum Factsheet 28, National Children's Bureau Publications: London.

Reay, D. (1998) 'Rethinking social class: Qualitative perspectives on class and gender', *Sociology*, **32**(2) pp. 259–75.

Reay, D. (2001) '"Spice girls", "nice girls", "girlies" and "tomboys": Gender discourses, girls' cultures and femininities in the primary classroom', *Gender and Education*, **13**(2): 153–66.

Redman, P. (1994) 'Shifting ground: Rethinking sexuality education', in Epstein, D. (ed.) *Challenging Lesbian and Gay Inequalities in Education*, Buckingham: Open University Press.

Redman, P. (1996) 'Curtis loves Ranjit: Heterosexual masculinities, schooling, and pupils' sexual cultures', *Educational Review*, **48**(2):175–82.

Redman, P. (1997) 'Invasion of the monstrous others: Heterosexual masculinities, the "Aids carrier" and the horror genre', in Steinberg, D. L., Epstein, D. and Johnson, R. (eds) *Border Patrols: Policing the Boundaries of Heterosexuality*, London: Cassell.

Redman, P. (2000) 'Tarred with the same brush: "homophobia" and the role of the unconscious in school-based cultures of masculinity', *Sexualities*, vol. 3, no. 4, pp. 483–99.

Redman, P. and Mac an Ghaill, M. (1997) 'Education Peter: The making of a history man', in Steinberg, D.L., Epstein, D. and Johnson, R. (eds) *Border Patrols: Policing the Boundaries of Heterosexuality*, London: Cassell.

Redman, P., Epstein, D., Kehily, M. and Mac an Ghaill, M. (2002) 'Boys bonding: Friendship and the production of masculinities in a primary school classroom', *Sexualities*, special issue: Re-theorising Friendship in Educational Settings, **23**(3): 179–91.

Renew, A. (1996) 'Acting like a girl: Lesbian challenges to constructions of gender and schooling' in Laskey, L. and Beavis, C. (eds) *Schooling and Sexuality*, Geelong, Victoria: Deaking University Centre for Change.

Renold, E. (1997) '"All they've got on their brains is football": sport, masculinity and the gendered practices of playground relations', *Sport, Education and Society*, **2** (1): 5–23.

Renold, E. (1999) 'Presumed innocence: An ethnographic exploration into the construction of sexual and gender identities in the primary school', unpublished Doctoral dissertation, Cardiff, University of Wales.

Renold, E. (2000) 'Coming out: Gender, (hetero)sexuality and the primary school', *Gender and Education*, **12**(3): 309–26.

Renold, E. (2001a) '"Square-girls", femininity and the negotiation of academic success in the primary school', *British Education Research Journal*, **27**(5): 577–88.

Renold, E. (2001b) 'Learning the "hard" way: Boys, hegemonic masculinity and the negotiation of learner identities in the primary school', *British Journal of Sociology of Education*, **22**(3): 39–385.

Renold, E. (2002a) '"Privacies and privates": Researching sexuality in the primary school', in Pugsley, L. and Welland, T. (eds) *Ethical Dilemmas in Qualitative Research*, Aldershot: Ashgate.

Renold, E. (2002b) 'Close encounters of the "third kind": Researching children's sexual cultures in the primary school', in Walford, G. (ed.) *Doing a Doctorate in Educational Ethnography: Studies in Educational Ethnography* 7, Oxford: JAI Press.

Renold, E. (2002c) '"Presumed Innocence": (hetero)sexual, homophobic and heterosexist harassment amongst children in the primary school', *Childhood*, **9** (4): 415–33.

Renold, E. and Allan, A. (2004) 'Bright and beautiful: High-achieving girls and the negotiation of young 'girlie' femininities'. Paper presented at *British Educational Research Association Annual Conference*, 16–18 September 2004, UMIST, Manchester, UK.

Rhedding-Jones, J. (1994) 'Girls, subjectivity and language: From four to twelve in a rural school', unpublished PhD thesis, La Trobe University: Bundoora.

Rhedding-Jones, J. (1996) 'Researching early schooling: Poststructural practices and academic writing in an ethnography', *British Journal of Sociology of Education*, **17**, pp. 21–39.

Rich, A. (1983) 'Compulsory heterosexuality and lesbian existance', *Signs*, **5**(4): 631–60.

Richardson, D. (ed.) (1996) *Theorising heterosexuality: Telling it straight*, Buckingham: Open University Press.

Richardson, D. (2000) *Rethinking Sexuality*, London: Sage.

Robinson, K. (2002) 'Making the invisible visible: Gay and lesbian issues in early childhood education', *Contemporary Issues in Early Childhood Education*, **3**(3): 415–34.

Ross, C. and Ryan, C. (1990) *Can I Stay in Today Miss?: Improving the School Playground*, Stoke on Trent: Trentham Books.

Rousseau, J-J. (1762) *Émile* (1911 edn), translated and annotated by Allan Bloom, London: Penguin .

Rossiter, A.B. (1994) 'Chips, coke and rock 'n' roll: Children's mediation of an invitation to a first dance party', *Feminist Review*, **46**: 1–19.

Russel, R. and Tyler, M. (2002) 'Thank heaven for little girls: "Girl heaven" and the commercial context of feminine childhood', *Sociology*, **36**(3): 619–37.

Scott, S., Jackson, S. and Backett-Milburn, K. (1998) 'Swings and roundabouts: Risk anxiety and the everyday worlds of children', *Sociology*, **32**(4): 689–705.

Sears, J.T. (1999) 'Teaching queerly: Some elementary propositions', in Letts IV, W.J. and Sears, J.T. (eds) *Queering Elementary Education: Advancing the Dialogue about Sexualities and Schooling*, Lanham, MD: Rowman and Littlefield.

Sedgwick, E.K. (1990) *Epistemology of the Closet*, Berkeley: University of California Press.

Sedgwick, E.K. (ed.) (1997) *Navel Gazing: Queer Readings in Fiction*, Durham, NC: Duke University Press.

Sharp, R. and Green, A. (1975) *Education and Social Control: A Study in Progressive Primary Education*, London: Routledge and Kegan and Paul.

Silin, J. (1995) *Sex, Death and the Education of Children: Our Passion for Ignorance in the Age of AIDS*, New York and London: Teachers College Press.

Sinfield, A. (1994) *Cultural Politics, Queer Reading*, London: Routledge.

Singh, P. (1993) 'Institutional discourse and practice: A case study of the social construction of technological competence in the primary classroom', *British Journal of Sociology of Education*, **14**(1): 39–59.

Skeggs, B. (1997) *Formations of Class and Gender*, London: Sage Publications.

Skelton, C. (1996) 'Learning to be tough: The fostering of maleness in one primary school', *Gender and Education*, **8**(2): 185–197.

Skelton, C. (2000) '"A passion for football": Dominant masculinities and primary schooling', *Sport Education and Society*, 5(1): 5–18

Skelton, C. (2001) *Schooling the Boys: Masculinities and Primary Education*, Buckingham: Open University Press.

Skelton, C. (2003) 'Male primary teachers and perceptions of masculinity', *Educational Review*, **55**(2): 195–211.

Skelton, C. and Francis, B. (eds) (2003) *Boys and Girls in the Primary School*, Berkshire: Open University Press.

Smith, D. (1987) *The Everyday World as Problematic: A Feminist Sociology*, Boston: Northeastern University Press.

Smith, P. and Sharp, S. (eds) (1994) *School Bullying: Insights and Perspectives*, London: Routledge.

Stein, N. (1996) 'Sexual harassment in school: The public performance of gendered violence', *Harvard Educational Review*, **65**(2): 145–62.

Sunnari, V., Kangasvuo, J. and Heikkinen, M. (2002) *Gendered and Sexualised Violence in Educational Enviroments*, Oulu, Finalnd: Oulu University Press.

Swain, J. (2000) '"The money's good, the fame's good, the girls are good": The role of playground football in the construction of young boys' masculinity in a junior school', *British Journal of Sociology of Education*, **21**(1): 95–109.

Swain, J. (2002a) 'The right stuff: Fashioning an identity through clothing in a junior school', *Gender and Education*, **14**(1): 53–6.

Swain, J. (2002b) 'The resources and strategies boys use to establish status in junior school without competitive sport', *Discourse: Studies in the Cultural Politics of Education,* **23**(1): 91–107.

Swain, J. (2003) 'How young schoolboys become some*body*: The role of the body in the construction of masculinity', *British Journal of Sociology of Education*, **24**(3): 299–314.

Thorne, B. (1980) 'You still takin' notes?: Fieldwork and problems of informed consent', *Social Problems*, **27**(3): 284–97.

Thorne, B. (1987) 'Revisioning women and social change: Where are the children?', *Gender and Society*, **1**(1): 85–109.

Thorne, B. (1993) *Gender Play: Boys and Girls in School*, Buckingham: Open University Press.

Thorne, B. and Luria, Z. (1986) 'Sexuality and gender in children's daily worlds', *Social Problems*, **33**(3): 176–90.

Tobin, J.J. (1997) 'The missing discourse of pleasure and desire', in Tobin, J. J. (ed.) *Making a Place for Pleasure in Early Childhood Education*, New Haven: Yale University Press.

Valentine, G. (1997) '"Oh yes you can". "Oh no you can't": Children and parents' understandings of kids' competence to negotiate public space safely', *Antipode*, **29**(1): 65–89.

Valentine, G. and McKendrick, J. (1997) 'Children's outdoor play: Exploring parental concerns about children's safety and the changing nature of childhood', *Geoforum*, **28**(2): 219–35.

Vance, C. (ed.) (1992) *Pleasure and Danger: Exploring Female Sexuality* (2nd edn), London: Pandora.

Walden, R. and Walkerdine, V. (1985) *Girls and Mathematics: From Primary to Secondary Schooling,* London: Institute of Education, Bedford Way Papers.

Walker, J.C. (1988) *Louts and Legends: Male Youth Culture in an Inner City School*, Sydney: Allen and Unwin.

Walkerdine, V. (1981) 'Sex, power and pedagogy', *Screen Education*, Spring, 38.

Walkerdine, V. (1989a) 'Femininity as performance', *Oxford Review of Education*, **15**(3): 267–79.

Walkerdine, V. (1989b) *Counting Girls Out*, London: Virago Press Ltd.

Walkerdine, V. (1990) *Schoolgirl Fictions*, London: Verso.

Walkerdine, V. (1996) 'Popular culture and the eroticization of little girls', in Curran, J., Morely, D. and Walkerdine, V. (eds) *Cultural Studies and Communications,* London: St. Martin's Press Inc.

Walkerdine, V. (1997) *Daddy's Girl: Young Girls and Popular Culture*, Hampshire: Macmillan Press Ltd.

Walkerdine, V. (1999) 'Violent boys and precocious girls: Regulating childhood at the end of the millenium', *Contemporary Issues in Early Childhood*, **1**(1): 3–23.

Walkerdine, V. (2004) 'Developmental psychology and the study of childhood', in Kehily, M. (ed.) *An Introduction to Childhood Studies*, Buckingham: Open University Press.

Walkerdine, V., Lucey, H. and Melody, J. (2001) *Growing Up Girl: Psycho-social Explorations of Gender and Class*, Basingstoke: Palgrave.

Walkowitz, J. (1992) *City of Dreadful Delight: Narratives of Sexual Danger in Late-Victorian London*, London: Virago Press.

Wallis, A. and Van Every, J. (2000) 'Sexuality in the primary school', *Sexualities*, **3**(4): 409–23.

Walton, D., Weatherall, A. and Jackson, S. (2002) 'Romance and friendship in pre-teen stories about conflicts: "We decided that boys are not worth it"', *Discourse and Society*, **13**(5): 673–91.

Warner, S. (1993) 'Constructing femininity: Models of child sexual abuse and the production of "woman"', in Burman, E. (ed.) *Challenging Women: Psychology's Exclusions and Feminist Possibilities*, Buckingham: Open University Press.

Warwick, I., Rivers, K., Aggleton, P., Ruxton, L., Turney, L. and Tyrer, P. (2002) *The Sex and Relationship Education Teaching Pilot: An Investigaion of Key Stakeholder Perceptions*, Research Report (No. 376) for DfES.

Watney, S. (1991) 'School's out', in Fuss, D. (ed.) *Inside/Out: Lesbian Theories, Gay Theories*, London: Routledge.

Weedon, C. (1987) *Feminist Practice and Poststructuralist Theory*, London: Basil Blackwell Ltd.

Weeks, J. (1981) *Sex, Politics and Society: The Regulation of Sexuality Since 1800*, Harlow: Longman.

Weeks, J. (1985) *Sexuality and its Discontents*, London: Routledge.

Weeks, J (1986) *Sexuality*, London: Routledge.

Weems, L. (1998) 'Pestalozzi, perversity and the pedagogy of love', in Letts IV, W.J. and Sears, J.T. (eds) *Queering Elementary Education: Advancing the Dialogue about Sexualities and Schooling*, Lanham, MD: Rowman and Littlefield.

Welsh Assembly Government (WAG) (2002) Sex and relationships education in Schools. Wales: Welsh Assembly Government.

White, P., Young, K. and McTeer, W.G. (1995) 'Sport, masculinity and the injured body', in Sabo, D. F. and Gordon, D. F. (eds) *Men's Health and Illness: Gender, Power and the Body*, London: Sage Publications Ltd.

Williams, R. (1977) *Marxism and Literature*, Oxford: Oxford University Press.

Willis, P. (1977) *Learning to Labour: How Working Class Kids Get Working Class Jobs*, Farnborough: Saxon House.

Wilton, T. (1996) 'Genital identities: An idiosyncratic foray into the gendering of sexualities', in Adkins, L. and Merchant, V. (eds) *Sexualising the Social: Power and the Organisation of Sexuality*, London: Macmillan Press Ltd.

Wilton, T. (2004) *Sexual (Dis)orientation: Gender, Sex, Desire and Self-fashioning*, Basingstoke: Palgrave.

Wolpe, A. M. (1988) *Within School Walls: The Role of Discipline: Sexuality and the Curriculum*, London: Routledge.

Wood, J. (1984) 'Groping towards sexism: Boys' sex talk', in McRobbie, A. and Nava, M. (eds) *Gender and Generation*, London: Macmillan.

Woodhead, M. and Faulkner, D. (2000) 'Subjects, objects or participants? Dilemmas of psychological research' in Christensen, P. and James, A. (eds) *Research With Children*, London: Falmer.

Woodhead, M. and Montgomery, H. (eds) (2003) *Understanding Childhood: An Interdisciplinary Approach*, Chichester: John Wiley and Sons.

Woods, P. (1976) 'Having a laugh: An antidote to schooling', in Hammersley, M. and Woods, P. (eds) *The Process of Schooling: A Sociological Reader*, London: Routledge and Kegan Paul.

Woods, P. (1981) 'Understanding through talk', in Adelman, C. (ed.) *Uttering, Muttering, Collecting, Using and Reporting Talk For Social and Educational Research*, London: Grant McIntyre.

Wright, J. (1996) 'The construction of complementarity in physical education', *Gender and Education,* **8**(1): 61–79.

Wulff, H. (1988) *Twenty Girls: Growing Up, Ethnicity and Excitement in a South London Microculture*, Stockholm: University of Stockholm.

Index